But suppose God didn't quite finish by closing time of the afternoon of the sixth day? We know today that the world took billions of years to take shape, not six days. The Creation story in Genesis is a very important one and has much to say to us, but its six-day time frame is not meant to be taken literally. Suppose that Creation, the process of replacing chaos with order, were still going on. What would that mean? In the biblical metaphor of the six days of Creation, we would find ourselves somewhere in the middle of Friday afternoon. Man was just created a few "hours" ago.

When Bad Things Happen to Good People
Harold Kushner

The dripping blood our only drink,
The bloody flesh our only food;
In spite of which we like to think
That we are sound, substantial flesh and blood—
Again, in spite of that, we call this Friday good.

"East Coker"
T. S. Eliot

He descended into Hell.
The Apostles' Creed

THE SUFFERING OF LOVE:

Christ's Descent into the Hell of Human Hopelessness

Regis Martin

ST. BEDE'S PUBLICATIONS
Petersham, Massachusetts

Imprimatur: +Giovanni Marra,
                           Auxiliary, Vicariate of Rome
31 May 1988

The *Imprimatur* is an official declaration that a book is considered to be
free of doctrinal and moral error. It is not implied that those who have
granted the *Imprimatur* necessarily agree with the contents, opinions or
statements expressed.

Library of Congress Cataloging in Publication Data

Martin, Regis, 1946-
    The suffering of love : Christ's descent into the Hell of human
hopelessness / Regis Martin.
        p.   cm.
    Includes bibliographical references.
    ISBN 1-879007-14-2
    1. Jesus Christ—Descent into hell.   2. Suffering—Religious aspects—
Christianity.   3. Suffering of God.   4. Incarnation.   5. Holocaust
(Christian theology)   6. Christianity and antisemitism. 7. Catholic
Church—Doctrines.   I. Title.
BT470.M35   1995
231'.8—dc20   95-21586
                                                         CIP

Published by: St. Bede's Publications
                P.O. Box 545
                Petersham, MA 01366-0545

CONTENTS

For Roseanne

Without whom this,
and much besides,
(especially our eight children)
would not be

PROLOGUE

Ecce Homo

Whose is this horrifying face,
This putrid flesh, discoloured, flayed,
Fed on by flies, scorched by the sun?
Whose are these hollow red-filmed eyes
And thorn-spiked head and spear-struck side?
Behold the Man: He is Man's Son.

Forget the legend, tear the decent veil
That cowardice or interest devised
To make their mortal enemy a friend,
To hide the bitter truth all His wounds tell,
Lest the great scandal be no more disguised:
He is in agony till the world's end,

And we must never sleep during that time!
He is suspended on the cross-tree now
And we are onlookers at the crime,
Callous contemporaries of the slow
Torture of God. Here is the hill
Made ghastly by His spattered blood

Whereon He hangs and suffers still:
See, the centurions wear riding-boots,
Black shirts and badges and peaked caps,
Greet one another with raised-arm salutes:
They have cold eyes, unsmiling lips;
Yet these His brothers know not what they do. ...

He who wept for Jerusalem
Now sees His prophecy extend
Across the greatest cities of the world,
A guilty panic reason cannot stem
Rising to raze them all as He foretold;
And he must watch this drama to the end. ...

Not from a monstrance silver-wrought
But from the tree of human pain
Redeem our sterile misery,
Christ of Revolution and of Poetry,
That man's long journey through the night
May not have been in vain.

David Gascoyne
From *Poems 1937-1942*

With the promulgation of *Nostra Aetate* in October 1965,[1] a significant milestone in Roman Catholic relations with non-Christian religions was finally reached. As regards Judaism in particular, a historic threshold had been crossed, over which not a few timorous churchmen at the time had hesitated to venture. Quite understandably, too, given so many centuries of impacted silence marked by episodic outbreaks of violence between the two traditions. "Since the foundation of the Church," observed Hans Urs von Balthasar in his book on Martin Buber published the year before the Council opened, "a dialogue between Jew and Christian has always been rare and invariably brief. Judaism shut itself off from Christianity, and the Church turned its back on the people which rejected it."[2] Can it be cause for wonder that, in the circumstances, relations between the two should inspire so little hope or confidence?[3]

But the events of the Council were intended to change all that. In the great work of renewal launched by the Second Vatican Council, Mother Church, the whole People of God, were to return to the roots and springs of their past; there the encounter with Judaism was inescapable, rich, and full of promise. Exactly ten years before *Nostra Aetate* was to crystallize so much of what the Church had rediscovered of her origins relating to Judaism, Fr. John Oesterreicher, in a trail-blazing first volume of Judeo-Christian studies called *The Bridge*, in fact anticipated the aims of the conciliar declaration.[4] Setting forth the journal's statement of purpose, he wrote: "A bridge links two shores, spans an abyss, opens a road for communication; it is thus an instrument of peace, as is this bridge, its editors hope." In other words, both he and the Council were pledged, in the terms set out by *The Bridge's* editors, "...to show the unity of God's design as it leads from the Law to the Gospels—the unbroken economy of salvation. Never can the Church forget that the Rock on which she stands is embedded in the revealed wisdom of patriarchs and prophets and in the mighty events which dominate the history of the children of Israel."[5]

The Second Vatican Council was intended to enshrine, and thereupon deepen and extend, precisely this sort of understanding and respect for the shared patrimony of Jew and Christian. That the conciliar effort was one of unprecedented ambition may be judged by the comment of Johannes Cardinal Willebrands who, writing some twenty years after the event at which he had been a participant, recalls the bracing and singular quality of the experience: "Never before has a systematic, positive, comprehensive, careful and daring presentation of Jews and Judaism been made in the Church by a Pope or Council. This should not be lost sight of."[6]

Clearly the event's significance has not been lost on the part of the present Pope, John Paul II, whose extraordinary visit to the Major Temple on the other side of the Tiber in April of 1986 marked the first time ever that a Roman Pontiff had actually entered a Jewish synagogue. (Even his saintly predecessor, John XXIII, had only stopped his car one morning to bless the Jews as they were leaving the Temple.) Addressing this oldest community of the Diaspora, between whom profound and perduring bonds exist, the Universal Pastor of the Catholic Church is reported to have marveled at how *Nostra Aetate* succeeded in midwifing "the decisive turning point" in the relationship between Christians and Jews. "On these convictions," the Pope stated, having in mind the short yet incisive paragraph four, "rest our present relations. On the occasion of this visit to your Synagogue, I wish to reaffirm and to proclaim them in their perennial value. For this is the meaning which is to be attributed to my visit to you, the Jews of Rome."[7]

It is worth inquiring, certainly, into the nature of those convictions which drew the Bishop of Rome across the Tiber and into a Jewish synagogue where, to recall the headline in *L'Osservatore Romano*, he gave thanks to God for the rediscovery of a common fraternal love. What does that love mean? At the very least, it implies an affinity between two peoples on the strength of which the old deicide charge cannot apply; thank God, that ancient canard of a specific Jewish complicity in the Crucifixion was finally laid to rest at the Council. While, to be sure, conceding that there were Jewish authorities conspiring against Jesus, seeking therefore to conscript the passions of the mob so as to pressure Pilate into killing him, the text of *Nostra Aetate* is perfectly plainspoken in reminding us that "neither all Jews indiscriminately at that time, nor Jews today, can be charged with the crimes committed during his passion."

If we must speak plainly here, and here above all for the conversation with Judaism is charged with an eternal meaning, it was never Judaism which drove Christ to the Cross but human sin and God's answering love. "It is not Israel who crucified Jesus," writes Jean Daniélou, "it is the infidelity of Israel. And consequently, what caused the death of Jesus is, in the final analysis, sin. But then it is no longer Israel alone who bears the responsibility for the death of Jesus; rather it is the 'iniquity of the world' that it had taken upon itself. Before the cross of Jesus, we must, we too, strike our breast like the centurion."[8] Here we are asked to accept an affinity with Judaism in which there can be no question of arrogant superiority but rather that complete and perfect solidarity in sin which Christ came and suffered to remove. "At this depth of mystery," concludes Daniélou, "all men are equal at the foot of the cross, just as all are equal in the salvation that comes through the cross."[9]

Under the circumstances, Christians are solemnly enjoined not to speak of the Jews as an accursed or rejected race, as if Holy Scripture had mandated one to do so. In fact, to so vilify the Jews amounts to an act of dishonor against Almighty God himself, for whom the Children of the Covenant are to remain forever a sacrament of his fidelity, the deepest, most abiding pledge that God's promised word, once given, will never be withdrawn. Here the conciliar text cites the Apostle Paul, kinsman by race to this people whom he would gladly have suffered for—yes, even unto final separation from Christ!—were the Father only to ask it; Paul's insistence on the truth of Israel's continuing proximity to God is absolutely unambiguous. It was God, he said, the very One who, from the beginning, called her to be his own: "For the gifts and the call of God are irrevocable" (Rom. 11:29).[10] In other words, if it once be thought odd of God to choose the Jew, i.e., the scandalous particularity of *this* people and not another, why should it not seem equally so that, having thus chosen, he would never revoke his word, the clearest and dearest sign of his eternal solicitude towards this People of the Promise?

The glory of Israel is neither ethnic nor racial but fundamentally religious: that for two millennia all the revelations of God were entrusted to it. Can such a thing be said of any other people in the history of the world? And not just the words of God were handed over to Israel; the unheard of enfleshment of God's very Word took place within Israel, within the womb of the Jewish maiden Mary. No other people can say that from the loins of its very life there once sprang into human being the Eternal Word and Son of the Father. "In this alone," says Daniélou,

> there is a greatness that staggers our imagination and reason. All other earthly greatness is passing. The great empires of antiquity have sunk into oblivion; their monuments—attempts to defy time—are merely tombstones of bygone civilizations. The great powers of today will decline in their turn, but Jesus Christ will live eternally and will be eternally Jewish by race, thereby conferring a unique, eternal privilege on Israel.[11]

But, it is sometimes asked, are there not then two Peoples of God? No, there is only the one Covenant; and Catholic Christianity, thanks to the blood of Jesus Christ, has been mercifully grafted onto its salvific trunk. "If the dough offered as first fruits is holy," announced St. Paul in a sublime passage touching on this mystery lying at the heart of things, "so is the whole lump; and if the root is holy, so are the branches" (Rom. 11:16). It cannot be well, therefore, for a mere wild shoot so engrafted to go about boasting of its good fortune at the expense of branches broken away; but if you must boast, adds Paul, "remember it is not you that support the root, but the root that supports you" (Rom. 11:18).[12] Abraham, in other words, is to be revered as our common father in faith; it is he who, humanly speaking, remains the source of that immense spiritual patrimony which joins our two destinies. How well the Holy Father traced this point of origin the evening of his fraternal visit! "The Church of Christ," he told the Jewish community, "discovers her own 'bond' with Judaism by 'searching into her own mystery,' [cf. *Nostra Aetate*]. The Jewish religion is not 'extrinsic' to us, but in a certain way is 'intrinsic' to our own religion. With Judaism, therefore, we have a relationship which we do not have with any other religion. You are our dearly beloved brothers and, in a certain way, it could be said that you are our elder brothers."[13]

This is why, at the profoundest level, the sin of anti-Semitism stands condemned; why it is not lawful for anyone, especially not for the Christian, to visit contempt upon the Jew, or to countenance the least persecution by others against him. *Spiritually we are all Semites!* Which is why, moreover, that whatever the vicissitudes of history now sadly dividing us—two disparate communities, nevertheless rooted in a common revelational source—the designs of our mutual Father in heaven cannot suffer lasting defeat.[14] "For if their rejection means the reconciliation of the world," to quote those infinitely mysterious words of St. Paul, "what will their acceptance mean but life from the dead?" (Rom. 11:15).[15]

Notwithstanding all this, there exist between Abraham and *Nostra Aetate* two horizon-shattering events which, for many, would thwart even the superintending Providence of Almighty God. These are the Cross and the Holocaust.[16] How, in the teeth of all the seemingly intractable differences of theology and history presently confounding our two communities, might these two events be joined in some creative and daring way, the nexus of which could well empower Jew and Christian alike to move as kindred souls in a common school of suffering? "Ultimately," writes von Balthasar of the mystery of Israel and Church, "they are two chambers of the one heart which beats, which indeed beats on the cross of the world, where the dividing wall was broken down and all hate was overcome in the flesh of the suffering Christ, so that in his person, the two are made one, in the single new man who is our peace (Eph. 2:14-15)."[17]

Could not the Cross, then, paradoxically understood as the axis point of history, its very shape stretched toward the sheer limit of the world, provide really the key to an understanding of Jewish travail in our time, and indeed, the travail of Everyman at any time? Might not the Cross, its very configuration signifying solidarity,[18] serve thus to illuminate the Holocaust of six million Jews, their sufferings representing (*re-presenting*, as it were) the sum and horror of all human abandonment which cries out in every age to God for redeeming relief? Is it possible, in other words, speaking at the deepest exegetical level of textual interpretation of history—at the level, that is to say, of *anagogical* meaning—to see in the countless events of literal human suffering, their horrors achieving a kind of infernal apotheosis in the Holocaust, the startling and mysterious presence of Christ, and thus the co-inherence of Christ's flesh in their flesh and their own annealed to his? Not as mere metaphor but as that deepest signification possible between what other-wise would eternally remain so many disparate and meaningless events in history.[19] Again, the Apostle Paul presses us to remember the high destiny of his kinsmen, a destiny thanks to which the whole human race has been raised to the dignity of a sacrament, that because they are Israelites, "to them belong the sonship, the glory, the covenants, the giving of the law, the worship, and the promises; to them belong the patriarchs, and of their race, according to the flesh, is the Christ, who is God over all, blessed forever" (Rom. 9:4-5). From the body of one nation only, shaped and kneaded from the beginning, the Son of the Most High was made Man: Son of Mary, Daughter Zion, he arose into Jewish manhood awaiting, with full prophetic expectation, that Cross by which we are all made whole.[20] And, to be sure, what the Lord did not assume, so the Fathers tell us, he could not redeem.

What does this testify to but that the self-same God has been count-less times tortured to death. Once on a hill and now in a Holocaust. *Six million crucifixions*, to use words aptly chosen by John XXIII in attempting to fix the equation between Golgotha and the grisly events of our time. And the point surely remains that, in each instance, we have all con-spired to crucify him: by our sins we raised Christ atop Calvary, and by those same sins inflicted countless times upon the Jew—the Jew whose countenance is that of Everyman and today bears the same tortured and sorrowful look of Christ—we stoked the fiery ovens of the Third Reich.[21]

Is it not fitting, then, that we take as our own act of reparation the one which Pope John XXIII wrote out for the whole Church when he was its Chief Shepherd? "We are conscious today," it begins, that many centuries of blindness have cloaked our eyes so that we can no longer see the beauty of Thy chosen people, nor recognize in their faces the features of our privileged brethren. We realize that the mark of Cain stands on our foreheads. Across the centuries our Brother Abel has lain in blood which we drew, or shed tears we caused, forgetting Thy love. Forgive us for crucifying Thee a second time in their flesh. For we knew not what we did.[22]

Can it still be possible, one wonders, for anyone to ask, "Whose is this horrifying face," on which hangs the weight of the world's sin?

Behold the Man: He is Man's Son.

How infinitely wide, then, must be the wounds of this world! "We think that Paradise and Calvary," says the poet John Donne,

Christ's Cross and Adam's tree, stood in one place;
Look, Lord, and find both Adams met in me;
As the first Adam's sweat surrounds my face,
May the last Adam's blood my soul embrace.[23]

Or, in still more rhapsodic verse, the Jesuit Gerard Manley Hopkins, exultantly expressing how it can be that, in God's eye, so perfectly and analogically exact is it, we are all Christ:

...for Christ plays in ten thousand places,
Lovely in limbs, and lovely in eyes not his,
To the Father through the features of men's faces.[24]

Alas, faces not always so lovely to look upon. When prolonged, unendurable sufferings encamp about us, the human face can seem a frightful thing. So frightful, in fact, that even death itself might not seem to be any real deliverance. And, yet, here too is place enough for Christ to play because, as the Gospel narratives reveal, Christ's features once wore that same look of death, only worse. Who, for example, on reading Dostoevsky's account in *The Idiot* of the dead Christ—the body freshly removed from the Cross with its face all shorn of beauty—has not felt, like Horatio on seeing the ghost of Hamlet's father, harrowed with fear and wonder? "It is," recounts Dostoevsky,

in every detail the corpse of a man who has endured infinite agony.... Nothing is rigid in it yet, so that there's still a look of suffering in the face of the dead man, as though he were still feeling it. Yet the face has not been spared in the least. It is simply nature, and the corpse of a man, whoever he might be, must really look like that after much suffering.... But, strange to say, as one looks at this corpse of a tortured man, a peculiar and curious question arises; if just such a corpse (and it must have been just like that) was seen by all his disciples, by those who were to become his chief apostles, by the women that followed him and stood by the cross, by all who believed in him and worshipped him, how could they believe that that martyr would rise again? The question instinctively arises: if death is so awful and the law of nature so mighty, how can they be overcome? How can they be overcome when even he did not conquer them, he who vanquished nature in his lifetime, who exclaimed, "Maiden, arise!" and the maiden arose—"Lazarus, come forth!" and the dead man came forth? ...The people surrounding the dead man must have experienced the most terrible anguish and consternation on that evening, which had crushed all their hopes, and almost their convictions. They must have parted in the most awful terror.... And if the Teacher could have seen himself on the eve of the crucifixion, would he have gone up to the cross and died as he did?[25]

A look of such suffering in the face of the dead man, *as though he were still feeling it.* These are terrible words indeed. But for all the terrors which they inspire, is there anything here that Holy Scripture has not already anticipated, exceeded even, in its own terrifying account of the Cross? It is, we often forget, in the Gospels themselves that the deadliest arguments against the Gospels are to be found, And if, asks Dostoevsky, Christ had seen himself on the eve of his own crucifixion, what then? But he had seen himself, in Gethsemane, and from the sheer stupefying extremity of that horror his sweat became, we are told, like so many drops of blood falling upon the ground. What else is Gethsemane but a vision of Golgotha, of anguish so awful it is likened unto death? In other words, the cry in the garden points beyond itself, to the place of the skull, to the hill where it will be heard no more. And three times, no less, will the Son's prayer go out to the Father unanswered; three times will he ask to forego the chalice, and as often as he asks he will be refused. The only prayer in the New Testament which was not granted; has ever a petition existed more heart-felt than his? "It is not just the sum," comments von Balthasar,

> but the surpassing, of all the abandonment that men could suffer. For only the "I" that was so close to the divine "I"—"the Word was with God...the Father loves the Son and shows him all that he does...my food is to do the will of him who sent me"—only this "I" can know what it really means to be abandoned by God.[26]

For all that the Lordship of the Son lays claim to the universe the Father made, and he remains the Word without whom there could not ever be anything made that was made, in the end there is only silence. And if Gethsemane points to Golgotha, to what then does Golgotha point? To Easter? Yes, most certainly it does, but it will not do to get there any sooner than Christ our Lord. (One must never, warned Plato, move too fast from the many to the one.)[27] So where does Christ go, then, if not directly to Easter? He goes into the silence of all that falls between—between, that is, Death and Resurrection—into the deepest silence of all, the state which marks the last, unspeakable limit to his descent. Christ goes, in a word, to hell.[28]

Thus baldly put, the proposition at once strikes the modern mind as a warhead, so utterly discordant is it with all that modernity finds fitting and true. In fact, of all the articles drawn from that Creed whose singular antiquity invites the title Apostolic,[29] this is surely the one with which most people, and not a few of them theologians, are fairly blithely prepared to dispense; it is simply thought of as wholly and completely unbelievable.[30] In an age of the electric light bulb, to recall a common enough example of progress and enlightenment (indeed, one which Rudolf Bultmann triumphantly seized upon as rendering twentieth-century man incapable of *turning on* to the miracle fables of the New Testament), what could be more fanciful and farfetched than the assertion that, yes, Jesus Christ had once died and gone to hell? What self-respecting member of the Secular City is likely to credit the claim that what, in the Old Testament, went by the name of "the grave," "the shades," "Sheol," now means that state of utter and ultimate God-forsakenness which in the New Testament has been parlayed into meaning "hell," into whose horror Christ descended for the world's salvation?[31]

And yet, to recall the clarity of language with which the German Bishops' Conference describes the event of Christ's descent, no outdated worldview is implied in the doctrine at all; indeed, their own position would seem to be highly suggestive of the lines of inquiry which the present study aims to take up in its grappling with the mystery of Holy Saturday. "When it is said of Jesus that he descended into the realm of death, this does not mean only that he entered into our common fate of death. It means that he also entered into the whole abandonment and loneliness of death, that he took upon himself the experience of meaninglessness, of the night, and—in this sense—of the hell of being human." Yes, to be sure the doctrine does draw upon the imagery of what we, strait-jacketed within our smug modernities, choose to dismiss as so many mythologized fables, but it does so only in order "to describe a permanent, profound dimension in man, one that does not lie only in the beyond but already begins in the midst of this life."[32]

Are these statements the product of pre-critical innocence, I wonder? Are they merely offered up in the pious hope that a credulous faithful may believe them? If that were the case, then, of course they would invite, not scholarly explication, but ridicule. But to think that is really to imagine a modern intelligence so worm-eaten with skepticism and methodic doubt that the whole meaning of the descent would thereby be lost, and with it the Easter hope and joy on which it ultimately is fixed.

And, of course, the trouble with men whose minds have been swept thoroughly clean of all the imagined dogmatic cobwebs of yesteryear, is that as a result of such leveling exercises most of us are forced to inhabit an unreal world, i.e., one whose metaphysical topography has been rendered more or less flat as a map. In other words, with the fashionable refusal to accept as an article of the faith something seen to be dependent for its validity upon antique cosmology—to wit, that three-tiered universe science was widely thought to have smashed all to bits—the world has suddenly become, in our century, very complicated and dangerous indeed. This is because an understanding shaped by rationalist and positivist categories alone (the results of which, warned Aldous Huxley, would be a world wrapped in cellophane), simply leaves a man helpless in the face of certain phenomena—namely, the encounter with evil. So, what is to become of the experience of people for whom the collision with evil in our century has opened up depths far below the topography we'd all been happily instructed was all flattened out? People who have drawn swords against God and man for permitting events to happen of sheer metaphysical wickedness; an abyss of evil, no less, which neither God can redeem, nor any man escape. There does not exist, they are saying, any theodicy by which we might acquit God of such enormities, nor any anthropology by which the myth of man's goodness could survive, say, a single Nazi death camp. (There is no cellophane so resistant to the revelations of our time in which to wrap the world at all.) "O the mind," wrote Hopkins,

> mind has mountains; cliffs of fall
> Frightful, sheer, no-man-fathomed. Hold them cheap
> May who ne'er hung there. Nor does long our small
> Durance deal with that steep or deep.[33]

It is one thing to acknowledge the experience of that horror, something else again to give it meaning. What follows is an attempt to anchor that meaning in the Christ who freely chooses to remain in agony until the world's end, so that, as the poet Gascoyne put it in words used to adorn this text, "man's long journey through the night / May not have been in vain." It is, in short, to provide an answer raised by the horror of the Holocaust (and all the horrors of meaningless misery which have overtaken the race in its long journey); the cry of anguished men who deserve to know where God was, for instance, while his people perished in the death camps of the Third Reich. The whole argument of this book, of course, is (that God *was* there,) amid the sufferings and death of so many millions; that precisely in and through the mystery of Jesus' descent into hell—and it is an event which the Church solemnly honors in her Creeds—the deepest salvific meaning of the Holocaust and numberless other human horrors may yet be found. Thus, for example, between the experience of Jesus' own abandonment on the Cross, his mysterious descent into Sheol, and the experience of abandonment by the Jewish inmates of the death camps, there remains the profoundest possible nexus.

The march of the argument will be as follows: Chapter One, in the Thomistic spirit of the *disputatio*, will present the argument of those who hold, more or less, that because of the Holocaust, and other horrors too numerous to mention, *all* human discourse is suspended, including that which presumes the existence of a good and all-powerful God. Chapter Two will attempt to disarm the force of that argument by suggesting that the alleged silence culpably imputed to God may in fact be seen as the deeper silence of the Son sent into that state of lostness and apparent final God-forsakenness in order, paradoxically, to redeem its hellish and everlasting hold. Chapter Three, the final chapter, will seek to deepen the sense of this mystery, which is the mystery of Holy Saturday, the deepest point of the kenotic emptying of the Son of God on the Cross. An Epilogue will follow which, like the *coda* to a symphony, attempts a brief recapitulation of the themes set out in the text, using in particular the examples of St. Maximilian Kolbe and Blessed Edith Stein. I will conclude the book by trying to situate the meaning of their sacrifice within the larger Christic context of self-emptying for the sake of the other.

NOTES

1. For the full text of the Conciliar statement see Austin Flannery, O.P., general editor, *Vatican II: The Conciliar and Post-Conciliar Documents*, (Northport, NY: Costello Publishing Co., 1981), pp. 738-742.

2. Hans Urs von Balthasar, *Martin Buber and Christianity: A Dialogue Between Israel and the Church*, (New York: Macmillan, 1961), p. 12.

3. And yet, von Balthasar reminds us, notwithstanding all the centuries of silence during which these two have lived entirely apart, "without ever coming face to face or trying to see what sort of person the other might be," their very existence "involves them in a conversation which it is not in their power to terminate," (*ibid.*, p. 7). If the conversation to which, inescapably, Jew and Christian are joined, is to bear fruit which will last, "its range must therefore be such as to reckon with heaven and earth, and so it will always hark back to the conversa-

tion held on the Mountain of the Transfiguration, when the Son of Man conversed with Moses and Elijah...," (*ibid.*). How could the Jewish-Christian dialogue, cast at such a sublime level, not then succeed in resolving our mutual difficulties?

4. John M. Oesterreicher, ed., *The Bridge: A Yearbook of Jewish-Christian Studies*, vol. I, (Pantheon Books, 1955).

5. See "A Statement of Purpose," *The Bridge*, vol. I.

6. Johannes Cardinal Willebrands, "Christians and Jews: A New Vision," *Vatican II: By Those Who Were There*, Alberic Stacpoole, ed., (London: Geoffrey Chapman, 1986), p. 222.

7. "Let us thank God for the rediscovery of our fraternal love," headline in *L'Osservatore Romano*, 21 April 1986, pp. 6-7.

8. Jean Daniélou, S.J., *Dialogue with Israel*, (Baltimore-Dublin: Helicon Press, 1968), p. 85. See also St. Augustine (*Enarratio in Psalm.* 65,5; PL 36.790-791), quoted in "The Mysterious Destinies of Israel," *The Bridge*, vol. II, (1956), p. 61. Writes Augustine, "My brethren...we beg you to be on your guard: you who are in the Church, do not insult those who are not; rather pray that they may be in it. 'For God is able to graft them back' [Rom. 11:23]. It is of the Jews that the Apostle said this, and so it happened to them. The Lord rose and many believed. They did not know Him when they crucified Him. But later they believed in Him, and that great offense was forgiven to the *homicides*. I do not say *deicides*, 'for had they known it, they would not have crucified the Lord of glory' [1 Cor. 2:8]. The slaying of an innocent was forgiven them, and the blood they had shed while out of their minds they later drank by grace. Say then to God: 'How tremendous are your deeds!' [Ps. 65:3]."

9. Daniélou, *Dialogue with Israel*, p. 85. For a striking confirmation of the above, see Jean-Marie Cardinal Lustiger's *Dare to Believe: Addresses, Sermons, Interviews—1981 to 1984*, (St. Paul Publications, 1986), pp. 33-94. Himself born and raised a Jew, he reflects deeply upon this mystery of shared iniquity in which all men, from Pilate to the apostles to the ordinary people, remain silent. "Everybody was compromised, including the disciples who were afraid and ran away. Such is the universal dimension of the cross of Christ. The Passion of Christ serves as an instrument of revelation of the totality of evil which exists in the world and in each one of us," p. 87.

10. Romans 9–11 remains as profound and luminous a presentation of God's word as any three chapters of Sacred Scripture. Von Balthasar, in his book on Buber, speaks of "the dazzling eschatological light that falls on Israel from the eleventh chapter of the Epistle to the Romans..." (p. 12). A light, however, "which had hardly been mirrored in the works of Origen before it was once again obscured," and no longer noticed at all. Perhaps the, as yet, unharvested hope of the Council will restore something of that light and so illumine the dialogue with its bright promise.

11. Daniélou, *Dialogue with Israel*, p. 7. "The greatest saints of Christianity," he continues, "are Jewish: above all, the Virgin Mary, daughter of David and

mother of God; John the Baptist, the precursor; Joseph, the adoptive father of Jesus and protector of the Church; Peter, Paul and all the apostles."

12. "...the common link between the Jewish and the Christian understanding of faith reveals the following law: There can be no Christianity which is not *a priori* and inwardly, related in a deeply sympathetic manner to the 'holy tree,' as the branch is related to the root. Christianity is only the fullness if it is the fulfillment of something...," von Balthasar, *Martin Buber*, p. 23.

He puts it in its strongest possible form on pp. 108-109, where he asserts the following: "Jewish-Christian history is, at any rate from a Christian point of view, an indivisible unity. There is no greater unity in the world, according to God's plan, than that between the Old and New Covenant, except the unity of Jesus Christ himself who embraces the unity of the two covenants in his own unity.... Christianity when separated from the Old Covenant is always in danger of degenerating into Gnosticism, Marcionism or some form of Hitlerism."

13. See again, *L'Osservatore Romano*, 21 April 1986.

14. Von Balthasar in his study of Buber provides an apt illustration of the point. "In *Two Forms of Faith* M. Buber...carried his lonely dialogue up to the point at which, in his opinion at least, the only intelligible attitude was silence. His final conclusion was that the two forms of faith are irreconcilable. That judgment is acceptable in the world, but it is not one that *invokes the grace of God*" (emphasis mine).

15. For a superbly rich exegesis of the above, see von Balthasar's *Church and World*, (Herder & Herder, 1967), pp. 166-176. His extraction of Paul's three theses from Romans 9–11 is particularly helpful. "First: Israel's obduracy enters incontestably into God's plan of salvation in its historical working characterized by election and reprobation.... Second: The reprobation of Israel serves to the election of the Gentiles who, as the elect, are the spiritual Israel and have their lasting roots fixed in the old Israel.... Third: Israel's rejection, as a factor of salvation history, points to an eschatological salvation common to it and the Church, in which rejection and election are brought into equilibrium."

16. Throughout the book the use of the term "Holocaust" will refer to the historical event of Nazi Germany's attempted destruction of European Jewry between the years 1939 and 1945. Millions of Jews were targeted for extermination merely because of one man's murderous contempt for them. Concerning the specificity of this crime, i.e., that Jews perished precisely as Jews, it is important that it be remembered in all its ghastly particularity. In other words, while any number of things about the Holocaust remind us of other horrors, and men of the twentieth century have supped full on the flesh of their brothers, this particular horror is entitled to its own distinctive mark of atrocious human behavior. In fact, it is its very shocking singularity which provides the setting for the argument of this book. Nevertheless, for all its uniqueness and unrepeatability, the Holocaust is not, alas, so inclusive an event or instance of human iniquity that there can remain nothing left of man's inhumanity for us to lament; nothing of that iniquity the cumulative impact of which in our time threatens to undermine

belief in the saving Providence of Almighty God. Yes, the Holocaust remains (in my judgment certainly) *the* salient symbol and expression of demonic destructiveness in our time; yet it plainly fails to exhaust all the possibilities of human sin and suffering which continue to bedevil the human condition. Therefore, while the march of my argument particularly focuses upon the Holocaust as the chief symptom and example of that which needs most deeply to be redeemed, because other atrocities of our time as well evince that same need for healing grace which Christ came to confer, they too will fall within the ambit of the book.

17. Balthasar, *Church and World*, p. 176. And not only Jew and Christian. Is not membership in the school of human suffering expansive enough to embrace every category of pain, including even those expressions of cosmic futility and despair which characterize much of twentieth-century literature? One thinks, for instance, of that doomed poet who fell in the First World War, Wilfred Owen, who left lines of such hopeless and bitter lacerating intensity that they amount to a kind of anthem of existential anguish and despair. "Futility" is a typical example of the genre, and the bitter question posed at the end absolutely cries out for an answer, one which—so the argument of the book will advance—only Christ in his descent can give. "Move him into the sun...," it begins,

> Gently its touch awoke him once,
> At home, whispering of fields unsown.
> Always it woke him, even in France,
> Until this morning and this snow.
> If anything might rouse him now
> The kind old sun will know.
>
> Think how it wakes the seeds,—
> Woke, once, the clays of a cold star.
> Are limbs, so dear-achieved, are sides,
> Full nerved—still warm—too hard to stir?
> Was it for this the clay grew tall?
> —O what made fatuous sunbeams toil
> To break earth's sleep at all?

The Norton Anthology of Poetry, (New York: W. W. Norton and Company, 1970), p. 1037.

18. See also von Balthasar, *Heart of the World*, (San Francisco: Ignatius Press, 1979), p. 13. The Cross, he writes, "extending out into the four winds...*means* solidarity: its out-stretched arms would gladly embrace the universe." The book's thesis is at once applicable to the issues under review here, namely, that Christ is the true form or configuration of the world's sorrow and salvation. Indeed, as von Balthasar argues with great ardor and acuity, Christ *is* the world's heart.

19. Such has been the mature fruit of a Christian sensibility steeped in the habits of medieval exegesis, with its four levels of images, to wit, the literal, alle-

gorical, moral and anagogical. For a brilliant discussion of what Fr. William F. Lynch, S.J. has called "thinking and imagining according to a Christic dimension," see his *Christ and Apollo*, (New York: Sheed and Ward, 1960). "In brief, the question can be put thus: in our terms of analogy the act of existence has descended and keeps descending into every created form and possibility, adapting itself to every shape and form and difference. Is it true or not that the natural order of things has been subverted and that there has been a new creation, within which the one, single, narrow form of Christ of Nazareth is in process of giving its shape to everything? To think and imagine according to this form is to think and imagine according to a Christic dimension. It would also make every dimension Christic. However, like analogy itself, this would not destroy difference but would make it emerge even more sharply," p. 183. In other words, we are to bore right through the successive layers of literal and historical fact relating to the Holocaust, which itself serves as a symbol of modern suffering and what men take to be its meaningless obscenity, and there at the deepest point possible situate its meaning within the participatory folds of the eternal *anagoge*, Jesus Christ, who forever remains mysteriously present to its pain and loss. Thus, in the book, whenever reference is to be made to the genuinely redemptive meaning of this or that atrocity of our time, particularly the events surrounding the Holocaust which so many have felt bereft of meaning at all, the intent is always the same: to think and imagine Christologically, so that even the worst descent of our time into the blood and beastliness, despair and hopeless death, is always encompassed within that infinitely deeper descent of the Son of God into hell.

20. "Israel can only really become conscious of its role in the Kingdom of God to the extent to which it allows itself to be saved in Christ; then it can receive the mission towards which it has always been drawn, the role which it abandons when it denies the transcendent character of the resurrection and the ascension. Israel before Christ knew that transcendence and looked towards those realities; its prophets and the prayers of its faithful were filled with that spirit. But the Israel of today has lost its sense of transcendence and only thinks of the here and now; and that strong feeling for the earth with its eschatological agnosticism, its refusal to think of the 'hereafter' as well as the 'here,' is quite unbiblical," von Balthasar, *Buber*, p. 109.

21. See, for example, the extraordinary portraits of the Jewish artist Marc Chagall, for whom the figure of the Crucified One so entirely absorbed his attention over the years. "All these centuries, the Crucified has been hanging over the ghettos with His outstretched, waiting arms, and hardly anyone has seen Him there. Now Marc Chagall has looked up and seen Him," write Cornelia and Irving Sussman in an admiring essay from *The Bridge*, vol. I, p. 104. Why does he do it? they ask. "To the Jew, though he does not know it, Christ is always there, crucified. Chagall, who has apprehended this, has thus become the recording artist of the Jew in the diaspora...he is the recording artist of the

'Jewish subconscious' since Calvary. He has looked deep into the Jewish soul and seen Christ crucified and what he has seen he has painted," p. 105.

22. Cited by John X. Evans, "After the Holocaust: What Then Are We To Do?" *Center Journal*, Winter, 1984, p. 81.

23. John Donne, "Hymn to God My God, In My Sickness," *The Complete Poetry and Selected Prose of John Donne*, ed. by Charles M. Coffin, (New York: Random House, 1952), pp. 271-272.

24. Gerard Manley Hopkins, Number 34, *Poems and Prose*, edited by W. H. Gardner, (New York: Penguin Books, 1953), p. 51. Still another stirring, lyric confirmation of Christ's laying hold of the human and turning it all to grace and glory, is his "That Nature is a Heraclitean Fire and of the Comfort of the Resurrection," of which the following is characteristic:

> Across my foundering deck shone
> A beacon, an eternal beam. Flesh fade, and mortal trash
> Fall to the residuary worm; world's wildfire, leave but ash:
> In a flash, at a trumpet crash,
> I am all at once what Christ is, since he was what I am, and
> This Jack, joke, poor potsherd, patch, matchwood, immortal diamond,
> Is immortal diamond.

25. Fyodor Dostoevsky, *The Idiot*, (New York: Bantam Books, 1960), pp. 395-396.

26. Balthasar, "Why I am Still a Christian," *Two Say Why*, (Chicago: Franciscan Herald Press, 1971), pp. 48-49.

27. Plato's admonition ought to prove especially cautionary to exegetes of Psalm 21 (22) inasmuch as here the movement from the many to the one, if too hastily conducted, will result in the exegete having reached Easter Resurrection long before the Suffering Servant himself. On hearing the note of abandonment struck at the beginning—"My God, my God, why hast thou forsaken me?"—the exegete must not, in his haste to hear the trumpet of deliverance on which the hymn triumphantly concludes, miss any of the intervening music. What is to become, in other words, of those manifold miseries which Christ has steeled himself to pass through in his complete bearing of human iniquity, right to the last extremity of pain and loss? Is Christ's lament, which runs nearly from first to last in the 32 verses of the psalm, to count for nothing? Consider: a full 17 verses having elapsed since the initial note of abandonment is spoken from the Cross, and Christ is only now numbering the bones which hold together his pierced hands and feet! No credible application of Christ's real solidarity with human sinners and their suffering, I am saying, will permit undue haste here. See, for instance, Augustine's explanation in which he confronts the cry of abandonment in terms of that profound unity between the Head and the members of one Body. "It is the voice of Christ," he says, "but it speaks for the members." And he asks, "Why has God forsaken the son...if not because he recognized the voice of the sinner in the flesh of our infirmity?" Cited by Stanislas Lyonnet and Leopold

Sabarin, *Sin, Redemption, and Sacrifice: A Biblical and Patristic Study*, (Rome: Biblical Institute Press, 1970), p. 214. Or, again, Gregory Nazianzen, whose application of the solidarity principle to the words of abandonment spoken by Christ, is assessed as follows: "In this situation, he (Gregory) explains, Christ was representing us. We were abandoned, but by the sufferings of the impassible we were assumed and saved. Because he has appropriated our madness and our disorder, he pronounced the rest of Psalm 22.... As the Word he is neither obedient nor disobedient. But made slave and servant of slaves, he became someone else, carrying me in himself, all that I am and that I represent, to consume in himself evil, as fire consumes wax or the heat of the sun absorbs the vapors of the earth," p. 200 in Lyonnet and Sabarin text.

28. It is imperative to determine with theological exactitude just what is meant by the expression, "He descended into hell." Both the Symbol of Rufinus, who comments in the early fifth century on the creed used in Aquilaea, and the famous Roman Order of Baptism, which is destined to achieve authoritative status throughout the Western Church, speak of a descent *ad inferna*: "He went down to the dead." While at the Fourth Lateran Council (1215), the operative phrase is *ad infernos*: "He went down to the underworld." In each case, however, Christ is understood as descending to a place, or state, of the dead and departed, that is, Hades. He does not enter the place or condition of the damned, that is, Gehenna; failure to distinguish the two produces the distorting mirror whereby Christ is made to suffer the penalties of eternal torment, i.e., the errors of Calvin and, in modified form, Karl Barth. See *The Christian Faith in the Doctrinal Documents of the Catholic Church*, eds., J. Neuner and J. Dupuis, (New York: Alba House, 1982), pp. 4-15. See also W.J. Dalton, *Christ's Proclamation to the Spirits*, (Rome, 1965), who, on the basis of meticulous research of the scriptures, concludes that, "In the New Testament, the descent of Christ to the world of the dead is a way of insisting on the fact that He really died," p. 184. Likewise J.N.D. Kelly, who in his monumental *Early Christian Creeds*, (London: Longman, 1972), ventures the following, namely that the descent represents "no more than the natural corollary of Judeo-Christian ideas about the condition of the soul after death. To say that Jesus Christ had died, or that He had been buried, was equivalent to saying that He had passed to Sheol," p. 380. And he cites Tertullian's *De anima* (55) wherein it is alleged that Christ "did not ascend aloft to heaven until He had gone down to the regions beneath the earth."

But is there nothing more signified in the descent than the plain meaning of the words that he died? And are these words really so plain, so transparent, after all? Certainly as regards any work or activity performed by Christ among the dead, both Dalton and Kelly—along with J. Daniélou, whose *Théologie du Judeo-Christaninise*, (Tournai, 1958), Dalton approvingly quotes, p. 8—agree that there is nothing in the New Testament to warrant such belief. "As for the development in later Christian literature," writes Dalton, "in which Christ brings the tidings of redemption to the souls of the just, or overcomes Satan by a 'harrowing of hell' " —to mention the two other possibilities in addition to the fact of Christ's simply having died, which represent the usual range of interpreting the descent—"these go beyond the text of the New Testament," p. 184. Nevertheless, Dalton admits, on the strength of the descent's first credal appearance in 359 (i.e., the Fourth Formula of Sirmium, which Kelly documents as well, pp. 281-291, 378-379) that a distinct activity is intended, namely the "harrowing of hell." The Sirmium text reveals very clearly that Christ, having been crucified and died, "descended to hell, and regulated things there, whom the gatekeepers of hell saw and shuddered..." (see Kelly, p. 289). And so the question one is left with is this: Is it possible to pin real salvific meaning to the Sirmium text, always consistent of course with the Church's traditional credal language, despite the apparent silence of scripture concerning such activity as preaching to the saved or "harrowing" the servants of Satan? In other words, if one excludes either the kerygmatic interpretation, or the "harrowing of hell" view, what really remains of the descent? And will it retain sufficient relevance to speak to the condition of futility and despair which characterize, say, the events of the Holocaust? What follows is an attempt to answer these questions. It is not to enter into speculation about either the kerygmatic or "harrowing" interpretations, however interesting they may be; rather the book seeks to flesh out all that is really and salvifically significant in the fact that Christ, in his desolation and death upon the cross, entered fully into the human condition, and thus "He descended into hell."

29. "The Apostles' Creed," says Henri de Lubac, "is the simplest and oldest of the creeds still in use in the Church, the one which even today all Christian sects in the West claim as their own, the one which every Christian child learns in the catechism, the one which his godparents recited in his name the day he was baptized." See de Lubac's *The Christian Faith: An Essay on the Structure of the Apostles' Creed*, (San Francisco: Ignatius Press, 1986), p. 19. And notwithstanding the legendary claim according to which each article was crafted by an apostle, thus resulting in the necessary twelve credal propositions or articles of faith, both its origin and legitimacy trace all the way back to that "Rule of Faith" established by Christ and held to and later transmitted by the holy apostles; it was they who thereupon handed it on to us. "Let us believe in the Apostles' Creed," exhorts St. Ambrose as far back as the fourth century, "which the Roman Church keeps and always preserves intact." It is a striking testimony to the strength and antiquity of that creed which, as I hope to show, enshrines in a special and luminous way the Church's belief and hope in the Mystery of Holy Saturday contained in the words, "He descended into hell." Cited by de Lubac, p. 20. See also *The Christian Faith in the Doctrinal Documents of the Catholic Church*, eds. J. Neuner and J. Dupuis, pp. 1-2.

30. Concerning the descent of Jesus Christ into the realm of death, to cite a recent compilation of Catholic doctrine put out by the German Bishops' Conference, it is precisely due to the failure of Christians to understand its real meaning that the truth which it enshrines is now largely forgotten. "It is unintelligible and foreign to most Christians, who find the present version particularly unpalatable: 'descended into hell.' This declaration reminds us of a three-story world

view that we find antiquated. Perhaps we even see in it mythical motifs of the descent of the gods into the underworld. What are we to do today with such declarations?" *The Church's Confession of Faith: A Catholic Catechism for Adults*, (San Francisco: Ignatius Press and Communio Books, 1987), pp. 162-163. And, to be sure, not only garden-variety Christians do not believe it but very learned theologians as well. "Many modern theologians," writes Herbert Vorgrimler, "including some Catholic ones, are a little too ready to look on present-day theology mainly as a process of constant clearing and cleaning. It is possible that unconsciously they have given the impression that the biblical texts about the descent into hell were purely mythological and that we are now in a condition to dispense with it. But if we look a little more closely into the matter we see that from the way the Fathers developed it, this theological question points in the opposite direction." "Christ's Descent into Hell—Is It Important?" *Concilium: An International Review of Theology*, vol. 1, no. 2, Jan. 1966, p. 76. Fr. Vorgrimler, in fine heuristic fashion, shows that "Christ's descent into hell is a decisive juncture at which the main lines of any Christian theology converge. It is a point which lies at the center of theology, not on the periphery." Why this should be is, of course, the point of this book.

31. Not F.W. Beare, certainly, who dismisses the idea as "a fantastic dream." See A.T. Hanson's definition in *A New Dictionary of Christian Theology*, ed. by Alan Richardson and John Bowden, (London: SCM Press), p. 154. Also, the reader is left to wonder what, if anything, is to remain of the descent as a result of Hanson having fairly stripped it (in my judgment) of its distinctive meaning. Referring to 1 Peter and the theme of rescue which it introduces, he writes, "The doctrine of the descent helps to answer the question: 'What of those who have died before the incarnation?' This is undoubtedly how we should interpret the article in the Apostles' Creed, 'He descended into hell.' " Maybe so. But, as has been seen, this view lacks any ballast at all from scripture in order to lend it credibility. In addition, the question Hanson asks of the descent, is it really the central thrust of what the doctrine intends to communicate to men today? That answering faith brought to men forced to endure the hell of meaninglessness is hardly the one suggested by Hanson's reference to those who died before Christ came to save them.

32. *The Church's Confession of Faith: A Catholic Catechism for Adults*, (San Francisco: Ignatius and Communio Books, 1987), pp. 162-163.

33. Hopkins, Number 42, *The Poems*, R.K.R. Thornton, (London: Edward Arnold Publishers, 1973), p. 61.

I

THE SHAME OF MEN AND
THE SILENCE OF GOD

THE TENTH STATION
Jesus Is Stripped of His Garments

What is shame?
The mystery of the body is but a poor allegory.
What *this* body makes visible
is the twisted shape of hearts,
created for love, chosen for love,
that yet offer every insult unto love,
attempt every abuse of its secret and holy nakedness.

White scourged limbs stripped of allurement.
Blood risen to the head where all sense of shame is gathered.

And what is this game with the loincloth?
Will they cover him?
Or will they—it is more likely—tear the cloth away?
It makes little difference.
The whole body shouts shame,
has become the utter shame of mankind;
and nothing can conceal that shame any longer.

Look at him or look away—it is all the same.
For there *you* are, my friend.
That is how you really look.

Hans Urs von Balthasar[1]

The Holocaust:
Unique and Symptomatic Horror

When Sir Kenneth Clark, author of an acclaimed television series entitled *Civilisation: A Personal View*,[2] stepped out from behind the archival shadows where so many stylized impressions of the past had flitted across our screens, he found himself face to face with an unfinished, vastly unsettled present. And sounding a theme which had been implicit throughout the thirteen week series, he confessed "that it is lack of confidence, more than anything else, that kills a civilization. We can destroy ourselves by cynicism and disillusion just as effectively as by bombs." Recalling the oft-quoted lines from William Butler Yeats ("more like a man of genius than anyone I have ever known"), Clark gloomily concludes with the observation that the world is in a most awful fix. "Things fall apart," the apocalyptic Yeats had written,

> the center cannot hold;
> Mere anarchy is loosed upon the world;
> The blood-dimmed tide is loosed, and everywhere
> The ceremony of innocence is drowned;
> The best lack all conviction, while the worst
> Are full of passionate intensity.

For all the good that may abound even in the best of men, said Clark, "the trouble is that there is still no center. The moral and intellectual failure of Marxism has left us with no alternative to heroic materialism, and that isn't enough. One may be optimistic, but one can't exactly be joyful at the prospect before us."[3]

A quarter of a century having elapsed since Lord Clark's somewhat lugubrious summing-up, and with no apparent increase in confidence in sight, the outlook for the future would indeed seem to be bleak and foreboding. In fact, it is arguable, given the manifest growth in cynicism and disillusion over the intervening years, our situation is perhaps pronouncedly worse than ever before. In any case, concerning this alleged center, the sense of whose absence now haunts the emptiness and futility of our time, it is a thesis of this book that whatever the particular complex of events one might lay hold of to explain civilization's collapse—and the data of disintegration, again, would appear to lie all about us—clearly the attempted extermination of European Jewry between the years 1939 and 1945 remains a vivid and salient expression of it. Is it not, in point of fact, the single event of our time most profoundly, shockingly symptomatic of that center's disappearance; with the result that, to quote Yeats, "the blood-dimmed tide is loosed, and everywhere the ceremony of innocence is drowned"?

Certainly the sheer scale of slaughter renders the event almost unprecedented in the annals of human suffering and loss. For those Jews living in circumstances of complete Nazi domination, there was virtually no escape. According to figures taken from Lucy Dawidowicz's *The War Against the Jews, 1933-1945* (New York: 1975),[4] the following numbers perished: 3 million Polish Jews, 228,000 from the Baltic countries, 210,000 from Germany and Austria, 80,000 from the Protectorate of Bohemia and Moravia, 1,352,000 from White Russia, the Ukraine and Russia. Other countries, too, took part in the orgy of annihilation: 105,000 from the Netherlands, 54,000 from Greece, 90,000 from France, thousands more from Slovakia, Hungary, Belgium, Yugoslavia, Rumania, Norway, Bulgaria, Italy, and Luxembourg.

Leaving aside for the moment the issue of complicity in the face of so vast and systemic a destruction of human beings, by its very nature the Holocaust remains an event absolutely central to Jewish experience, Jewish expectations. "The destruction cut so deeply that it is a question whether the community can recover from it," writes Irving Greenberg, long-time student and professor of Jewish Studies in America. The whole pre-war life source of European Jewry having been nearly eviscerated at one stroke (over 80% of Jewish scholars, Rabbis, and full-time students and teachers of Torah alive in 1939, he says, would not survive the war), "the fundamental existence of Jews and Judaism is thrown into question by this genocide. For this reason alone, the Holocaust cannot be overcome without some basic reorientation in light of it by the surviving Jewish community."[5] And where there is no Covenant People, where is the Covenant to be found?[6]

"In each generation," writes Bruno Bettelheim, who survived the horrors of Nazi incarceration before going on to establish an international reputation as a scholar and writer, "one event more than any other makes this lesson (that we ought to care for the other) especially pertinent, as it gives it a characteristic specific to that age. For this century I believe this event is the extermination of the European Jews in the gas chambers."[7] Quite apart from Bettelheim's own involvement in the event, which probably accounts for a certain heightened awareness of its singularity, the event itself invites unique attention insofar as here were a People, millions of whom were destined for destruction solely because they were Jews, and meanwhile just about the whole world stood by in

HOLOCAUST – HAPPENS WHEN THERE is no more MORALITY

silence.[8] In the circumstance, nothing seems nearly so hideously instructive to contemplate as the Holocaust of the Jews.

Progress and Perfectibility: The Vanished Dream

But not merely in terms of a grisly summary of its human victims, the six or more million innocents ruthlessly sacrificed on altars of racial and religious hatred. Civilization itself, no less than those human beings it failed so conspicuously to defend, seems not to have survived intact the genocidal passions loosed by Adolf Hitler and his Third Reich. What is being suggested here is that more than just Jews became fuel for gas ovens. Ideals, too, went up in smoke, their make-believe substantiality consumed like so many tufts of cotton in the fire. Foundations, no less, of an entire order of being, trapped beneath the weight of so many murdered dead ("so many, I had not thought death had undone so many"[9]), suddenly seemed to great numbers of people to be no more than a scaffolding of lies. And thus that cynicism and disillusion of which Lord Clark spoke, i.e., a thing more lethal even than atom bombs, began for the first time in the West on a massive scale to set in and proceed to poison the wells of human hope and confidence. Ideals, for example, of man's vaunted progress, of the infinite and benign perfectibility of human beings and their institutions, suddenly shattered on the basis of so immensely brutal and programmatic an enterprise of contempt for some men by other men. "The Terrible Twentieth" it was called by Winston Churchill. "Until it opened," writes historian Barbara Tuchman, "the idea of progress had been the most firmly held conviction of the nineteenth century. Man believed himself both improvable and improving. Then, twice in twenty-five years, or the space of one generation, came the Gadarene plunge into world war, accompanied the second time by the Germans' actual physical killing—pursued with fanatic zeal for more than five years amidst the simultaneous demands of foreign war— of six million people in the area they occupied." We are obliged to listen whether we want to or not, she says in her review of *Justice in Jerusalem*, Gideon Hausner's account of his successful prosecution of Adolf Eichmann, a book which grimly compiles the total German program for the elimination of the Jews; "for Mr. Hausner's book has to do not simply with Germans and Jews, with war crimes and unimaginable atrocities but, like the tale of the Ancient Mariner, fundamentally with the human soul. We must listen because what we are confronting here is the soul of man in the twentieth century."[10]

It does not seem to have mattered that one have been even directly involved in the event itself to feel, and thus to recoil from its ghastly effects. François Mauriac, for example, in recalling the terrible years of German occupation, of storm troopers in his beloved Paris, confesses that nothing he had ever seen during those melancholy years left so harrowing an impression as that which he did not see, namely row upon row of Jewish children boarding trains to the East where, almost certainly, they would die. "Yet," admits Mauriac,

> I did not even see them myself! My wife described them to me, her voice still filled with horror. At that time we knew nothing of Nazi methods of extermination. And who could have imagined them! Yet the way these lambs had been torn from their mothers in itself exceeded anything we had so far thought possible. I believe that on that day I touched for the first time upon the mystery of iniquity whose revelation was to mark the end of one era and the beginning of another. The dream which Western man conceived in the eighteenth century, whose dawn he thought he saw in 1789, and which, until August 2, 1914, had grown stronger with the progress of enlightenment and the discoveries of science—this dream vanished finally for me before those trainloads of little children. And yet I was still thousands of miles away from thinking that they were to be fuel for the gas chamber and crematory.[11]

For some, then, it is the whole mythology of progress, of increasing, unending universal peace and brotherhood (what one might scornfully wish to call the superstitions of secular liberalism) which, under the burden of the mystery of boundless human iniquity opened up in our century, reveals itself as being fundamentally illusory, as morally and intellectually corrupting to those who hold fast to it. "Most of us know, now," observes the critic and poet Randall Jarrell, "that Rousseau was wrong: that man, when you knock his chains off, sets up the death camps. Soon we shall know everything the eighteenth century didn't know, and nothing it did, and it will be hard to live with us." Jarrell's point is strategically placed, i.e., a review of Robert Penn Warren's *Brother to Dragons: A Tale in Verse*, which consists of an imaginative retelling of an atrocious murder of a black slave by the children of Charles and Lucy Lewis, brother-in-law and sister, no less, to Thomas Jefferson, "who," acidly comments Jarrell, "spoke and believed that Noble Lie of man's innocence and perfectibility."[12]

The tragic sense, it would seem, has once more become a matter of stern practical necessity for twentieth-century man. It is the sense of mounting doom and horror which, for instance, fills so much of Elizabethan theater with an atmospheric despair well nigh impossible to escape; in its mortal coils not a few of Shakespeare's characters have been caught. One thinks of the anguished cry of Gloucester from *King Lear*, his innocent eyes freshly plucked from their sockets: "As flies to wanton

Enlightment — Rousseau.
absence of God is darkness (Prof)

boys are we to the gods;/they torture us for their sport."[13] Here is ample and articulate re-working of that earlier and ancient Greek ethos—"the foremost contribution of the Greek genius to our legacy," it has been called[14]—the dramatic formula for which is that life is a thing irremediably tragic. A walking shadow, Macbeth called it in a scene of unbearable tragic bitterness;

> a poor player
> That struts and frets his hour upon the stage
> And then is heard no more. It is a tale
> Told by an idiot, full of sound and fury,
> Signifying nothing.[15]

not just post-modern phenomena.

is there another way to live?

Something of the same attitude persists, of course, in those immemorial accents of resignation which issue forth from the bent and gnarled figures of Castillian peasantry; men and women for whom *No hay remedio* bespeaks a fatalism owing more to Lucretius perhaps than to Christianity.[16] But Homer remains the prototypical tragedian, the one creative mind in whom so many of the motifs and images of tragedy have set like granite over the course of some thirty centuries.[17] "Much has been talked of the melancholy of Virgil," says C.S. Lewis, "but an inch beneath the bright surface of Homer we find not melancholy but despair. 'Hell' was the word Goethe used of it. It is all the more terrible because the poet takes it all for granted, makes no complaint."[18]

The sense of life understood as tragedy then—in which, as George Steiner puts it, "Things are as they are, unrelenting and absurd. We are punished far in excess of our guilt"[19]—would seem thus to be an indispensable aid in traversing the peculiar landscape of horror which marks our time. And not to have this sense, to sentimentalize life as though one were living it between the covers of a P.G. Wodehouse novel (i.e., replete with picture-postcard perfection where, thanks to an omniscient and omnibenevolent Jeeves, nothing terribly untoward *ever* happens to anyone), is really to invite disaster. It is to welcome, in fact, the hellish places of Auschwitz and Dachau.

The End of Literature

For those of still more exacting fastidiousness, however, it is not only civilization and the myth of progress which it enshrines that collapse into irrelevance beneath the weight of the Holocaust; it is literature itself, the whole disinterested life of mind and sensibility it gives expression to, which, because so many millions failed to survive Auschwitz and Dachau, have no right to survive either. At least not in those forms of

How do we as Christians embrace this mystery.

holocaust — emperils literature
is despair the only road for humanity after holocaust?

28 / *The Suffering of Love*

ultimate optimism in which they presently function, i.e., on the basis of various humanistic ideals of classical art (from catharsis in Aristotle, sublimity and beauty in Longinus, to the suspension of disbelief in Coleridge and emotion recollected in tranquillity in Wordsworth). Such paradigms can no longer be taken for granted in a post-Holocaust universe where the imaginative faculty as such stands uprooted by the ineffable enormity of six million dead. "Stunned by the awesomeness and pressure of event," writes Alvin Rosenfeld, "the imagination comes to one of its periodic endings."[20] The point is, how does one come to credit "a view of literature as an unqualifiedly constructive act of the imagination,"[21] which is the view undergirding the existing canons of humanistic art, when just around the corner lurks the sheer unspeakable otherness of the Holocaust? Can an event so unimaginably destructive be assimilated at all? Ought it to be subject to the artist's *muse* as suitable material for representation?[22]

If the answers are no, that such aesthetic strategies are wrong and indecent, then the grim pronouncement of Theodore Adorno would seem to follow, to wit, "No poetry after Auschwitz." For Adorno, the mere composition of a sonnet becomes a barbaric act in the aftermath of the Death Camps. A severe judgment, to be sure, but one which George Steiner, among others, records approvingly in a rueful collection of his essays entitled *Language and Silence.*[23]

"Has civilization," asks Steiner, "by virtue of the inhumanity it has carried out and condoned…forfeited its claims to that indispensable luxury which we call literature?" How, he wonders, is it possible to sustain without complete loss of intellectual and moral integrity, those elements of high humanistic culture in which, say, the civilizing influence of a Matthew Arnold found expression (teaching our children only the best that had been thought and said), when the plain fact is that "a man can read Goethe or Rilke in the evening, that he can play Bach and Schubert, and go to his day's work at Auschwitz in the morning?"[24]

The maintenance of high literary culture, argues Steiner, is no longer tenable in a world where such places "of literacy, of philosophy, of artistic expression. became the setting for Belsen."[25] Better by far, one would think, the silence of dumb, uncomprehending animals than the harnessing of language in a world given over to the triumph of the inhuman, the demonic. "After such knowledge," asks T.S. Eliot, "what forgiveness?"[26] Indeed, suggests one Yiddish poet, Aaron Tsaytlin, "Were Jeremiah to sit by the ashes of Israel today, he would not cry out a lamentation…. The Almighty Himself would be powerless to open his well of tears. He would maintain a deep silence. For even an outcry is now a lie, even tears are mere literature, even prayers are false."[27]

where do the actions of man point to?
Germans were Christian people.

no only Christians, but artists etc... agreed with naziism.

"It is not only the case," continues Steiner, sharpening the edge of his polemic, "that the established media of civilization—the universities, the arts, the book world—failed to offer adequate resistance to political bestiality; they often rose to welcome it and to give it ceremony and apologia."[28] Again:

> Not only did the general dissemination of literary, cultural values prove no barrier to totalitarianism; but in notable instances the high places of humanistic learning and art actually welcomed and aided the new terror. Barbarism prevailed on the very ground of Christian humanism, of Renaissance culture and classic rationalism. We know that some of the men who devised and administered Auschwitz had been taught to read Shakespeare or Goethe, and continued to do so.

Under the circumstances, he concludes forlornly, "we must countenance the possibility that the study and transmission of literature may be of only marginal significance, a passionate luxury like the preservation of the antique."[29] As W.H. Auden once put it, "In the end, art is small beer." Would our century have been laid out any differently had Dante or Michelangelo or Cervantes never existed to lend its contours literary and artistic shape? Was anything written or said against Hitler which decisively worked to save a single Jew?[30]

The End of Religion

Thus far we have put both liberalism and literature—politics, poetry and culture—provisionally to the test. And, the fact must be faced, neither one appears to have survived altogether intact the strictures of those who, in some unspeakable way, suffered the event of the Holocaust. What remains then but religion? Belief in both progress and poetry having sustained grievous losses in credibility as a result of organized wickedness on so humanly colossal a scale, what is left but faith in that which, because it claims issuance from Almighty God, precisely transcends all the impacted terrors and bestiality of recent history? Surely— the argument might be made—the substance of true religion, of belief legitimized and enlivened by eternity and the pure God who serenely reposes therein, sitting in majestic judgment upon the evil and folly of men, surely all that will effortlessly lift us above the oppressions of our time and place?

However, even here (especially here!) one finds reproduced the identical predicament, i.e., the same strictures which, assailing the provinces of politics and poetry, have left them ravaged and broken by all too recent events. Susan Shapiro, writing in *Concilium's* volume on "The Holocaust as Interruption" (itself a provocation to existing categories of understanding), argues that *all* discourse is in ruins, shattered by the event of the Holocaust; but most particularly discourse about God. Three related experiences have led to this sundering of language, she says:

> The first experience is the Holocaust's victims' pervasive sense of having been abandoned by God. "Theirs was the kingdom of night. Forgotten by God, forsaken by Him, they lived alone, suffered alone, fought alone" (Elie Wiesel, "The Holocaust as Literary Inspiration," *Dimensions of the Holocaust*, ed. Lacey Baldwin Smith, [Evanston, IL: 1977, p. 7]). The second is the purposeful attempt by the Nazis to dehumanize their victims totally before exterminating them. The third experience was the Jews' virtually complete abandonment by the rest of the world to its fate. ("Alone. That is the key word, the haunting theme. Alone with no allies, no friends, totally, desperately alone.... The world knew and kept silent.... Mankind let them suffer and agonize and perish alone. And yet, and yet, they did not die alone, for something in all of us died with them" (Elie Wiesel, p. 7).[31]

Having deduced from all this massive testimony of negation—"Negation in language, negation of language"—a state of religious rupture within both Judaism and Christianity, what follows is fairly clear, namely an indictment to be drawn up against God, against too his putative servants, far deadlier than any mere philippics hurled against the world (whether its politics or its poetry). But especially against the God of Christianity, conventional claims on behalf of whom simply will not survive—it is argued—the fact of extermination camps on soil where the seeds of Christendom had once fallen and were fed. "The question is," asks well-known ecumenist and Temple University religion professor, Dr. Franklin Littell, "How could Jesus be the Messiah if His followers feel that they must torment other men? How could this have happened in the heartland of the Reformation, in the heart of Christendom?"[32] Or Alan T. Davies, a leading scholar of Christian anti-Semitism, who argues that only a "daring and heretical, and a true theological response to the post-Auschwitz situation," can liberate Christianity from its fundamental and inherent denigration of the Jewish people:

> Auschwitz has altered the criteria of theology forever. The beliefs and doctrines of Christianity must be weighed not solely for their inner logic, but immeasurably more for their human ramifications. Never again, one trusts, will the church dogmatize abstractly about human themes without pre-testing its conclusions in the crucible of the flesh-and-blood world....[33]

Not to put too fine a point on it, much of the fallout from recent theological literature seems uncommonly polemical, full of shrill disputatiousness concerning, in particular, the question of an intrinsic Christian faith connection with an anti-Semitism whose most virulent forms took

expression in the gas chambers of the Third Reich. Frequently, allega-
tions of systemic Christian anti-Semitism commence with the Gospels
(particularly John) and St. Paul, then branch out to include Origen, John
Chrysostom, Augustine, Aquinas, Luther, Calvin, et al.[34] The governing
assumption here is not that anti-Semitism is a pathology which is likely
to afflict Christians grown insensible to the moral requirements of the
Gospel; after all, a man is never sick so long as sickness sickens him.[35]
No, what is imputed rather is this, that a Christian anti-Semitism derives
from the very centrality of New Testament faith and life; it is not therefore a species of moral sickness accidental to Christianity at all but
fundamentally indispensable to it. "The roots of Hitler's final solution,"
says Paul Van Buren, "are to be found...in the proclamation of the very
kerygma of the early Christians."[36] Or Gregory Baum's claim that Auschwitz is an entirely special "sign of the times, in which God empowers the
Church to correct its past teaching, *including its central dogma* [his italics],
to the extent that it distorts God's action in Christ and promotes human
destruction."[37] A position pushed to the point of polemical extremity, it
would seem, in Rosemary Reuther, whose persisting claim has been that
wholesale relativizations are in order of all the distinctive Christian
elements; nothing less will do, she argues, if relations between Christians
and Jews are to improve. Such radical diminution of the Christian
deposit would perforce begin with seeing Christ as "only a significant
beginning...a first installment" of an eschatological deliverance yet to
arrive.[38] "Reuther joins the other dialogue theologians," reports John
Pawlikowski, "in rejecting any contention that the Messianic age came to
pass in the Christ event.... For her, human history remains every bit as
much, perhaps even more, mired in ambiguity, sickness, sin, and death,
as was the case prior to the coming of Jesus. If the Church persists in
affirming that the term 'Christ' signifies the Messiah of Israel's hope,
then it must likewise appreciate that, to quote Reuther,

> ...from the standpoint of that faith of Israel itself, there is no possibility of
> talking about the Messiah having come (much less of having come two
> thousand years ago, with all the evil history that has reigned from that time
> until this) when the reign of God has not come.[39]

The logic is of course unassailable given the premise that, according
to Reuther, no Jewish tradition can view the Messiah's coming apart
from the Golden Age it promises to produce; no such Age having come,
it follows that no Messiah has come. To invest Jesus with the aura of a
Golden Age, the very Messianic future somehow infused into history, is
a "historicizing of the eschatological," to use an idea central to Reuther's
thought.[40]

WAS CHRIST REALLY THE MESSIAH ?

The whole matter of theodicy has thus been raised anew by the Holocaust; in ways which, for all the speciousness of earlier arguments, cannot be so easily dismissed. It is one thing to unmask the pretensions of literary critics like Leonard Woolf;[41] or art historian Sydney Cockerell who, replying to a friend's conversion, demands to know: "But *how* can you believe in a creative, all-good, all-wise God, knowing that you have an appendix, which is a totally useless organ and can prove dangerous?"[42] An epistemology of atheism deserves better and the fact of so much unmerited suffering has got to be faced. "Either we are not free and God the all-powerful is responsible for evil," says Camus, "or we are free and responsible but God is not."[43] Lewis, in *The Problem of Pain*, has nicely captured the classic formulation:

> If God were good, He would wish to make His creatures perfectly happy, and if God were almighty He would be able to do what He wished. But the creatures are not happy. Therefore God lacks either goodness, or power, or both.

This, concludes Lewis, is the problem of human pain in its simplest and most stark form.[44]

In its simplest form, yes. But because of the singular and widespread prevalence and depth of evil in our time—so the argument runs—no resolution of the problem can be found which will acquit God of complete complicity in so wicked a world. In other words, what Maritain, commenting on two texts in St. Thomas, has called "the fundamental certitude, the rock to which we must cling in the question of moral evil, (namely) the *absolute innocence of God,*"[45] is precisely being called into question by the existence of the Death Camps. "After the dreadful horrors our century has seen," notes Walter Kasper in his discussion of the fact, "post-Auschwitz theology believes it now impossible to speak responsibly of a God who is both omnipotent and good."[46] To borrow an apt phrase from Lewis, God himself has now been placed in the dock.[47] And who, surveying all the evidence, would dare to move for an acquittal?

Not Emil Fackenheim, to take an emblematic example of the lengths to which the aggrieved will go in pressing the argument against God. Fackenheim, a survivor of the Sachsenhausen Concentration Camp, is a man for whom the Holocaust represents something altogether, irreducibly *special*; an event which encompasses evils quite beyond anything previously imagined. To enter the Death Camps, he tells us in book after book determined on the religious meaning of modern Jewish experience, amounts to a kind of revelation, a disclosure of the way things really are in this world; we are all captives of a world steeped in sorrows purely

THEODOCY :

metaphysical, in which the basic fact confronting us is that of one vast Nazi Concentration Camp. On this view of things, who can claim vindication? Neither God, who made so radically wretched a world, nor men, who behave so barbarously to one another in it. "Fackenheim demands that the Holocaust be understood philosophically," says Hyam Maccoby, an admiring critic of his works, "as a manifestation of radical evil that is part of the metaphysical fabric of Being itself."[48] *(part of God)*

Here, then, is a canvas on which the brush strokes of iniquity would appear to have covered just about everything, leaving not a whit of blessed being free from infestation.[49] "Jews are forbidden," warns Fackenheim, "to grant posthumous victories to Hitler."[50] Presumably even a theodicy whereby God himself is spared condemnation must, on that basis, says Fackenheim, amount to a sort of victory for him. A strange way, one would suppose, for setting about redressing wrongs committed in this century by, after all, human beings.[51] But then Fackenheim's point is not judicial at all, i.e., an attempt to obtain retroactive justice for the Jews who suffered at the hands of Nazi sadists fifty-some years ago. No, his point is precisely the metaphysical one which emerges as a result of a harrowing personal and philosophic collision with 'absolute' evil. An abyss of pure unrelieved human and cosmic wickedness had suddenly opened up in our age—*the theological tremendum*, Arthur Cohen has called it[52]—and so frightful and earthshaking is it that it is all a man can do to try and register the awesome seismic shock of the thing, then reel despairingly from the meaning which it discloses to those who follow.[53]

For the meaning of Auschwitz, again, is that it has no meaning; "the one place on earth," writes William Styron, "most unyielding to meaning or definition."[54] There the unleashing of the 'raw demonic,' athwart even the will of Almighty God, has worked its transmogrifying poison; as a result of which this "nightmare of our own century...its unspeakable monstrousness—one is tempted to say its unbelievability—continues to leave us weak with trauma, haunting us as with the knowledge of some lacerating bereavement."[55]

And who ultimately is responsible for Auschwitz, for the sheer absurdity of its horror and death which deprives it of any meaning whatsoever? "It is to no avail," writes Eliezer Berkovits, "to seek to exonerate God by loading all the blame upon human beings. Men are culpable, of course. But the ultimate responsibility for the evil of this world is God's, for the plain reason that it is he who made the world and it is he who permits monstrous suffering to take place."[56] How dare God, as it were, evade responsibility for having made a world where men are free to make history! After Auschwitz, says William Jay Peck, "the very being of God is tied up with the problem of murder."[57]

indictement

Towards an Absolute Atheism of Despair

This is not garden variety atheism according to which a man cannot bring himself to believe because he sees only an obscene grimace which, nevertheless, he hopes and prays is but a mask obscuring what otherwise will be bathed in beauty and light.[58] No, this is simon-pure rejection of any good God whatsoever; it is the metaphysical rebellion of men prepared to impute evil to God out of misplaced rage at its presence in and among men. There is a sense in which, as Maritain has put it, the absolute atheist is *not atheist enough;* only the saint is prepared to strike at the root of the world's wickedness,[59] and not at the world's root which is God (whom, as St. Thomas tells us, "is absolutely not the cause of moral evil, neither directly nor indirectly"[60]). No, this bedrock atheism exists in those who, like Nietzsche, the self-styled "destroyer par excellence" who dreamed of a company of like-minded souls bent on the practice of "active nihilism," have come to shape much of the modern attitude to life.[61] Its premier literary forebear is, to be sure, the character Ivan in Dostoevsky's *The Brothers Karamazov,* who urges upon the innocent Alyosha an atheism of absolute despair.

In the novel, Ivan tells his younger brother the heart-rending story of the peasant child who struck the master's dog while playing. Thereupon the master ordered the child to be seized and the following morning hunted and torn to pieces by his hounds before the child's own mother's eyes. Ivan asks:

> And what sort of harmony is it, if there is a hell? I want to forgive. I want to embrace. I don't want any more suffering. And if the sufferings of children go to make up the sum of sufferings which is necessary for the purchase of the truth, then I say beforehand that the entire truth is not worth such a price. I do not want a mother to embrace the torturer who had her child torn to pieces by his dogs. She has no right to forgive him. And if that is so, if she has no right to forgive him, what becomes of the harmony? I don't want harmony. I don't want it out of the love I bear mankind. I want to remain with my suffering unavenged. Besides, too high a price has been placed on harmony. We cannot afford to pay so much for admission. And therefore I hasten to return my ticket of admission.... It is not God that I do not accept, Alyosha. I merely most respectfully return him the ticket. I accept God, understand that, but I cannot accept the world that he has made.[62]

The same piercing, exigent note of metaphysical anguish leading to revolt is struck throughout Camus' novel, *The Plague,* one of a handful of shattering tales to come out of post-war Europe, in which, to take a single example, a priest and a physician watch helplessly while a young child is literally tortured to death. They had seen much of death already; it was nothing new in a city torn in two by plague. But until now they had been spared so long a vigil in the presence of one child's agony.

> And just then the boy had a sudden spasm, as if something had bitten him in the stomach, and uttered a long, shrill wail. For moments that seemed endless he stayed in a queer, contorted position, his body racked by convulsive tremors; it was as if his frail frame were bending before the fierce breath of the plague, breaking under the reiterated gusts of fever.... When the spasm had passed, utterly exhausted, tensing his thin legs and arms on which, within forty-eight hours, the flesh had wasted to the bone, the child lay flat, racked on the tumbled bed, in a grotesque parody of crucifixion.

The priest falls to his knees and in the midst of the death-cry itself, "the angry death-cry that has sounded through the ages of mankind," calls out to God to spare the child.

> But the wail continued without cease.

When, at last, it is all over and nothing more can be done, the doctor confesses bitterly, "there are times when the only feeling I have is one of mad revolt." The priest appears to understand: "That sort of thing is revolting because it passes our human understanding." But, he counters, perhaps one should then try to love what one cannot understand. To which the doctor replies, witheringly, "No, Father. I've a very different idea of love. And until my dying day I shall refuse to love a scheme of things in which children are put to torture."[63]

Here, one supposes, is what Henry Adams must have meant by *the last lesson*, really the sum and term of a man's education, a phrase Adams used to describe his own painfully acquired education one fateful summer in the year 1870 when he was just thirty. "He had passed through," says Adams, speaking of himself years later in the autobiography,

> thirty years of rather varied experience without having once felt the shell of custom broken. He had never seen Nature—only her surface—the sugar-coating that she shows to youth. Flung suddenly in his face, with the harsh brutality of chance, the terror of the blow stayed by him thenceforth for life, until repetition made it more than the will could struggle with; more than he could call on himself to bear. [64]

Here Adams is remembering, years later, the horrible death of a beloved sister who, thrown from a cab and injured, soon develops lockjaw and dies. She lay amid fiendish tortures for ten days, says Adams, while outside her sick-room a rich and sensuous Italian summer unfolded. "For many thousands of years, on these hills and plains, Nature had gone on sabring men and women with the same air of sensual pleasure."[65] In the face of inconsolable loss, Adams discovers the frailty of every human thing we love; and the futility of trying our best to shore up against such ruination as, in the end, no mortal has the ability to resist anyway. *relieve pain*

> The usual anodynes of social medicine became evident artifice. Stoicism was perhaps the best; religion was the most human; but the idea that any personal deity could find pleasure or profit in torturing a poor woman, by accident, with a fiendish cruelty known to man only in perverted and insane temperaments, could not be held for a moment. For pure blasphemy, it made pure atheism a comfort. God might be, as the Church said, a Substance, but He could not be a Person. [66]

Leaving aside Adams' (inadvertent?) truncation of the central mystery of Trinitarian life, i.e., that God as both One and Three is to be understood precisely as Substance *and* Person,[67] we are nevertheless left with Ivan's question, namely the sort of God who would countenance a world in which little children, and all those whom we most love, are permitted to die, and not infrequently in circumstances horrifyingly cruel. Who would not, then, like Ivan, wish to return his ticket? We are confronted here with what Irving Greenberg has called his "working principle" for any post-Holocaust theology: "No statement, theological or otherwise, should be made that would not be credible in the presence of burning children."[68]

Thus we need, more urgently than ever before, to know the following: Is our God a gracious God, or is he not? Has he in fact counted the hairs on our head and will he thus help cushion our falls, having himself suffered in mysterious anticipation of all human catastrophe his own unique fall into Sheol where, Psalm 139 assures us, he awaits our headlong descent?[69] Or have we rather all been sent, simply by being born into this wretched world, to Kafka's Penal Colony, that horribly apt symbol of arbitrary cruelty where, beneath the Harrow prepared for us from all ages, we learn through pain our individual sentence of death?[70]

"How quiet a man grows at just about the sixth hour!" exclaims the executioner as he sets about exhaustively explaining to the stranger each detail and function of the machine.

> Enlightenment comes to the most dull-witted. It begins around the eyes. From there it radiates. A moment that might tempt one to get under the Harrow oneself. Nothing more happens than that the man begins to understand the inscription.... You have seen how difficult it is to decipher the script with one's eyes; but our man deciphers it with his wounds. To be sure, that is a hard task; he needs six hours to accomplish it. By that time the Harrow has pierced him quite through and casts him into the pit, where he

pitches down upon the blood and water and the cotton wool. Then the judgment has been fulfilled, and we, the soldier and I, bury him.[71]

The last lesson. It is, to be sure, a hard lesson to be learned. And if the *teaching* pedagogy be ultimately God's own whereby we learn wisdom through our wounds—never mind the fact that the only wisdom we ever learn is that there is no wisdom and that to learn it is to die[72]—what then of his putative servants and ministers who pass on to the rest of us the infinite and brutal deception about his alleged graciousness? What sort of reckoning ought these Grand Inquisitors to face for the lies they speak to our face?

In an essay on Pope Pius XII's "complicity" with agents of Nazi genocide (one of a number of pieces stitched together on the theme of Rolf Hochhuth's *The Deputy*, the controversial play which baldly advances the indictment against the Church[73]), Arthur Cochrane, among others, argues that what is fundamentally at stake here is the very possibility of faith in a world surrounded by human and institutional depravity; where the Church herself, Christ's own Body extended in time and history, seems culpably aloof from all that oppresses and degrades man. "The last scene of the play," he comments,

> is entitled "Auschwitz, or Where Are You God?" Realizing that the neutrality of the Vatican is bound to continue, young Father Fontana decides to become a "real substitute" and joins a group of Roman Jews who are arrested under the windows of the papal palace and are carried off to the gas chambers of Auschwitz. There, as he watches Jewish men, women, and children being "led as sheep to the slaughter," a cynical Nazi doctor taunts him: "Now, Father, after all you have seen, do you still believe in God?" Ricardo Fontana replies: "I am in a narrow room. I am suffocating...and no one cares. O God, help me! Help me!"[74]

But there is no one to help at all, leaving the theater-goer with the appalling prospect of an eternity, no less, of silence in the face of absolute evil. Which eventuality, of course, is the whole point of the play: the silence of a complicity with evil stretching between Church and God, each implicated in the indifference of the other. For instance, Act Five takes up in a fully explicit way the whole question of God's silence. Its expressed aim is that of sheer forensic demonstration of evil, a satanic wickedness which, due to the silence of God and Church, is free to triumph. Why does God fall strangely silent before the cries of his People? Why does not the Church speak out against these outrages? The Death Camps are thus understood, given the logic of Hochhuth's drama, as so many harmonious parts of an engine engaged upon vast and routinized murder; the machinery harnessed to the demonic task of undoing

the work of a good creation. And neither God nor Church seem sufficiently stirred by the event to try and rescue a humanity writhing
beneath the fascist boot. Only the devils remain at large, their efforts
yielding an immense harvest of misery and death.

Poor Father Fontana: constrained thus to co-operate with instruments
of devilish terror, he feels himself as one "burning God himself." And at
every turn he is taunted by the sinister figure, Doctor Mengele, who,
with a punctilio positively satanic, presides over each detail involving
the incineration of human flesh.

> Fr. F: Why...why? Why do you do it?
>
> Dr. M: Because I wanted an answer! And so I've ventured what no man
> has ever ventured since the beginning of the world. I took the vow to chal-
> lenge the Old Gent, to provoke him so limitlessly that he would have to give
> an answer.... Well, hear the answer: not a peep came from heaven, not a
> peep for fifteen months, not once since I've been giving tourist tickets to
> paradise.... The truth is, Auschwitz refuses creator, creation, and the crea-
> ture. Life as an idea is dead.[75]

The Holocaust and Hell

Here is nihilism plain and simple. Here commences that "Season in
Hell" concerning the topography of which George Steiner, in a more
recent and concentrated work, has given us so acute and searing a
report.[76] We now know, he informs us, with the blueprints of those who
built them, the documented anguish of so many who endured them, that
the Death Camps constituted a complete, coherent world.

> They had their own measure of time, which is pain. The unbearable was
> parceled out with pedantic nicety. The obscenities and abjections practiced
> in them were accompanied by prescribed rituals of derision and false
> promise. There were regulated gradations of horror within the total, concen-
> tric sphere. *L'univers concentrationnaire* has no true counterpart in the secular
> mode. Its analogue is Hell. The camp embodies, often down to minutiae, the
> images and chronicles of Hell in European art and thought from the twelfth
> to the eighteenth centuries. It is these representations which gave to the
> deranged horrors of Belsen a kind of "expected logic."[77]

And the finality of so vast and systemic and sinister a torture of
human beings? In short, the whole hellish system was mounted and
sustained in order to rid the world of a special vermin called Jewry. The
Holocaust, says Robert McAffee Brown in his Foreword to A. Roy
Eckardt's *Long Night's Journey Into Day*, must never be seen "simply as
one further instance of the enormity of evil, but an event absolutely

without parallel. Let it be forever registered on the human consciousness that Jews were killed not for *doing* what they did but for *being* who they were."[78] This, at any rate, has been Emil Fackenheim's point, the spearhead of his challenge thrown up before the Gentiles. "More than any other writer," asserts Maccoby his faithful exegete, "he brings out the uniqueness of the Holocaust, and refutes the attempts that have been made to assimilate it to other horrific massacres...." It was only the Jews whom the world sought to destroy, he insists; not for anything they did or were thought to have done, "but simply because they *were*, a people whose very existence was considered an evil which it was meritorious to annihilate, in an action analogous to the eradication of malaria."[79]

However, the campaign of eradication proceeded with this decisive difference, says Maccoby; and here Hyam Maccoby breaks ranks with Fackenheim's analysis on the grounds that it is not nearly radical enough to suit the polemic which he, Maccoby, is anxious to press. The analogy with malaria breaks down, he insists, because men do not ordinarily torture and degrade bugs before deciding to dispatch them. But with the Jews, there was precisely this concerted effort not merely to kill as many as possible but to revile and demoralize and humiliate in every way the victim *before killing him*. "Nothing in history," Maccoby tells us,

> has been like a Nazi Death Camp, with its creation of a vast community of suffering and its proliferation of techniques—including covering inmates in excrement—by which the victims' torture could be protracted and concentrated.... There is only one possible analogy in human experience, or rather in human imagination, and that is with the supreme place of torture: Hell, as created by Dante and other Christian writers and preachers.[80]

Yes, however extensive or formidable the literature of the Holocaust—an entire industry, as it were, pursuant to examining the pathology of human pain—there is nothing in it nearly equal to the fullness or depth to be found in Dante—the same Dante derisively dismissed by another poet, Charles Péguy, who charges the Florentine with having merely passed through hell as a tourist.[81] Notwithstanding this criticism, it is true that while Dante is never actually part of the hellish landscape he wanders across, he does reveal permanent details about its condition. And because the reality he imagined can be replicated in so many particulars within the world of the Death Camps, *L'univers concentrationnaire*, not a few of the cantos from his *Inferno* furnish that key to understanding the hell of the Holocaust; for example, Canto 33. "Whoever can grasp," says Steiner, "the full meaning of 'The very weeping there forbids to weep/And grief finding eyes blocked with tears/Turns inward to make agony greater' will, I believe, have grasped the ontological form of the camp world."[82]

In other words, argues Steiner, wherever the Death Camps are to be found in this century, or under whatever regime their horrors happened to be sanctioned, it is always the same principle: "*Hell made immanent.* They are the transference of Hell from below the earth to its surface."[83] In a word, they are the *enactment* of every imagined Dantesque detail of the place where the damned have been sent to suffer everlasting torment. Meanwhile, centuries of rationalist enlightenment having set in since the time of Dante, all but collapsing into quaint superstition the very idea of a literal hell, we now find it paradoxically necessary to re-read the *Commedia* in order to learn something of the quality of our time. "Much has been said of man's bewilderment and solitude after the disappearance of Heaven from active belief," Steiner concludes provocatively:

> We know of the neutral emptiness of the skies and of the terrors it has brought. But it may be that the loss of Hell is the more severe dislocation. It may be that the mutation of Hell into metaphor left a formidable gap in the coordinates of location, of psychological recognition in the Western mind. The absence of the familiar damned opened a vortex which the modern totalitarian state filled. To have neither Heaven nor Hell is to be intolerably deprived and alone in a world gone flat. Of the two, Hell proved the easier to recreate. (The pictures had always been more detailed.)…
>
> Needing Hell, we have learned how to build and run it on earth. A few miles from Goethe's Weimar or on the isles of Greece. No skill holds greater menace. Because we have it and are using it on ourselves, we are now in a *post-culture*. In locating Hell above ground, we have passed out of the major orders and symmetries of Western civilization.[84]

The Death of Hope

It is supremely tempting (is it not?), to give in, meekly submitting to the nihilist tocsin which sounds so well the terrible depths of all that we now know. It is, after all, what so much of our best literature and the arts invite us to think about God and man in our time. Or, for that matter, any time.[85] We live not only in an Age of Anxiety, oppressed by an omnipresent bomb (What would happen to us should it decide to go off?), but an Age of Absurdity as well, whose characteristic theme is, Well, it may not go off at all, but man will remain wretched forever just the same.

> Man hands on misery to man,
> It deepens, like a coastal shelf.

Get out as early as you can
And don't have any kids yourself.[86]

In a scene from Ingmar Bergman's *The Seventh Seal*,[87] a haunting story set sometime near the end of the medieval world, we watch while a hapless young wisp of a girl is brutally seized and sentenced to die; and we follow behind the cart in which the child is drawn into the dark wood, the soldiers led by a sinister and hooded figure who shows himself as Death; and, helpless and horrified, we witness the burning of a witch. "What does she see? Can you tell me?" The Squire pleads with Antonius Block, his Lord and Knight, lately returned from the Crusades; a good and honorable man who, alas, not knowing either, remains throughout her sufferings likewise tormented by that which he cannot know, and cannot reconcile with what he does know. "You don't answer my question," the Squire persists. "Who watches over that child? Is it the angels, or God, or the Devil, or only the emptiness? Emptiness, my Lord!"

But the Knight cannot bear that it be so. And the Squire exhorts him to look again at her eyes, and there see the emptiness under the moon which they register. "We stand powerless," he tells him, "our arms hanging at our sides, because we see what she sees, and our terror and hers are the same. That poor little child," he bursts out. "I can't stand it, I can't stand it...." [88]

Earlier that same day we observe the Knight on his knees, attempting to pray before a small altar; the darkness meanwhile, cool and musty, lies all about him. Hearing a noise from the confessional, he goes toward the box; the face of Death is within but the Knight, unaware of who it is, kneels in silence, about to address the voice behind the grill:

> Knight: I want to talk to you as openly as I can, but my heart is empty.
> Death doesn't answer.
> Knight: The emptiness is a mirror turned toward my own face. I see myself in it, and I am filled with fear and disgust.
> Death doesn't answer.
> Knight: Through my indifference to my fellowmen, I have isolated myself from their company. Now I live in a world of phantoms. I am imprisoned in my dreams and fantasies.
> Death: And yet you don't want to die.
> Knight: Yes, I do.
> Death: What are you waiting for?
> Knight: I want knowledge.
> Death: You want guarantees?
> Knight: Call it whatever you like. Is it so cruelly inconceivable to grasp God with the senses? Why should he hide himself in a mist of half-spoken promises and unseen miracles?

Death doesn't answer.

Knight: What is going to happen to those of us who want to believe but aren't able to? And what is to become of those who neither want to nor are capable of believing?

The Knight stops and waits for a reply, but no one speaks or answers him. There is complete silence.

Knight: Why can't I kill God within me? Why does he live on in this painful and humiliating way even though I curse him and want to tear him out of my heart? Why, in spite of everything, is he a baffling reality that I can't shake off? Do you hear me?

Death: Yes, I hear you.

Knight: I want knowledge, not faith, not suppositions, but knowledge. I want God to stretch out his hand toward me, reveal himself and speak to me.

Death: But he remains silent.

Knight: I call out to him in the dark but no one seems to be there.

Death: Perhaps no one is there.

Knight: Then life is an outrageous horror. No one can live in the face of death, knowing that all is nothingness.

Death: Most people never reflect about either death or the futility of life.

Knight: But one day they will have to stand at that last moment of life and look toward the darkness.

Death: When *that* day comes...[89]

And when, finally, at film's end, Death does come, he comes to claim them all: Knight, Squire, and those others whose appointed hour has struck. "From our darkness, we call out to Thee, Lord," cries the Knight, his anguished face hidden in his hands. "Have mercy on us because we are small and frightened and ignorant." But the Squire, of course, will suffer none of this pious pleading and his voice, full of bitterness and scorn, cries out: "In the darkness where You are supposed to be, where all of us probably are.... In the darkness You will find no one to listen to Your cries or be touched by Your sufferings. Wash Your tears and mirror Yourself in Your indifference." It is a speech of sheer blasphemous dismissal, of the sort one is inclined to attribute to the damned, fraught with an eternity of spite. How different it sounds from that note of sustained, almost desperate poignancy with which the Knight implores salvation for himself and those whom he loves. "God," he pleads, "You who are somewhere, who *must* be somewhere, have mercy upon us."[90]

But why *must* he have mercy upon us? Because, in our fear, we fashion an image and call *that* God? It is hardly enough, is it, in establishing his existence, that we merely wish him to be? "For we mortals are hedged about by feelings of dread and awe because we are spectators of multiform phenomena in earth and sky to which we are unable to assign

WHY NOT DESPAIR ?

visible and comprehensible causes and for whose explanation we have recourse to some concept of deity."[91] To move from the optative to the declarative mood is just that, a mood; it is not a metaphysical demonstration, as the argument from Lucretius indicates, spoken in accents of high pagan melancholy amid the twilight of the ancient world. Lucretius did not shrink before the fact of all that lay at the end of noble human striving—namely death, horror and nothingness—why then should we? If nothing can come from nothing, to sound the keynote of Lucretian gloom, then everything is destined for extinction. And to believe otherwise on the ground of some vain human hope, or out of fear before the void, amounts to an epistemological stolen base. Thus having forfeited the game, we find ourselves back where we started from. Who then can resist on the strength of the Squire's scorn—silenced in the end, yes, but only under protest—the inner logic and dynamism of despair? The nightmare conviction that life and faith are all false, dead-ends from which no man may turn because all life runs just that way right from the beginning?[92]

In other words, God is simply dead, and his name, I Am Who Am, delivered out of a burning bush to some hallucinating Hebrew on a mountaintop long ago—to wit, the Book of Exodus 3:1-15—was merely a lie meant to assuage his people's thirst for assurance while traversing a desert. He didn't appear then, and he hasn't appeared since.[93]

Under the circumstances, the only explanation for the terrible silence of heaven across the centuries of human suffering is the nihilist one, that it is simply empty. Thus to bleat on and on with noble sounding pathos the cry, "God, You who are somewhere, who *must* be somewhere, have mercy upon us," is no better than sifting through the entrails of dead animals in search of solutions to the riddle of the cosmos. "... Superstition, like belief, must die," murmurs the anonymous "Church-goer" in Philip Larkin's poem, who wanders idly about the cavernous interior of empty churches,

> Wondering what to look for; wondering, too,
> When churches fall completely out of use
> What we shall turn them into...
> And what remains when disbelief has gone?

he asks. Only

> Grass, weedy pavement, brambles, buttress, sky...

And having no place to go when you die.[94]

"Faith is a torment," the Knight tells the condemned child, "did you know that? It is like loving someone who is out there in the darkness but never appears, no matter how loudly you call."[95] Faith is like the cry of the dying nun at the center of Hopkins' immortal "Wreck of the Deutschland," the tall frail Franciscan destined to perish alongside her exiled companions (driven from Germany by the Falk laws of 1874, their ship capsizes off the English coast), calling loudly and often, "O Christ, come quickly!"[96] But he does not come. Or even the poet himself, recording in one of his "terrible sonnets" the grief felt in the wake of his Beloved's forsaking him:

> cries like dead letters sent
> To dearest him that lives alas! away.[97]

We are all forsaken (to continue the rhetoric of despair) because, finally, there is no one anywhere on whom we can call or depend. Or, if there be Someone somewhere, the essential *apatheia* of his being radically precludes the least interest in or regard for our own; so much finite and limited being outside his own infinite and self-perfected Being. As that which is purely perfect, what have we to offer him? Our poverty? Why should One perfectly fulfilled in Himself have need of anything or anyone? Certainly he cannot have the least need of our friendship or love. "Friendship occurs," says Aristotle, "where love is offered in return. But in friendship with God there is no room for love to be offered in return, indeed there is not even room for love. For it would be absurd if anyone were to assert that he loved Zeus."[98] Is it not unseemly, then, to speak of God as one's *dearest*? One is reminded of the unnamed lay assistant in the Orthodox Church whose tragic end Whittaker Chambers recounts in one of his letters.[99] About to be arrested and shot by Marshall Tito, he pens the following note to his wife before hanging himself: "I have gone to remind God of a world he has forgotten. This is our reality."[100] Indeed it is, on the basis of the shrill notes of despair sounded throughout this chapter. Which is to say, there is either no God to go to at all, or, already blissfully aware of all that he's forgotten, it becomes perfectly pointless for anyone to want to go to him.

Again, how tempting the whole business of despair becomes. Why not succumb, handing over all one's innate optimism about the goodness of being, abdicating altogether the common wisdom concerning their sheer convertibility, i.e., that goodness is and that it is good to be? Why should a man exult, say, with St. Augustine, who first framed the proposition which has since shaped the patrimony of Western Christian culture, that "Because He is good, we are, and inasmuch as He is, we are good"? Not to mention that entire *ecstatic* culture raised up as a result of men free to rejoice over so many gifts they could never themselves have given?[101]

There is nothing to rejoice over, goes the argument rooted in nihilist despair, Belsen and Buchenwald, Auschwitz and Dachau prove that. See, it is said, these places of death cancel out at once all our facile, unearned, Pickwickian optimism about the universe. How could life ever be conceived in terms other than those of an obscene joke told at the expense of the living.[102] "Don't let yourself be fooled with illusions," the young Elie Wiesel is admonished in the Death Camp by the faceless neighbor when they hear the sound of distant guns:

> "Hitler has made it very clear that he will annihilate all the Jews before the clock strikes twelve, before they can hear the last stroke." I burst out: "What does it matter to you? Do we have to regard Hitler as a prophet?"
>
> His glazed, faded eyes looked at me. At last he said in a weary voice: "I've got more faith in Hitler than in anyone else. He's the only one who's kept his promises, all his promises, to the Jewish people."[103]

The Witness of Elie Wiesel: Seeing Wickedness Beyond Words

"From the depths of the mirror," notes child-protagonist Elie Wiesel, "a corpse gazed back at me. The look in his eyes, as they stared into mine, has never left me."[104] We have come to the bitter end of *Night*, a searing and unforgettable memoir forged out of the fires of this century's Holocaust; its message put into words by one extremely wary of words, of the terrible ease with which men have prostituted their use. (Words, he would say years later, are like whores: they give themselves to anyone.) So, properly suspicious of them, Wiesel waits ten long years before committing his own to the creation of *Night*.[105]

The corpse staring at him out of the depths is, of course, his own, as blank and silent a thing to behold as the God whose countenance he once longed to look upon. But no longer:

> My eyes were open and I was alone—terribly alone in a world without God and without man. Without love or mercy. I had ceased to be anything but ashes....[106]

Without doubt the single most shattering narrative to emerge from the experience of the Holocaust, the book recounts the whole terrible ordeal of capture, torture, and death which overtakes Wiesel's family, hellishly trapped in the nightmare world of a Nazi concentration camp. Scarcely a child himself at the time, he must watch in mute horror while his mother and sister are led away to die, their corpses consumed in gas ovens. He is then forced to witness, day by day, the slow degradation of his own father, a process which culminates in a death described so over-poweringly that it is almost too painful to read. "Listen to me, boy," the child is brutally told while attempting to revive his stricken father. "Don't forget that you're in a concentration camp. Here, every man has to fight for himself and not think of anyone else. Even of his father. Here, there are no fathers, no brothers, no friends. Everyone lives and dies for himself alone. I'll give you a sound piece of advice—don't give your ration of bread and soup to your old father. There's nothing you can do for him. And you're killing yourself. Instead, you ought to be having his ration."[107] But Wiesel offers the ration anyway; only, of course, it is too late; his father has died.

Will there be prayers at his grave? No, there will be no prayers offered up, nor candles lit to his memory. "His last word was my name. A summons, to which I did not respond. I did not weep, and it pained me that I could not weep. But I had no more tears."[108]

But there will be no forgetting either. Not this child who, at age twelve, had believed so simply, so deeply; studying by day the Talmud, while at night running off to the synagogue to weep over the ruin of the Temple. An entire boyhood spent in ardent, unceasing pursuit of God; in fasting so that the Messiah's long expected arrival might somehow be quickened. This same child who, en route to Auschwitz, a name no one had ever heard of, will discover for the first time that "the world was a cattle wagon hermetically sealed." So many Jews crammed into one car! "There are eighty of you in the wagon," barked the German officer. "If anyone is missing, you'll all be shot, like dogs...."[109] No, there can be no forgetting any of this:

> Never shall I forget that night, the first night in camp, which has turned my life into one long night, seven times cursed and seven times sealed. Never shall I forget that smoke. Never shall I forget the little faces of the children, whose bodies I saw turned into wreaths of smoke beneath a silent blue sky.
> Never shall I forget those flames which consumed my faith forever.
> Never shall I forget that nocturnal silence which deprived me, for all eternity, of the desire to live. Never shall I forget those moments which murdered my God and my soul and turned my dreams to dust. Never shall I forget these things, even if I am condemned to live as long as God himself. Never.[110]

There are numberless nights besides this, their horrors all duly recorded; but there is none like the death of the "sad-eyed angel" whose story lies at the heart of *Night*. A quintessential innocent, a child hardly a day older than Wiesel himself, he has been singled out by the Gestapo and, for reasons horrifyingly capricious, sentenced to die by hanging; the entire camp, meanwhile, has been conscripted to witness this unspeakable iniquity. It will be from the memory of this event, this singular murder of innocence, that Wiesel will not ever be allowed to escape. This, above everything else, will leave him permanently, metaphysically bereft.

On the morning set for the child's death, the "sad-eyed angel" is brought before the camp and, at once, it becomes evident to all that he will not die quickly, for the child is far too light for mere rope to do its work well. And while he dangles horribly in front of the whole camp, Wiesel hears a man call out, "Where is God? Where is God now?" Thirty minutes later, the grisly business at last at an end, the prisoners silently file by the corpse. Again, Elie Wiesel hears the cry, "Where is God?" Only now he hears himself answer in a whisper which none can overhear, "Here he is, here is God."[111]

The theology to which Wiesel's equation points, like the memoir itself which surrounds and encases it, is a deeply shocking one, to wit, that both God and the child at the end of the rope are dead. Indeed, their fates literally fit into the same noose. In other words, there cannot be a shred of hope to be found in these two corpses conjoined at the end of a rope; to suppose otherwise is to falsify Wiesel's whole argument that God and man perished together in the Holocaust. Talk of deepening the literal level in order that it somehow mysteriously yield up an imagined anagogical deliverance by way of the fourfold method of medieval exegesis is sheer theological legerdemain; it is, moreover, exactly the sort of "magical" exegesis which, Wiesel would argue, his books are not about to indulge. Professor Fackenheim, too, who recounts the hanging episode in his own text (*God's Presence in History: Jewish Affirmations and Philosophical Reflections*, New York: New York University Press, 1970, p. 75), is positively ferocious in his defiant refusal to read a scintilla of redemption into the scene. For that to happen, he says, "A Jew, in short, would have to become a Christian. But never in the two thousand years of Jewish-Christian confrontation has it been less possible for a Jew to abandon either his Jewishness or his Judaism and embrace Christianity."[112]

Not long after (to continue the narrative of Elie Wiesel's *Night*), we come to the eve of Rosh Ha-shanah, the last night of the Hebrew year, lived out in an accursed time and place. Thousands of Jews have gathered in silence for the evening meal, their faces completely stricken. And yet, recalls Wiesel, "the whole camp was electric with the tension which was in all our hearts. In spite of everything, this day was different from any other. The last day of the year. The word 'last' rang very strangely. What if it were indeed the last day?" But, of course, it will be no different from all the rest, all the other days and nights of ceaseless torture, degradation, and death.

> "What are You, my God," I thought angrily, "compared to this afflicted crowd, proclaiming to You their faith, their anger, their revolt? What does Your greatness mean, Lord of the Universe, in the face of all this weakness, this decomposition, and this decay? Why do You still trouble their sick minds, their crippled bodies?"[113]

Suddenly, however, the night air is strangely rent with the exultant cry of so many thousands of voices, Jewish men lifting their stout hearts to heaven, and to God. "Blessed be the Name of the Eternal!" is the inexplicable cry which these wretched souls raise aloft to God.

> Why, but why should I bless Him? In every fiber I rebelled. Because He had had thousands of children burned in His pits? Because He kept six crematories working night and day, on Sundays and feast days? Because in His great might He had created Auschwitz, Birkenau, Buna, and so many factories of death? How could I say to Him: "Blessed art Thou, Eternal Master of the Universe, who chose us from among the races to be tortured day and night, to see our fathers, our mothers, our brothers, end in the crematory. Praised be Thy Holy Name, Thou who hast chosen us to be butchered on Thine altar"?[114]

Notwithstanding every nihilist objection which mounts relentlessly within Wiesel's throat, each bitter bead told against a silent, unseeing God, still the idiot praise of the Almighty continues. Amid so many tears and sighs, despite programmatic tortures of every sort to dispossess human beings of their dignity, their lives, an entire camp world will be at worship this last day of the year. For, in spite of all, this night was indeed different from any other. "All the earth and the universe are God's," they cry. Wiesel, meanwhile, the rhapsodic melody choking in his throat, thinks bitterly to himself:

> "Yes, man is very strong, greater than God. When You were deceived by Adam and Eve, You drove them out of Paradise. When Noah's generation displeased You, You brought down the Flood. When Sodom no longer found favor in Your eyes, You made the sky rain down fire and sulphur. But these men here, whom You have betrayed, whom You have allowed to be tortured, butchered, gassed, burned, what do they do? They pray before You! They praise Your name!"
>
> "All creation bears witness to the Greatness of God!"
>
> Once, New Year's Day had dominated my life. I knew that my sins grieved the Eternal; I implored His forgiveness. Once, I had believed pro-

foundly that upon one solitary deed of mine, one solitary prayer, depended the salvation of the world.

    This day I had ceased to plead. I was no longer capable of lamentation. On the contrary, I felt very strong. I was the accuser, God the accused. My eyes were open and I was alone—terribly alone in a world without God and without man. Without love or mercy. I had ceased to be anything but ashes, yet I felt myself to be stronger than the Almighty, to whom my life had been tied for so long. I stood amid that praying congregation, observing it like a stranger.[115]

How—the question persists—is it possible for anyone to give an adequate response to places like Auschwitz, Birkenau. Buna...and so many other factories of death scattered across Europe? Is not the Holocaust, in its sheer unspeakability as event, beyond the reach of words, of art, of imagery, even of faith? And if so, does not the very aesthetic or religious undertaking to explain the event reduce to triviality the sufferings of those who were forced to endure it? In a moving piece Wiesel wrote for *The New York Times* several years ago, reacting adversely to yet another cinematic treatment of the Holocaust (*Sophie's Choice*, as it happens, based on William Styron's novel), he asks that very question. And answers: "Between the dead and the rest of us there exists an abyss that no talent can comprehend." The Holocaust demands, at the very least, an admission of honesty, he says. "Since we are incapable of revealing the Event, why not admit it. And so the admission itself becomes an integral part of testimony. This is what I have been doing in my own work. I write to denounce writing. I tell of the impossibility one stumbles upon in trying to tell the tale. I need only to close my eyes for my words to desert me, repudiate me." And speaking of the survivors, those who alone "know what it meant to be in Auschwitz," he confesses that, even here, "What we really wish to say, what we feel we must say cannot be said." The essay concludes with deep poignancy:

> We read, we laugh, we drink our wine, we enjoy music and literature, and yet, there is always this strange feeling that accompanies us: the feeling of some final, irreplaceable loss.[116]

Conclusion

In his acute study of *The Liberal Imagination*, literary critic Lionel Trilling notes: "Before what we now know the mind stops; the great psychological fact of our time, which we all observe with baffled wonder and shame, is that there is no possible way of responding to Belsen and Buchenwald."[117] What words, what forms of the imagination, could possibly encompass these events? It is precisely *The Holocaust As Interruption* of all else that we need to understand.[118] An experience so crushing, so cosmic in its oppressiveness, so singularly and hellishly distinct, that it quite reduces all of humankind to silence. "At Auschwitz, did the grave win the victory after all, or, worse than the grave, did the devil himself win?"[119] For if the devil having had the last decisive word, God himself is silent before such a cry of anguish thrown up by his own People, the very Children of his Heart—whose promise of an eternally steadfast love is the absolute rock of Israeli identity[120]—can any of us dare to be other than silent as well? Silent, that is, out of sheer shame at God's own prior and persisting silence?

NOTES

1. Hans Urs von Balthasar, "The Last Five Stations of the Cross," *Theologians Today*, selected and edited by Martin Redfern, (London and New York: Sheed and Ward, 1972).

2. Kenneth Clark, *Civilisation: A Personal View*, (British Broadcasting Corporation and John Murray, 1969).

3. *Ibid.*, p. 347.

4. Cited by Mary Knutsen, "The Holocaust in Theology and Philosophy: The Question of Truth," *Concilium: The Holocaust As Interruption*, ed. by Elisabeth Schussler Fiorenza and David Tracy, (Edinburgh: T&T Clark, 1984), p. 68.

5. Irving Greenberg, "Judaism and Christianity After the Holocaust," *Journal of Ecumenical Studies*, Special Issue on "Jews and Christians in Dialogue," vol. 12, no. 4 (Fall, 1975), pp. 522-523.

6. "One thing is certain," writes von Balthasar, "the continued existence of Israel...has a *meaning*. It lies, as always, in the unbreakable correspondence between promise and fulfillment with God." See his *Martin Buber and Christianity: A Dialogue Between Israel and the Church*, (New York: Macmillan, 1961), pp. 93-94. But what is to ensure the continued existence of Israel as such, never mind its meaning? And what becomes of this putatively unbreakable bond when there is no People to give it force at this end? This explains Eichmann's boast, "I laugh when I jump into the grave because of the feeling I have killed five million Jews." (Quoted by Greenberg [see above n. 5], p. 523.) Here is the very point of mounting a "Final Solution," as a result of which the enemies of Jewry are entitled to that derisive laughter, there being no Jews left to kill.

7. Bruno Bettelheim, *Encounter*, (December, 1978). Quoted by Alan Ecclestone, *The Night Sky of the Lord*, (London: Darton, Longman and Todd, 1980), p. 7.

8. "Lest this horrifying word 'Auschwitz' lose its historical concreteness, and with it, its horror, let us start by *stating the reality* it symbolises as baldly as possible: the systematic torture and murder of millions upon millions of Jewish children, women and men has in fact occurred, carried out with relentless sin-

gleness of purpose, with the active or tacit complicity of untold thousands and the silence of the whole world, in the heart of the cultural, social and historical reality which is broadly Christian, European civilisation. In every country of Hitler's Europe, with the sole exceptions of Denmark and Finland, millions of human beings, from infants to the aged, were hunted down, often physically tortured, and killed, whose sole crime was that, as 'racially' defined Jews, they were still human beings, and alive," Mary Knutsen (see above, n. 4), p. 68.

9. T.S. Eliot, "The Waste Land," lines 62 and 63, from the *Selected Poems,* (London: Faber, 1954).

10. Barbara Tuchman, "The Final Solution," *Practicing History,* (New York: Knopf, 1981), pp. 118-119. Apropos the soul of man in the twentieth century, see her Address to the American Historical Association in December of 1966 in which the following progress report was issued: "Man in the twentieth century is not a creature to be envied. Formerly he believed himself created by the divine spark. Now, bereft of that proud confidence, and contemplating his recent record and present problems, he can no longer, like the Psalmist, respect himself as 'a little lower than the angels.' He cannot picture himself today, as Michelangelo did on the Sistine ceiling, in the calm and noble image of Adam receiving the spark from the finger of God. Overtaken by doubt of human purpose and divine purpose, he doubts his capacity to be good or even to survive. He has lost certainty, including moral and ethical certainty, and is left with a sense of footloose purposelessness and self-disgust which literature naturally reflects," pp. 52-53.

11. François Mauriac, Foreword to Elie Wiesel's *Night,* (New York: Avon, 1958), pp. 7-8. Again, see Tuchman's Address for a historian's confirmation of the artist's foreboding about our own century, particularly 1914, that watershed mark in its tragic unfolding. She notes how "the historical experience of the twentieth century has been since the First World War one of man's cumulative disillusionments in himself. The idea of progress was the greatest casualty of that war, and its aftermath was cynicism, confirmed by a second round of world conflict and by the implications of the Nazis' gas chambers," p. 52.

12. Randall Jarrell, "On the Underside of the Stone," *New York Times Book Review,* August 23, 1953. Warren's book, comments Jarrell, "is written out of an awful time, about an awful, a traumatic subject: sin, Original Sin, without any Savior...it wasn't happiness Warren was in pursuit of, but the knowledge of Good and Evil." The essay, among others of his written between 1935 and his death in 1964, appears in *Kipling, Auden & Co,* (New York: Farrar, Straus and Giroux, 1980), p. 177.

13. William Shakespeare, *King Lear,* Act IV, Scene 1. Shakespeare's play is powerfully illustrative of our theme, both in the predicament of Gloucester, "a plain man whose tongue's prose can not save him from descent into dumb-animal agony when his eyes are gouged out by Cornwall and he stumbles on in full knowledge of his injustice to Edgar (his son)"; and in the excruciating sorrow and death of its king, Lear, a man literally uprooted from every living thing. "And when he is convinced of his homelessness in either daughter's castle, he is ready for the final irony of his desire to go homeless among the elements. The

ruined king will become a ruined piece of nature too. Hamlet had been isolated in the society of Elsinore, but the King of Britain must be as naked in the universe as he is destitute of human love. The great wheel of Fortune...must grow for Lear into a wheel of fire that turns with him down into a hell of his own making," Mark Van Doren, *Shakespeare*, (New York: Doubleday, 1939), p. 205; pp. 210-211.

14. George Steiner, *The Death of Tragedy*, (New York: Knopf, 1963), p. 5.

15. William Shakespeare, *Macbeth*, Act V, Scene 5. The speech follows directly upon the news of Lady Macbeth's end, to which he remains entirely insensible having for too long "supped full with horrors."

16. Well, certainly as much anyhow. It is one thing to say with the sainted Teresa of Avila that life is like a night in a second-class hotel—that's stark Christian realism—something else again to hold that the accommodations get no better when you die. Legend declares that the stones of Avila where St. Teresa lived are the tears Christ shed over the poverty of the plains and mountains of the land of castles. But those who see only the stones, and a lifetime's purposeless drudgery in working a barren land, are, as a practical matter, more kindred with Lucretius, who held it as *his* working principle "that nothing whatever is produced from nothing by agency of the divine under any circumstances" (I.148ff., *On the Nature of the Universe*), than with Christianity.

17. "The *Iliad* is the primer of tragic art. In it are set forth the motifs and images around which the sense of the tragic has crystallized during nearly three thousand years of western poetry: the shortness of heroic life, the exposure of man to the murderousness and caprice of the inhuman, the fall of the City...the fall of Troy is the first great metaphor of tragedy.... The Homeric warrior knows that he can neither comprehend nor master the workings of destiny. Patroclus is slain, and the wretch Thersites sails safely for home. Call for Justice or explanation, and the sea will thunder back with its mute clamour. Men's accounts with the gods do not balance," Steiner, pp. 5-6.

18. Quoted by Professor Glenn Arbery, University of Dallas, *The Terrain of Comedy*, ed. with an Introduction by Louise Cowan (The Pegasus Foundation: The Dallas Institute of Humanities and Culture, 1984), p. 19. The example of typical Homeric horror cited by Lewis is the following from Book 8 of *The Odyssey*:

> As a woman throws herself weeping over her warrior husband, who fell fighting before his city and people...she sees him dying and gasping for breath and embraces his body keening loudly, while the enemy behind strike her on back and shoulders with their spears and lead her off into slavery to bear hard work and sorrow...(8. 523-527).

"This is a mere simile," Lewis remarks, "the sort of thing that happens every day."

19. "Tragic drama tells us that the spheres of reason, order, and justice are terribly limited and that no progress in our science or technical resources will enlarge their relevance," Steiner, pp. 8-9.

20. Quoted by Mary Gerhart in *Concilium: The Holocaust As Interruption*, p. 76. "In this century," her own article—"Holocaust Writings: A Literary Genre?"—begins, "there has been no greater challenge to the conventional understanding of literary genre than that brought to bear by Holocaust literature...(which) confronts and subverts our ordinary assumptions about the relationships between literature and history, literature and life, and the act of reading itself.... Not only in diverse forms, but as a body of texts, the literature of the Holocaust challenges the very assumptions of literature in general," pp. 75 and 77.

21. Gerhart, p. 78.

22. See, for example, Jewish writer Cynthia Ozick's three imperatives in writing about the Holocaust, as quoted by the editors of *Concilium: The Holocaust As Interruption*, pp. 85-86. "First, that it has no analogies, second that it is not a metaphor or 'like' anything else and, third, that it is not to be 'used' but only to be 'understood'. It generates 'lessons' to be learned or 'legacies' to be lived but it must not be 'used' in a partisan argument or polemical debate." However, if Elie Wiesel is to be believed, whom the editors warmly approve, "All (the writer) can possibly hope to achieve is to communicate the impossibility of communication," p. 7. What does that in effect leave for the writer to write, for the artist to render?

23. George Steiner, *Language and Silence*, (London: Faber, 1967), p. ix.

24. *Ibid.*, pp. 4-5.

25. *Ibid.*, p. ix.

26. T.S. Eliot, "Gerontion," *Selected Poems*, (London: Faber, 1954), p. 32.

27. Irving Howe, "Writing and the Holocaust," *The New Republic*, October 27, 1986, p. 28.

28. Steiner, p. ix.

29. *Ibid.*, p. 5.

30. "Christmas and Easter can be subjects for poetry," believed Auden, "but Good Friday, like Auschwitz, cannot." Quoted by William Styron in "Hell Reconsidered," *This Quiet Dust: And Other Writings*, (London: Jonathan Cape, 1983), p. 96.

31. Susan Shapiro, "Hearing the Testimony of Radical Negation," *Concilium: The Holocaust As Interruption*, pp. 3-4.

32. Quoted by Michael Schwartz, "Are Christians Responsible?" *National Review*, August 8, 1980, p. 956. For a fuller development of Littell's position, see his *The Crucifixion of the Jews*, (New York: Harper & Row, 1975), pp. 2 and 17. "The cornerstone of Christian Anti-Semitism," he writes, "is the superseding or displacement myth, which already rings with the genocidal note. This is the myth that the mission of the Jewish people was finished with the coming of Jesus Christ, that 'the Old Israel' was written off with the appearance of 'the New Israel.' To teach that a people's mission in God's providence is finished, that they have been relegated to the limbo of history, has murderous implications which murderers will in time spell out. The murder of six million Jews by baptized Christians, from whom membership in good standing was not (and has not been) withdrawn, raises the most insistent question about the credibility of Christianity.... Was Jesus a false messiah? No one can be a true messiah whose

followers feel compelled to torture and destroy other human persons who think differently."

33. Quoted by Norman Ravitch, "The Problem of Christian Anti-Semitism," *Commentary*, April, 1982, p. 46. Interestingly enough, Vatican Council II, in its lengthy Pastoral Constitution on The Church in the Modern World, proposes the most rigorous sort of Christian examination of conscience concerning the extent to which the Catholic faithful, by their own lives and distorted expression of the gospel, bear a certain amount of responsibility for the actual spread of an atheism which, not finding the face of God among them, forlornly concludes that God does not exist. See, for example, the final lines of paragraph 19, in which, among the origins of modern atheism is the following: "...a critical reaction against...the Christian religion in particular. Believers can thus have more than a little to do with the rise of atheism. To the extent that they are careless about their instruction in the faith, or present its teaching falsely, or even fail in their religious, moral, or social life, they must be said to conceal rather than to reveal the true nature of God and of religion."

34. See John X. Evans, "After the Holocaust: What Then Are We To Do?" *Center Journal*, Winter, 1984, pp. 75-98.

35. "The holy man is not sick because his sickness sickens him," says Lao-tzu. "Therefore he is not sick." See Josef Pieper, *In Tune with the World: A Theory of Festivity*, (Chicago: Franciscan Herald Press. 1973), p. 74.

36. Paul Van Buren, "The Status and Prospects for Theology," *CCI Notebook* 24, November 1974, p. 3.

37. Gregory Baum, *Anti-Semitism and the Foundations of Christianity*, ed. by Alan Davies, (New York: Paulist Press, 1979), p. 142.

38. Rosemary Reuther, *Faith and Fratricide: The Theological Roots of Anti-Semitism*, (New York: Seabury Press, 1979), pp. 15-16.

39. In other words, she unqualifiedly affirms that "what Christianity has in Jesus is not the Messiah, but a Jew who hoped for the kingdom of God and who died in that hope." Quoted by Fr. Pawlikowski in his book *Christ in the Light of the Christian-Jewish Dialogue*, (New York: Paulist Press, 1982), p. 26. And, what is more to the point, Fr. Pawlikowski would appear to agree. Early on (p. 3), he confesses to his growing conviction as a result of years spent in the dialogue, "that no lasting resolution of the historic Christian-Jewish tension is possible unless the Church is ready to significantly rethink its traditional interpretation of Christology. Rosemary Ruether's writings, especially her volume *Faith and Fratricide*, have brought the issue to a head for me...." It is difficult to resist the conclusion here that, in a word, Jesus is not the Christ. Is this the direction the 'dialogue theologians' would drive us to in their solution to the centuries-old split between Judaism and Christianity? And if so what becomes of the substance of hope then?

40. Cited by Pawlikowski in his text, p. 27.

41. "Thus, G.E. Moore had ceased to be a Christian simply from what he heard his elder brother say at table; Leonard Woolf, so he tells us, gave up God because He was not of much use if He did not produce rain when it was asked

for...." Quoted by Penelope Fitzgerald in her biography of *The Knox Brothers*, p. 72. She cites the case of Dilly Knox who, unlike most of his contemporaries at Cambridge, endured a great and protracted agony of loss over the disappearance of faith. The poet Houseman's prediction that all exact knowledge "pushes back the frontiers of the dark," thus consoling mankind for its discovery that "man does not come from the high lineage he fancied, nor will inherit the vast estate he looked for," proved scant consolation for him. But by his second year at Cambridge he'd thrown it all over. "In the Lent term of 1906," Mrs. Fitzgerald notes, "Dean Inge, who had himself been a Fellow of King's and was the most intelligent preacher that the Church could put into the field, had been asked to speak in chapel on the errors of intellectualism. The Dean appealed for a working faith, 'in fact, if not in name, Christian', evidently he was prepared to settle for this, but he failed to move the rationalists of King's," pp. 94-95. Surely we need to settle for a lot more than mere "muscular Christianity" in meeting the crisis of our century. That or we simply settle for nothing at all, that "vast estate" (i.e., Paradise) not impinging on our own vale of tears because it does not exist at all.

42. Quoted by Alec Guinness, who in fact was the alleged convert, in his memoir *Blessings in Disguise*, p. 99. Speaking of Cockerell, he says, "He enjoyed the derisions of his period, class, attainments and scholarship; blinkering himself, as so many of us do—but his generation particularly—with the worship of art and science and the hope of social change." Yet even such accomplishments as art, science and secular hope routinely serve up, "even the atheism for which this world is everything suffers shipwreck on the reef of suffering," writes Walter Kasper, *The God of Jesus Christ*, (London: SCM Press, 1983), p. 161. He then quotes Moltmann's telling comment: "For even the abolition of God does not explain suffering and does not assuage pain. The person who cries out in pain over suffering has his own dignity, which no atheism can rob him of." *The Crucified God: The Cross of Christ as the Foundation and Criticism of Christian Theology*, (London: SCM Press, 1974), p. 48.

43. Albert Camus, *The Myth of Sisyphus and Other Essays*, (London and New York, 1955), p. 42.

44. C.S. Lewis, *The Problem of Pain*, (London: Collins, 1940), p. 14.

45. See his essay on "The Innocence of God," in *A Maritain Reader*, edited with an Introduction by Donald and Idella Gallagher, (New York: Image, 1966), p. 124. On the following page Jacques Maritain quotes Lautreamont, who insisted at the end of his life, in violent retractation of his previous errors, that, "If one recollects the truth from which all other truths flow, *the absolute goodness of God and His absolute ignorance of evil*, the sophisms collapse of themselves. We do not have the right to interrogate the Creator about anything whatsoever," p. 125. Maritain corrects this to the extent that, yes, God is ignorant of evil but not absolutely speaking since He knows it, "and he knows it perfectly, *through the good* of which evil is the privation.... But God does not have the *idea* or the invention of evil. There is in God, as St. Thomas Aquinas teaches, no *idea*, no intelligible matrix of evil." Later on, it remains to be seen just how the knowl-

edge of evil, understood through the Incarnate Word's free assumption of human nature, permits his very mind and soul to be seared through and through by that fearful knowledge.

46. Kasper, *The God of Jesus Christ*, p. 159. He continues on the following page with how the impact of suffering has changed the whole nature of the theological enterprise. "Whereas modern theology's partner in dialogue used to be the enlightened unbeliever, the partner in dialogue of any contemporary theology is suffering man who has concrete experience of the persisting situation of disaster...all these experiences of suffering are not peripheral and residual aspects of existence, not the shadow side of human life, as it were; rather, they characterize the human condition as such.... A theology that taxes the human experience of suffering as its starting point starts, therefore, not with a borderline phenomenon but with the center and depths of human existence," p. 160.

47. See his essay "God in the Dock," *Undeceptions: Essays on Theology and Ethics*, edited by Walter Hooper, (London: Geoffrey Bles, 1971), p. 197.

48. Hyam Maccoby, "Theologian of the Holocaust," *Commentary*, December 1982, p. 37.

49. And it is surely crucial that we not lose sight of what is meant by so many "brush strokes of iniquity," i.e., that we not blink before the consequences of this radical pessimism which threatens to overturn the very foundations of that Christian metaphysic which sees being as a thing precisely "blessed." "To have joy in anything," writes Josef Pieper, quoting Nietzsche, "one must approve of everything." In other words, one must be willing to extend an absolute universal affirmation to the entire world, whose very being has been adjudged good. "And as the radical nature of negation deepens," continues Pieper, "and consequently as anything but ultimate arguments become ineffectual, it becomes more necessary to refer to this ultimate foundation...that, to reduce it to the most concise phrase, at bottom *everything that is, is good, and it is good to exist*.... Such affirmation is not won by deliberately shutting one's eyes to the horrors in this world. Rather, it proves its seriousness by its confrontation with historical evil. The quality of this assent is such that we must attribute it even to martyrs, at the very moment, perhaps, that they perish under brutal assault," *In Tune with the World*, pp. 20-21.

And in a subsequent chapter, he sharpens the observation, applying it precisely to the question which Fackenheim, among others, is wrestling with: "I really do not know how an incorruptible mind, faced with the evil in the world, could keep from utter despair were it not for the logically tenable conviction that there is a divinely guaranteed Goodness of being which no amount of mischief can undermine. But that *is* the point of view of the man who sees the world as *creatura*—not to speak of the believer who is confident of a salvation that infinitely surpasses all creature goodness. Perhaps it is only thanks to such superempirical certainties that man is able to assume the intellectually and existentially extremely demanding task of facing naked reality without resorting to the evasions either of euphemism or of slander.... What counts is truth. And might it not be the truth that the man who despairs, he in particular, has 'not yet received' certain 'tidings'?" p. 62.

50. Emil Fackenheim, "Jewish Faith and the Holocaust," *Commentary*, August 1968. Here Professor Fackenheim launched his celebrated warhead regarding the Jewish apostolate after Auschwitz. In a subsequent study, *God's Presence in History*, (New York: Harper Torchbooks, 1970), he reaffirmed his thesis that Auschwitz presents no salvific meaning at all but rather accosts the Jewish community with its 614th commandment that it survive. Yet, interestingly enough, for Fackenheim, the stunning Israeli victory of 1967 seems to have been salvific, "a moment of truth—a wonder at a singled out, millennial existence which, after Auschwitz, is still possible and actual," p. 96.

51. And even were it possible to draw up an indictment against Almighty God, even to execute sentence upon him for the slaughter of innocents at Auschwitz, would suffering thereby cease to disfigure the face of human experience? It calls to mind André Malraux's experience at a Writers' Congress in Moscow in the 1930s where, after listening to interminable speeches extolling the happiness of the Brave New World which Socialism was even now ushering in, one brave and disaffected delegate stood up to ask, "And what about the child run over by the tramcar?" After what seemed like hours of stunned silence throughout the vast hall, someone replied, and the entire assembly applauded its prescience: "In a perfect, planned socialist transport system, there will be no accidents." The story may be apocryphal but the point it makes is surely not.

52. See Arthur Cohen, *The Tremendum: A Theological Interpretation of the Holocaust*, (New York, 1981). He describes the phenomenon in terms of "an inversion of the divine, a demonic 'subscendence' countervalent to divine transcendence.... The Jewish People has become in our century the first and unique exemplum of the demonic possibility of a radical freedom severed from all transcendent controls." From his essay, "In Our Terrible Age: The *Tremendum* of the Jews," *Concilium*, pp. 11-16.

53. Really, there is nothing else that a sane man can do about it. The same Arthur Cohen, some half-dozen years after reflecting at length on the culpability of the divine at Auschwitz—due to whose fundamental incapacity the unleashing of the "raw demonic" was permitted in the first instance—in a letter to *Commonweal*, October 24, 1986, replied to those who would allow Polish Carmelite nuns to construct a convent at Auschwitz in order for them to help expiate evils committed in Poland. "What will the Carmelite nuns pray for?" he asked. "A divine change of heart? One hopes so, but believes otherwise. If for the benighted Jews, if for the salvation of the dead in Christ, if for the ultimate vindication of the church, it would be for Jews a blasphemy. How much wiser and more charitable to leave this unhallowed ground unhallowed, unsanctified, unmanipulated by sectarian interest. Auschwitz cannot be redeemed even with prayer," p. 574.

54. William Styron, *This Quiet Dust: And Other Writings*, p. 303.

55. *Ibid.*, pp. 95-96.

56. Quoted in *Long Night's Journey Into Day: Life and Faith After the Holocaust* by A. Roy Eckardt, with Alice L. Eckardt and Foreword by Robert McAffee Brown, (Detroit: Wayne State University Press, 1982), pp. 58-59.

57. Cited by the Eckardts on p. 67. They go on to quote, a couple of pages later, Richard Rubenstein's despairing pronouncement that, "If the God of history does not exist, then the Cosmos is ultimately absurd in origin and meaningless in purpose.... I have elected to accept what Camus has rightly called the courage of the absurd, the courage to live in a meaningless, purposeless Cosmos rather than believe in a God who inflicts Auschwitz on his people." Rubenstein goes on to make the point dogmatic, to wit, "God really died at Auschwitz...that nothing in human choice, decision, value, or meaning can any longer have vertical reference to transcendent standards. We are alone in a silent, unfeeling Cosmos.... Morality and religion can no longer rest upon the conviction that divinely validated norms offer a measure against which what we do can be judged," pp. 69-70. And yet, notwithstanding the apparent despair of his position, the Eckardts quote approvingly Rubenstein's following conclusion: "We Jews have tasted the bitterest and most degrading of deaths. Yet death was not the last word.... Death in Europe was followed by resurrection in our ancestral home." Does Israeli possession of the land in fact compensate the Jews for all the horrors of the Death Camps? Is that in any way a commensurate exchange, one wonders?

58. "There is another reason," says Walter Kasper, "why the question of God and the question of suffering belong together. We would not be able to suffer ...unless we had an at least implicit pre-apprehension of an undamaged, happy, fulfilled kind of existence; unless we were at least implicitly looking for salvation and redemption. Only because we as human beings are meant for salvation do we suffer at our disastrous situation and rebel against it," *The God of Jesus Christ*, p. 160. Kasper goes on to suggest a transcendent point of reference which the existence of evil precisely illumines; a point Aquinas made "with unparalleled intellectual boldness, by reversing the thesis that evil is an argument against God and saying: *quia malum est Deus est* (because evil exists, God exists) (*Summa contra Gentiles* III, 71). For hope in the face of despair is possible only in the light of redemption. It would be futile to seek an absolute meaning without God," p. 161.

And, to be sure, any meaning pitched lower than God is doomed altogether; which is to say, any human security anchored to some sense of relative redemption alone, prescinded from the God of Jesus Christ, cannot sustain its own hope of survival. But more of that anon.

59. See his sublime treatment of the theme in his essay on "The Meaning of Contemporary Atheism," *A Maritain Reader*, especially pp. 112-117.

60. Here, Maritain tells us, is the first of those two axioms which "in their simplicity sovereignly command the whole question, and which we should inscribe on our walls...." *Deus nullo modo est causa peccati, neque directe, neque indirecte* says Thomas in his *Summa Theol.*, I-II, 79, 1. And the second, according to the Common Doctor, is that it is always in ourselves that there exists that absence of grace which leads to moral evil: *Defectus gratiae prima causa est ex*

nobis, Summa Theol., I-II, 112, 3, ad 2. As Maritain comments, "it is in the creature that the *initiative* and the *invention* of sin have their origin." Quoted in his essay on "The Innocence of God," p. 126.

61. "Since the time of Nietzsche, who called himself 'the destroyer par excellence' and who dreamed of a company of men who would be called 'destroyers'—for almost three generations, then, the idea of 'active nihilism,' of the 'will to nothingness' and 'pleasure even in destruction,' has been part of the modern attitude toward life. And when someone comments that a myth like that of the Twilight of the Gods, which implies the shattering of the created world, in our time no longer belongs solely to the realm of imagination, we can scarcely disagree," Pieper, p. 61.

62. Fyodor Dostoevsky, *The Brothers Karamazov*, (Great Books of the Western World, Robert Hutchins, ed., Chicago, London, Toronto: Encyclopedia Britannica, 1952), p. 126. See especially Ch. 4, "Rebellion," from Book V.

63. Albert Camus, *The Plague*, (New York: Random House, 1948), pp. 193, 195, 196-197.

64. Henry Adams, *The Education of Henry Adams: An Autobiography*, vol. II, (New York: Time, Inc., 1964).

65. And not only does Nature present an air of insouciant indifference before the sufferings of men. See, for example, W.H. Auden's poem, "Musée des Beaux Arts," which begins:

About suffering they were never wrong,
The Old Masters: how well they understood
Its human position; how it takes place
While someone else is eating or opening a window
    or just walking dully along; ...

They never forgot
That even the dreadful martyrdom must run its course
Anyhow in a corner, some untidy spot
Where the dogs go on with their doggy life and the torturer's horse
Scratches its innocent behind on a tree.

From *Modern Poetry*, edited by Maynard Mack, Leonard Dean, and William Frost, vol. VII, (New Jersey: Prentice-Hall, 1961), p. 198.

66. Adams, pp. 27-28.

67. "Person is the pure relation of being related, nothing else," comments Ratzinger on the Creed's usage of the name *Father*. "Only in being-for the other is he Father; in his own being-in-himself he is simply God.... In this idea of relativity in word and love, independent of the concept of substance and not to be classified among the 'accidents,' Christian thought discovered the kernel of the concept of person.... 'In God [says Augustine] there are no accidents, only substance and relation,' " *Introduction to Christianity*, (New York: Seabury Press, 1969), pp. 131-132.

68. See his "Cloud of Smoke, Pillar of Fire: Judaism, Christianity, and Modernity after the Holocaust," cited in Eva Fleischner, *Auschwitz: Beginning of a New*

Era? (New York: Ktav, n.d.), p. 23. Ivan's question is a hard one indeed and, on the face of things, Greenberg's "working principle" certainly does narrow the range of answers to that pinpoint of anguished despair which no amount of Christian hand-wringing over the Holocaust will remove. One either returns the ticket or...or what? Without going into the matter at length as it bears on the following two chapters, perhaps an entirely different perspective on the issue of man in the presence of evil (which for Greenberg is symbolized by burning children) is in order. See, for example, the extraordinary meditation by the French poet Charles Péguy on *The Mystery of the Holy Innocents*. Cornelio Fabro, in an illuminating text on Péguy, "Ch. Péguy: *Il Mistero Dei Santi Innocenti*," (Roma: Il Veltro: Rivista Della Civilta Italiana, 1986), has written that, far from inducing disbelief in a God who appears unable to rid the innocent of their sufferings, such disbelief as, for instance, men like Camus and the character Ivan settled into—Péguy managed to penetrate right into and through such horrors to find therein a mysterious sign of the triumph of God's love and the very dawn of salvation's hope. Fabro concludes: "Cosi il mistero dei Santi Innocenti che aveva scandalizzato gli atei A. Camus e Ivan Karamazov, come mistero del male invincibile e prova dell'inesistenza di Dio, diventa per il convertito Péguy il segno del trionfo dell'amore di Dio e L'aurora di speranza della nostra salvezza," p. 6. It is not accidental that Péguy, unlike Dante who gave the Holy Innocents the lowest place in his celestial Rose, willingly accords them the very highest honor. God himself, says Péguy, gives ten reasons for his decision, one of which is that these children who enabled, by the shedding of their blood, the Child Jesus to flee from Herod, "were in a way his representatives." Thus they emptied themselves without in any way dissipating their innocence; and no one save Our Blessed Lady has been similarly set apart for so sublime a state and expression of purity. And the point? Again, without pressing a resolution which really awaits another two chapters to develop, we need at least to give the "working principle" more depth than perhaps Greenberg is able or willing to plumb.

    69. The relevant verses would seem to be 7 and 8:

> Whither shall I go from thy Spirit?
> Or whither shall I flee from thy presence?
> If I ascend to heaven, thou art there!
> If I make my bed in Sheol, thou art there!

In an essay entitled "May We Call God the 'Consoler'?" Hjalmar Sunden, Swedish Lutheran Pastor and theologian, throws the whole matter of the psalmist's question into starkest relief. "In the midst of their own desolation and suffering, many people have asked if it is not aberrant to pray to God as a consoling Spirit," he begins, and ends on this note: "Without the possibility of seeing God in the raw facts of history, I doubt whether we can pray to him as the Consoling Spirit. Only the undoubtable experience of the presence of God consoles—human words never," in *Concilium*, vol. 9, no. 4, November 1968. Thus the question is this: do the seemingly consoling words of the psalm signify a reality beyond the mere words, or are we left with nothing at all save the straws of pathetic human longing to which we vainly clutch? What T.S. Eliot calls "The crying shadow in the funeral dance,/The loud lament of the disconsolate chimera," *Four Quartets*, (New York: Harcourt, Brace & World, 1943), p. 19.

70. Franz Kafka, "In the Penal Colony," *The Complete Stories*, edited by Nahum N. Glatzer, (New York: Schocken Books, 1964).

71. *Ibid.*, p. 150.

72. "Do not delude yourselves with lies," writes the poet Bertolt Brecht. "Like the beasts man simply dies,/and after that comes nothing." Quoted by Joseph Ratzinger, *Seek That Which is Above*, (San Francisco: Ignatius, 1986), p. 34.

73. Rolf Hochhuth, *The Deputy*, (New York: Grove Press, 1964).

74. Arthur C. Cochrane, "Pius XII: A Symbol," from *The Storm Over The Deputy*, edited by Eric Bentley, (New York: Grove Press, 1964).

75. Hochhuth, Act V, Scene 2, pp. 247-248.

76. George Steiner, *In Bluebeard's Castle*, (New Haven: Yale University Press, 1971). Subtitled "Some Notes Towards the Redefinition of Culture," the book attempts to show that, "in regard to a theory of culture, western culture stands where Bartok's Judith stands when she asks to open the last door on the night." To open that door, Steiner suggests, is to risk seeing death which lies on the inside.

77. *Ibid.*, p. 53.

78. Eckardt, pp. 10-11.

79. Maccoby, p. 34. Which datum Eckardt confirms in his assertion, p. 52, that, "The Jew is the particular victim, but for no particular reason. That is to say, the Jew is not to be destroyed because he has done something specific, committed some specific crime. He is to be annihilated, not on the ground of doing, but on the ground of universal being—or, better, of non-being." "The intent," he says on p. 46, "was unparalleled in human history, most especially the intent to eradicate human compassion."

80. Maccoby, p. 34.

81. "Charles Péguy's mockery that Dante had passed through hell as a tourist is objectively true," notes Hans Urs von Balthasar. This is because Dante's encounters with the damned consist of highly restricted conversations amid an itinerary arranged for Dante himself to see the spectacle of the damned; under no circumstances does there exist any possibility of real solidarity with their sufferings. Dante, comments von Balthasar, "could look at hell as one looks at an objective painting; though he is 'in' it topographically, he does not share in its reality. The strange callousness which his poem shows in these parts—and not only in these—has nothing to do with the veiling of love in the 'dark night of the soul.' " Only in Christ, to anticipate somewhat the march of the argument, will the hellish predicament of the lost find its mysterious resolution. See von Balthasar's *The God Question and Modern Man*, introduced by John Macquarrie, (New York: Seabury Press, 1967), p. 136.

82. Steiner, p. 54.

83. *Ibid.*, p. 54.

84. *Ibid.*, pp. 55-56.

85. "Squalor, frustration, putrescence, downright futility and pointlessness—these are the characteristics of the world and of human life as they are presented to us by our novelists and dramatists...(they) witness to a conviction that human life, as it is experienced by many of our contemporaries, is basically unsatisfying and irrational," E.L. Mascall, *The Christian Universe*, (London: Darton, Longman & Todd, 1966), p. 28. Dr. Mascall quotes Martin Esslin who, in his Introduction to the Penguin series on *Absurd Drama*, notes: "There can be no doubt: for many intelligent and sensitive human beings the world of the mid-twentieth century *has* lost its meaning and has simply ceased to make sense...the firmest foundations for hope and optimism have collapsed. Suddenly man sees himself faced with a universe that is both frightening and illogical—in a word, absurd. All assurances of hope, all explanations of ultimate meaning have suddenly been unmasked as nonsensical illusions, empty chatter, whistling in the dark," pp. 28-29.

86. The last four lines of Philip Larkin's poem, "Dockery and Son," which for sheer bleak despair are hard to beat. "Doubtless he was sad," writes his friend A.N. Wilson, recalling the one poet of our time who "found the perfect voice for expressing our worst fears." Says Wilson, in an essay written the week of his death: "Larkin had an absolute conviction that death was nothing but extinction. It was a fact which filled him with terror and gloom. Religion was completely unable to console him. Last year he read through the Bible from cover to cover. When he had finished it, I asked him what he thought. 'Amazing to think anyone once believed it was true,' was his only comment," *The Spectator*, December 7, 1985.

87. From *Four Screenplays of Ingmar Bergman*, (New York: Simon and Schuster, 1960).

88. *Ibid.*, p. 148.

89. *Ibid.*, pp. 110-112.

90. *Ibid.*, p. 162.

91. So avers Lucretius in launching his exposition of what has since become the paradigmatic case for materialism, scientism, despair; see his *On the Nature of the Universe*, I.148ff.

92. "A blind God butts about the world with a pair of delicately malignant antennae to detect whatever is fit to live and an iron hoof to stamp it into the dust when found.... One's instinct that the world (as we know it) is governed by chance is almost shaken by the accumulating evidence that it is the best which is always picked out for destruction.... If one thinks at all (which rarely happens) one feels that we are all living so entirely on the edge of doom, so liable at any moment to fall in with the main procession, that the order of going seems less important, the only text that comes into my mind at these times is 'Let determined things to destiny take unbewailed their way'—I think from *Antony and Cleopatra*, isn't it?" See *Raymond Asquith: Life and Letters*, edited by John Jolliffe, (London: Collins, 1980), pp. 273-274. Killed in the Battle of the Somme, September 15, 1916, he figures most prominently in a great many books about the Great War; he was arguably the most promising, certainly he was the most conspicu-

ous—owing to his father being Prime Minister—of those who perished along the Western Front.

93. See John Courtney Murray, S.J., *The Problem of God*, (New Haven and London: Yale University Press, 1964), pp. 5-13, for his discussion of the importance of the Name on which the whole Israeli identity as a People—his People!, not just any disparate people wandering aimlessly about a desert—had come to depend. "To know the name of another was to know who and what the other was.... In the case of God, the Hebrew impulse was not to know his existence or essence; these were alien concepts. It was to know his Name, which was an operative entity in its own right. Knowledge of God's Name was empowering: one could address him as God, call on him, enter into community with him, make valid claims upon him," p. 7. Thus, says Murray, for this People to gain possession of the Name is tantamount to their coming into "God's possession and under his protection: 'Thou art in our midst, Yahweh; and we bear thy Name. Abandon us not' (Jer. 14:9)," p. 7.

94. Philip Larkin, "Church Going," *Modern Poetry*, p. 361. It is the last selection in the modernist canon, the location of which is highly significant in light of which poem had been situated first, namely Hopkins' "God's Grandeur." What could be more telling than a juxtaposition of the two, to limn the contours of growing disbelief in the modern age? The Jesuit ends his lyric with "the Holy Ghost over the bent / World brooding with warm breast and with ah! bright wings." While Larkin's effort ends with his anonymous Church-goer "gravitating...to this ground, / Which, he once heard, was proper to grow wise in, / If only that so many dead lie round."

95. *Bergman*, p. 137.

96. Hopkins, then a 31 year old Jesuit seminarian in Wales, hearing the account reported in the *Times*—"Five German nuns clasped hands and were drowned together, the chief sister, a gaunt woman, six feet high, calling out loudly and often 'O Christ, come quickly!' till the end came."—is moved to memorialize their heroism, and so one of the great poems of the language is born. *From Poems and Prose of Gerard Manley Hopkins*, ed. by W.H. Gardner, (New York: Penquin, 1953).

97. *Ibid.*, p. 62. From Number 44, one of a handful of sonnets—"a terrible pathos," his friend George Dixon found in them—which powerfully convey the poet's own experience of seemingly absolute separation from God. "I am gall, I am heartburn," the second stanza begins: "God's most deep decree / Bitter would have me taste: my taste was me...." To be sure, the sense here of spiritual loss, the intimation even of that hopelessness which is first cousin to despair ("I see," the sonnet ends, "The lost are like this, and their scourge to be / As I am mine, their sweating selves; but worse"), is also, the mystics assure us, an essential moment in the deified soul's ascent to God. And that Hopkins himself may have achieved ascent at the last, following upon the dryness and desolation of which the sonnets speak, is evident from his last words, spoken on his deathbed June 8, 1889: "I am so happy, so happy."

98. Aristotle, *Magna Moralia* II, 1208b, (London: Harvard University Press, 1935), pp. 649-651.

99. See *Odyssey of a Friend: Whittaker Chambers' Letters to William F. Buckley, Jr., 1954-1961*, edited with notes by Buckley and with a Foreword by Ralph de Toledano, (New York: G.P. Putnam's Sons, 1969).

100. *Ibid.*, pp. 133-134. It is not permissible, Chambers would tirelessly have added, *not* to attend to this reality. "It is forbidden us to turn away from the wound. You perhaps do not remember the mass graves of the First World War in Poland," he writes in his same letter of October 1956. "But you do remember the Katyn Forest. It is not just those bodies that lie heaped there. It is that we lie, smothering alive, under the heaps. We cannot know this and not ask, in our living voices, an ageless question. Who has not heard it? It is Odoacir's question. Trapped in Theodoric's court and cut down by Theodoric's sword, Odoacir cried: 'Where is God?'...I shall go on dogging this point past bearing. For, indeed, it is the only crucial point of our time, and all else, wars, peace, social and political systems, dwindle beside it."

Chambers seems to have been one of those rare spirits who actually dared to enter the seventh and forbidden chamber in Bluebeard's Castle, walking right through to stare death square in the eye. And survived to tell, too. In August 1954 he writes: "If you should see André Malraux, will you convey to him my great esteem and most kind feelings? After *Witness* appeared, he wrote to me: 'You are one of those who did not return from Hell with empty hands,' " p. 78. *Witness*, written in 1952, was Chambers' massive and eloquent account of his deep involvement with the Communist Party in the '30s and '40s, culminating in his sensational break with it and his courageous witness to the truth against it. It was the failure of Communism in organizing a world without God, not to make any humane provision for man which, for Chambers, proved finally disillusioning. Again, it was that ageless question about the wounded world; while Communism could effect no remedy whatsoever, Christianity might, so long as the figure of its wounded Incarnate Lord bore the world's wound, thus bringing solace and meaning to its misery. But, once again, this is to anticipate things.

101. "For man cannot have the experience of receiving what is loved, unless the world and existence as a whole represent something good and therefore beloved to him," Pieper, p. 20. That the world and existence as such, are seen to be good, indeed, are rendered infinitely better because of the blood of Christ, remains, of course, the animating idea behind a Christendom, i.e., a culture precisely understood under the aspect of the ecstatic (*ec-stasis*—standing outside of oneself) dimension of being. For confirmation see Frederick Wilhelmsen, *The Metaphysics of Love*, (New York: Sheed and Ward, 1962).

102. See, for instance, R. Griffiths' poem, "In Memoriam, Philip Larkin," the concluding stanza of which perfectly expresses this ethos of despair:

So Lord, if in the end you must exist,
be kindly to him now, whose only sin,
(remember, after all, he died unkissed)
was not to praise the muck you dropped him in. (*The Spectator*, Sept. 20, 1986)

A milder example, albeit one which is still steeped in a kind of metaphysical ingratitude, is Robert Frost's "Forgive me God the little jokes I play on Thee, / and I'll forgive the great big one Thou play'st on me."

103. Wiesel, *Night*, (New York: Avon, 1958), pp. 91-92.

104. *Ibid.*, p. 127.

105. "Only one of my books, *Night*, deals directly with the Holocaust; all the others reveal why one cannot speak about it." See *Concilium: The Holocaust As Interruption*, ed. by Elisabeth Schussler Fiorenza and David Tracy, (Edinburgh: T&T Clark, 1984), p. 7.

See also Wiesel's interview with Harry James Cargas, where the recent recipient of the Nobel Peace Prize stressed the importance of artistic reticence. "I don't want to be used, or to use, or to misuse, or to be misused by words," *Commonweal*, Oct. 24, 1986. One is reminded of Péguy's comment with which Wiesel would doubtless have agreed: "A word is not the same with one writer as with another. One tears it from his guts. The other pulls it out of his overcoat pocket."

106. Wiesel, *Night*, p. 79.

107. *Ibid.*, p. 122.

108. *Ibid.*, p. 124.

109. *Ibid.*, p. 34.

110. *Ibid.*, p. 44. Wiesel's numerological emphasis upon a life "seven times cursed and seven times sealed," is possibly deliberate and, at all events, by its use he overturns the joyous symbolism with which the number seven has been traditionally invested since the coming of Christ by the Church. See J. Ratzinger's "In the Evening Tears, But Joy in the Morning," where the point is made that Christian celebration is meant to recur for seven days and to be renewed on the eighth. "The seven days, completed by the eighth, symbolize the totality of time and its transcendence into eternity. The week-long feast encompasses a basic unit of human life and thus stands as a foretaste of the freedom of eternal life, a sign of hope and peace in the midst of earthly days of toil. The Church has endeavored to help us experience Easter as the feast of feasts, as the basic reason for all celebration and all joy, by causing the Easter octave to last for seven times seven days...which signify our breaking out of subservience to time into the boundless joy of the children of God, a joy uninterrupted by any striking of the hour," *Seek That Which Is Above*, (San Francisco: Ignatius, 1986), pp. 65-66. The contrast with Wiesel's rendering of that first unspeakable night in camp inaugurating a life "seven times cursed and seven times sealed," could hardly be more telling.

111. *Night*, pp. 74-76.

112. Not surprisingly, Fackenheim has dedicated his own book to Wiesel; the latter's work, he says, is "forcing Jewish theological thought in our time into a new dimension," p. v.

See also a more recent work by Wiesel, a re-working actually, of a Hasidic tale in which Abraham, Isaac and Jacob implore God to stop the Holocaust. "What kind of Messiah is a Messiah who demands six million dead before he reveals himself?" asks Abraham, the chief prosecutor in the Jewish case against God. In other words, the God who had promised Abraham, "Have no fear, I am your shield" (Gen. 15:1), will do nothing to resist the weapons of Nazi torturers. See *Ani Maamin: A Song Lost and Found Again*, (New York: Random, 1974), p. 29.

113. *Night*, p. 77.

114. *Ibid.*, p. 78.

115. *Ibid.*, p. 79.

116. *The New York Times*, April 17, 1983, p. 12. Nevertheless, as Wiesel himself points out elsewhere, "Anyone who does not actively, constantly engage in remembering and in making others remember is an accomplice of the enemy. Conversely, whoever opposed the enemy must take the side of his victims and communicate their tales, tales of solitude and despair, tales of silence and defiance," cited in *Concilium*, p. 5.

117. Lionel Trilling, *The Liberal Imagination*, (New York: Mercury Books, 1961), p. 265.

118. See, for example, the editorial introducing the theme: "As Christian theology moves past a concern for historical consciousness alone or even historicity alone into concrete history, it finds itself facing the frightening interruption of the Holocaust.

"History can no longer be understood as linearity nor continuity, much less evolutionary optimism. Theologically construed, history is concrete: here the concrete suffering of peoples trapped in the horror of the Holocaust. When facing *that* event, history theologically becomes interruption.

"Theologians come to the issue of the Holocaust not to 'explain' it but to face it—and to face it theologically," *Concilium: The Holocaust As Interruption*, p. xi.

119. "A good Christian suggests that perhaps Auschwitz was a divine reminder of the sufferings of Christ. Should he not ask instead whether his Master himself, had He been present at Auschwitz, could have resisted degradation and de-humanization? What are the sufferings of the Cross compared to those of a mother whose child is slaughtered to the sound of laughter or the strains of a Viennese waltz? This question may sound sacrilegious to Christian ears. Yet we dare not shirk it, for we—Christian as well as Jew—must ask: At Auschwitz, did the grave win the victory after all, or, worse than the grave, did the devil himself win?" Emil Fackenheim, *God's Presence in History: Jewish Affirmations and Philosophical Reflections*, (New York: New York University Press, 1970), p. 75.

120. John Courtney Murray, *The Problem of God*, p. 7.

II
THE SHAME AND THE SILENCE BECOME SALVIFIC

THE TWELFTH STATION
Jesus Dies On The Cross

The man who embraces the cross is always alone,
looking up at one who is not looking down,
but who is in turn looking upward
    towards the God who has forsaken them.
That is the important thing:
that he lifts our abandonment into his own greater abandonment.

Those words he spoke—
that the Father should forgive them;
that his soul is commended to God;
that another will share paradise with him;
that his mother is our mother;
that he thirsts;
that, truly, it has all been done—
having meaning only because he knows what abandonment is.

"The many" stand around;
some with magnificent gesture,
some alert, waiting, speculating,
all sensing that something may happen yet which concerns them...
Because there *is* one unanswered question here:
Is God ultimately revealed?

If yes,
it must be God's *love*
which makes him cry out with us to the One who has vanished,

"But why?"
"Why have you forsaken me?"

Let that be God's question to you.

Hans Urs von Balthasar[1]

The Witness of the Word:
Wordless Descent into Wickedness

In the wake of so vast a devastation wrought by the Holocaust, and, indeed, by all the accumulated horrors of human history which so mock our pretensions to hope and goodness, it would seem that silence and shame are alone to be the last word on the subject. And, to be sure, the aesthetic rendering of human desolation and despair—emotions which, by themselves, constitute that adequacy of response demanded by these events—remains thus the sole significant function of art and literature. But why must the obscene and the unspeakable be allowed to extend so far and to fill so much? Their blanket of black despair thrown across the age can only leave us, like the child-narrator of Wiesel's *Night*, bereft at the last of everything. Everything, that is, save only our sense of shame and silence before God and man. Are we really reduced, in other words, to saying only that we cannot believe in a Messiah since the One alleged to have come, apparently having left the world in the same state of hopelessness as before, forbids our ever believing in him again? "No, Gregor," pronounces the character Gavriel to his friend in Wiesel's *The Gates of the Forest*, "there can be no more hope. The Messiah came and the executioner goes right on executing. The Messiah came and the world is a vast slaughterhouse."[2]

Setting aside for the moment all the shame and the silence—or, better still, peering with deep intentness behind the facade of bleak hopelessness they present to the world—what if there actually were something hidden amid so many horrors which heretofore had completely escaped us? A truth more shattering even than the Holocaust which, for all their vaunted sensitivity, men like Trilling and Steiner, Wiesel and Fackenheim and Maccoby (and, of course, plays like *The Deputy* with its smug and deliberate adversarial relation to God, so fierce and shrill in its rectitude vis à vis the latter's countless shortcomings), had failed to notice before, or simply had not the capacity, humanly speaking, to notice at all? What if that silence and shame which they so insistently and eloquently urge upon us were a silence and shame once rendered truly, albeit mysteriously salvific? Not then the silence of the Father, mute seeming in its apparent eternal remoteness from men; the infuriating *apatheia* of, say, Aristotle's god, or the god of the Deists who, having wound the cosmic clock countless aeons ago, now retires bored and indifferent to his celestial study.[3] But the silence of the Son, who, fallen among wicked and twisted men free to do their worst, neither speaks nor hears that Word through which "all things were made...and without which was not anything made that was made."[4] The wordless descent of the Word into the world and onto the Cross; then into the strangest silence of all, the silence of Sheol. What if *that* were the silence in which all the shame and the slaughter, and the appalling silence therefrom, testified to in our century were to be enfolded: might it not then find its ultimate, indeed its only true meaning?

"And what the dead had no speech for when living," to recall the incomparable language of "Little Gidding," Eliot's profound and lyric meditation on the meaning of time and history in their unexpected collision with grace—"At the still point of the turning world"—the very *kairos* of Christ's coming, his descent into time and history, and into hell,

> They can tell you, being dead: the communication
> Of the dead is tongued with fire beyond the language of the living.[5]

For the Christian, at least, here is the ultimate center of gravity, namely the very ground and glory of that Triune love which lavished itself upon the world in the life and death of Jesus Christ. When, for reasons entirely gratuitous, God sent his only Son, as New Adam, to rescue and redeem the sons of the Old Adam. This very One who, St. Paul tells us in that sublime hymn of *kenosis*, "though he was in the form of God, did not count equality with God a thing to be grasped, but emptied himself, taking the form of a servant, being born in the likeness of men. And being found in human form he humbled himself and became obedient unto death, even death on a cross."[6] It is upon this single mystery that we must converge, to paraphrase the title of Fr. von Balthasar's little book,[7] if we are once again to find that Word who was with God from the beginning and yet who chose to empty himself of its manifold glories on our behalf.

"Today we must," he urges us, "investigate in what way the Christian wealth, without losses—such as a vanquished army leaves behind on the battlefield—relates to its origin: to the ineffable poverty of the divine, incarnate, crucified love."[8] For it is in this mystery alone that we see definitively revealed the majesty of God as sheer gratuitous, self-abandoning love. "God's majesty," writes Michael Waldstein, commenting here on the pivotal thesis of von Balthasar's monumental *The Glory of the Lord*,[9] "as expressed in the mission of Jesus, lies in the completeness, one might almost say, the recklessness, with which God gives himself for the salvation of the world. God effectively pours himself out in complete weakness. And this weakness is the most effective penetration of God's light into the darkest corners of creation."[10] Here is the last and most mysterious of secrets wrought in the silence of God which Holy Church, since at least the time of St. Ignatius Martyr, cries out to the world.[11] The spectacle of the Lord of Glory, Glory both Absolute and Triune, lacerated upon the Cross, this constitutes the supreme and paradoxical center of all faith in Christology.[12] And, to be sure, it is no less intended as the deepest truth about man, particularly in his brokenness and his bereavement.

Every statement, therefore, about God or man, grace or sin or death, absolutely depends for its meaning, its fullest intelligibility, upon the fact of Christ's being nailed to the Cross. Our questions are only answered here, if at all, at the foot of the Cross, beneath the pierced and crucified body of the Son of God. The Eternal Word of the Father, in other words, most profoundly consummates all discourse and deed when, stretched to the ends of the earth, he suffers himself to hang and to die, here, pinioned to this mysterious Tree of Life.[13]

In short, God as Man is born only to die, to endure the horror of his Passion's singular dereliction. The crucifixion is thus both an event in time, in history, upon which all perspectives rivet their meaning, and an event continually renewing itself throughout time, across the span of history. "True," concedes von Balthasar, "the Son no longer hangs bleeding on the cross. But since the three hours of agony between heaven and earth were already the breakthrough of time into the eternal, as of eternity into the temporal—hours which cannot be measured by any chronological time, by any psychological feeling of time ('Jesus is in agony until the end of the world'–Pascal)—so the divine-human suffering is the most precious relic that the resurrected Christ, now free of pain, takes with him from his earthly pilgrimage into his heavenly glory."[14]

The whole aim, one might almost say, of this world's evolution has been simply to raise up a hill called Golgotha, to grow the wood for God's cross, forge the necessary iron for his nails and, finally, to fashion a species from whose loins Christ would be born.[15] "The immutable God in himself," says Fr. Rahner,

> has no destiny and therefore no death. But he himself (and not just what is other than he) has a destiny, through the Incarnation, in what is other than himself.... And so precisely this death (like Christ's humanity) expresses God as he is and as he willed to be in our regard by a free decision which remains eternally valid...Jesus' death belongs to God's self-utterance.[16]

This is, of course, of incalculable importance because it is only through this particular *self-utterance* that, as von Balthasar puts it, the conditions of mankind become transparent to the conditions of the Word in its divinity. And in the Passion (which here leads to the kenosis of the Incarnation in its greatest intensity and obviousness), through the sufferings of humanity, are revealed both the victory and the power of God and the will of the divine person of the Son (and in him the will of the whole Trinity) to let himself be affected by this suffering. To be sure, von Balthasar reminds us, the subject of this suffering is the Word, who is himself a person; indeed, he adds, "the Son is the Word precisely as a divine person, not as a divine nature, which he shares with the Father and the Spirit, *even if he requires human nature in order to suffer*" (my emphasis).[17]

And so every human utterance, if it be faithful to Christ and the Father—faithful, too, to its own deepest meaning—must needs confront the death cry of the Son; to see in the Godforsaken One, the shattering cry of *his* abandonment, all the world's shame and silence converge. The fact is, God having chosen to lose, i.e., the Son "who knew no sin" yet moved by love unutterable "to be sin," man is now empowered to win.[18] He has redeemed us from the curse of the law—the punishment due to sin and the utmost horror of hell—by assuming the very curse itself.[19] And thus the liberation which the law could not of itself bring, so burdened were we with the sinful flesh of the First Adam, God has accomplished in and through the flesh of the Second Adam; the Son himself who, fallen into that same flesh—flesh to which he had completely assimilated himself—freed it from the weight and oppression of original sin and death.[20]

It is not mere ethical solidarity with sinners or sinned against which the Son's silent assumption of suffering, of sheer Godforsakenness, here evinces, but willingness to bear in his own broken body, shorn now of all speech and comeliness,[21] the full reality of sin, of its infinite and hateful violence against the good. All this, St. Paul reminds us in his Letter to the Colossians, he has done for us by the supreme act of nailing iniquity to the cross.[22] Most particularly the lie which is the deepest mark of sin, in its contempt for the good, for the truth of the real. All this, the whole hideously frightful actuality of sin, is to be sounded in the depths of the Son's mysterious descent into the silence. "The truth of sin," says von Balthasar, stressing particularly the form of the lie which it most egregiously takes,

> must be realized somewhere in the iron ruthlessness implied by the sinner's "No" to God and God's "No" to this refusal. And this could only be realized by someone who is so truthful in himself that he is able to acknowledge the full negativity of this "No": someone who is able to experience it, to bear it, to suffer its deadly opposition and melt its rigidity through pain.[23]

Towards the Trinity as Absolute
Foundation of the Cross

Who more profoundly and convincingly than Christ himself—the Word, the Son—can suffer the silence of one who *seems* no longer to speak the word, nor to beget the Son?[24] In Rainer Maria Rilke's "The Garden of Olives," the poet sees Christ go up under the gray foliage, and there lay his forehead that was full of dust

> deep in the dustiness of his hot hands.

> After everything, this. And this was the end.
> Now I must go, while I am turning blind,
> And why dost Thou so will, that I must say *Thou art,*
> when I myself do no more find Thee.

> I find Thee no more. Not within me, no.
> Not in the others. Not within this rock.
> I find Thee no more. I am alone.

> I am alone with all mankind's grief,
> which I through Thee to lighten undertook,
> Thou who art not. O nameless shame....

And so the poem ends, evoking sheer, blank, abysmal sorrow and loss; the fate of men "abandoned of their fathers/and shut out of their mother's womb."[25]

Notwithstanding the Son's experience of apparent eternal abandonment, there must remain the truth of love's essential exchange, i.e., the union of two hypostatically joined Persons whose very bond of relation is the Spirit; to neglect this is nothing less than to imperil the entire economy of salvation, a situation at risk whenever theology disturbs right relations within the Trinity. Particularly that species of theology which, driven by sheer rhetorical necessity, undertakes to convey the full horror of sin inflicted upon the Son; here the idea of the Father's wrath, poised to strike the innocence of the Son, fundamentally distorts the mystery of redemption. In his chapter on certain "distorting mirrors" of theological description, Philippe de la Trinité, OCD quotes Fr. Mersch, who, commenting on the phenomenon writes, "Christ answering before God for the world's sins appears as the total sinner, the damned among the damned, crushed under the most complete and utter divine wrath. But the truth is very different; for Jesus' work is diametrically opposed to Hell. Hell is hatred, opposition to God, oneself and humanity; Christ's work tends to love and union."[26]

We cannot, therefore, hold that between Father and Son there could exist a state of enmity, of war, such as to characterize the condition of the damned, for whom hell is an eternally fixed hatred and loathing for God. For theology even to ascribe the slightest velleity of irritation for the Father is forbidden. "In no way can substitution be understood," writes von Balthasar, advancing his own radical sense of the scriptural meaning of Christ's bearing the sin of the world, "as an identification of the crucified with the actual 'no' of sin itself" (which, according to Luther, rises up in Jesus and must be choked down by him).

> The manner in which Christ experiences the darkness of the state of sin cannot be identical with the manner in which sinners (who hate God) would have to experience it (if they were not saved from it by him).

Nevertheless, he insists in a conclusion fraught with a sense of the mystery we are left wrestling with ("Leaving one still with the intolerable wrestle / With words and meanings," says Eliot), "the darkness experienced by Jesus is deeper and darker than theirs, because it happens in the depth of the relations of the divine hypostases of which *no creature has as much as an inkling*"[27] (my emphasis).

On the Dangers of Docetism

Thus it remains entirely proper for theology to venture this breathtaking claim, namely that Christ freely suffered all the punishments intended for the unrepentant sinner, including even that condition of definitive separation from God which marks the soul of the damned forever.[28] How otherwise are we to understand the Pauline passages quoted above? Either our reconciliation with God means God taking the place of sinful man, putting himself in our shoes (sheer corruption cobbled onto the innocence of the Son), or it means nothing redemptive at all, and we are left with a Docetist Christology so etiolated and emptied of *passion* as to render the figure of Christ scarcely human at all. "The Docetic attempt to make Jesus' sufferings a mere surface illusion," writes Ratzinger, "was an option congenial to Stoic thought. But it must be clear to every unprejudiced reader of the Bible that such an option would attack the very heart of the biblical testimony to Christ, i.e., the mystery of Easter. It was impossible to excise Christ's sufferings, but there can be no passion without passions: suffering presupposes the ability to suffer, it presupposes the faculty of the emotions."[29]

And what is that place which Christ assumed in our stead if it is not the land of the lost, of the Godforsaken, of men cast out by sin from all that is living and true? "Cursed is he that dies on the cross," declare the Scriptures.[30] What happens to Christ is exactly what ought to have overtaken all of us. Not that Christ, in substituting for the sinner, is condemned to an everlasting forlornness by the Father, i.e., that he has been consigned to hell forever; again, to imply such a thing would amount to a state of detestation within the Godhead itself, for hell cannot be less than that, less than full hatred for Him who alone is Love. In Christ, therefore, even in his hour of blackest extremity when, on Golgotha, he bears all the sin of the world, there is not the least interruption of his will to do the Father's will. Only now, of course, it is done in complete absence of that joy and solace which would otherwise cause the working out of that will to be his very meat and drink.

"On the Cross," says von Balthasar, "he still does his will without realizing it anymore. With every fiber of his being he clings to the God whose presence he no longer feels, because now, in the name of sinners, he is to experience what it means to have lost contact with God."[31] What can this extraordinary statement possibly mean? Can it mean anything less than an abandonment singularly, unprecedentedly abysmal? "No one has ever dared to work out," writes von Balthasar elsewhere,

> a "logic" of the Passion: to face the fact that that Logos, in which everything in heaven and on earth is gathered and possesses its truth, descends into darkness, into fear, into non-feeling and non-knowledge, into the inescapable, into the abyss, into the absence of any relation to the Father who alone supports truth, and, therefore, into a hiddenness which is the exact opposite of the truth-revealing nature of being. One would then have to understand the silence of Jesus in the passion as a falling silent, a failure of the Word of God to say or answer anything. He would have to see the great flood dry up and become just drops, but also see how unspeakably precious these drops have become, condensed to the uttermost.[32]

Here, then, exists most assuredly, the deepest possible link between the Christian religion and the apparent endlessness of Judaism's travail. Here the strange configuration of the Cross becomes finally clear, i.e., the vertical descent of the Word, "from the highest height, deeper than a mere human word can descend, into the last futility of empty time and of hopeless death,"[33] is a descent precisely undertaken on our behalf; so that, in freely assuming our infirmities and diseases, our countless derelictions, all things might be nailed salvifically to the Word. The very Word of God awaits them in full, frightful expectancy of pain, fastened as he allows himself to be, to the wood of the Cross. "This Word does not poetically transfigure death, playing around it; he bores right through it to the bottom, to the chaotic formlessness of the death cry (Mt. 27:50) and the wordless silence of death on Holy Saturday. Hence, he has death in his grip: he dominates it, limits it, and takes from it its sting."[34] And thus the One who innocently bore our sorrows will join irrevocably his own unique (because mysteriously rooted to Triune reality) sorrow to those inflicted upon the Children of Abraham.

Where God Weeps, or The Suffering of Love

"We cannot know how much of humanity's endless suffering—the countless Auschwitz and Gulag Archipelagoes—has a direct relation to the Lord's expiatory suffering; if the latter were not in the background one would wonder how God could bear to behold it."[35] Under the circumstances—to answer the question posed by the hideousness of suffering recounted at such length in the last chapter—it becomes possible precisely to speak of a God after Auschwitz because he too is steeped in suffering, he is one acquainted from within with sorrow, infirmity, and loss. Franklin Sherman, in an essay entitled "Speaking of God after Auschwitz," writes that for Christianity, "the symbol of the agonizing God is the Cross of Christ. It is tragic that this symbol should have become a symbol of division between Jews and Christians, for the reality to which it points is a Jewish reality as well, the reality of suffering and martyrdom."[36]

Just how deeply it remains a Jewish reality, hidden away amid the prophetical riches of the Old Testament, the achievement of the late Abraham J. Heschel will attest. In his magisterial work *The Prophets*, fittingly dedicated "To the martyrs of 1940-45," he gives overwhelming evidence of God's intimate, unceasing association with his people.[37] The suffering of Israel becomes, quite literally, God's grief. Of Second Isaiah, the prophet who arose to announce the coming redemption, the lifting of captivity and sorrow, Heschel writes: "No words have ever gone further in offering comfort when the sick world cries."[38]

> For a long time I have kept silent,
> I have kept still and restrained Myself;
> Now I will cry out like a woman in travail,
> I will gasp and pant.   (Is. 42:14)

Think of it: *a woman in travail*. It is, says Heschel, "the boldest figure used by any prophet, convey(ing) not only the sense of supreme urgency of his action, but also a sense of the deep intensity of his suffering."[39]

> In all their affliction he was afflicted...
> In his love and in his pity he redeemed them
> He lifted them up and carried them all the days of old.[40]

How could so intimate and persisting a bond, profound affinity in affliction no less, take place between God and suffering humanity unless God were himself to assume that very burden of travail? "He will feed his flock like a shepherd," says Isaiah; "he will gather the lambs in his arms...and gently lead those that are with young."[41]

In a posthumous work, Heschel has recorded two views of Abraham's world: one in which he sees "infinity, beauty, and wisdom," and asks if it be possible for such grandeur to exist without God; the other view is of a "world engulfed in the flames of evil and deceit," which brings Abraham to ask, "Is it possible that there is no Lord to take this misfortune to heart?"[42] But what of the mysterious Servant of Isaiah, "Surely he has borne our griefs and carried our sorrows"?[43] And yet, we are reminded, we esteemed him not, he whom God had stricken; this Suffering Servant "wounded for our transgressions upon (whom) was the chastisement that made us whole...."[44] In other words, what does it really mean to speak of God as love except that he reveal this mysterious capacity to suffer with and in and for others. A God who can't do this, can't extend himself in this way, "is poorer than any man. For a God who is incapable of suffering is a being who cannot be involved. Suffering and injustice do not affect him. And because he is so completely insensitive, he cannot be affected or shaken by anything. He cannot weep, for he has no tears. But the one who cannot suffer cannot love either. So he is a loveless being."[45] He is no better than the god of Aristotle, the unmoved Mover whom no one is ever moved to love. Men may admire his perfected beauty, fear and tremble before his power, but in the end so loveless a being is more bereft than any potsherd of a man who suffers because, at least, he knows how to love.[46]

A God without love—understood less as attribute of divinity than as that which is most deeply constitutive of who God *is*—is a God forced by the very circumstances of all that he is not to leave his creation utterly vanquished and alone. And it was just this very rejection which, emphatically set out in the Christian creeds, broke the Aristotelian hold on the doctrine of God. "The one who is capable of love," says Moltmann,

> is also capable of suffering, for he also opens himself to the suffering which is involved in love, and yet remains superior to it by virtue of his love. The justifiable denial that God is capable of suffering because of a deficiency in his being may not lead to a denial that he is incapable of suffering out of the fullness of his being, i.e., his love.[47]

Who but Love freely responsible for the movement of the sun and the stars, would dare condescend to assume (not absorb!) human being beneath those same Dantean heavens which God's Word formed out of the dust; that "all-powerful love which, quiet and united, leads round in a circle the sun and all the stars"?[48] Who but that Love in whom Dante himself, at once fallen into a swoon of pure imaginative bliss at the close of his *Comedia*, suddenly espies his own face (a human countenance at the center of Triune reality!), would ever think to bestir himself on behalf of other men?[49] And yet, as Cardinal Joseph Ratzinger reminds us, "God comes to pass for man through men, nay, even more concretely, through *the* man in whom the quintessence of humanity appears and who for that very reason is at the same time God himself.... Can we cling at all to the straw of one single historical event? Can we dare to base our whole existence, indeed the whole of history, on the straw of one happening in the great sea of history?"[50] If we can, and if what Ratzinger has called in his foregoing analysis "the absolutely staggering alliance of *logos* and *sarx*, of meaning and a single historical figure" be true,[51] then it follows that only a God of love would presume to bother about thee and me, representatives of a paltry race of beings lost in the eternal silences of infinite space, to cite Pascal's profound meditation found in the *Pensées*.[52] Who, save the God of love alone, *could* accept responsibility for the world's dereliction? Who, asks von Balthasar in a sublime essay entitled "Only If," shall make up for all the losses of men? Who will redeem "the unthinkable sufferings and despair, the senseless, horrible, destruction of beings whose purpose for existence had to be contained in the narrow circle of birth and death?"[53]

Certainly no God of mere power, even the most gracious and creative exercise thereof, could possibly accept responsibility for the endless impacted miseries of his work. At most he might offer himself as that state of forgetful sleep on the other side of human suffering, the peace no less of the grave. But no amnesiac answer to our insupportably painful existence will do. And, of course, God would never as all-powerful Creator alone have consented really to do more, i.e., to endure the pain and the grief of complete Godforsakenness so that, from within, it might stand redeemed.[54] Who, then, to take up von Balthasar's question, will gather up the futilities and despairs?

> Who has so much compassion that he does not simply watch sympathetically (from his own freedom from suffering which he perhaps has achieved), nor wrathfully plan for redress (for the next time), but in solidarity bears the responsibility for all that cries to heaven, bears it in compassion (which must cry ever more frightfully to heaven)?...*only if* this one not only shares in the most terrible anguish but surpasses it by laying hold of it from below (for only God can know what it means to be truly forsaken by God), *only if* that Maximum coincides with this Minimum (both beyond our com-

prehension)—not in indifference, but in such a way that absolute power becomes one with absolute powerlessness in sheltering compassion....[55]

In the parable of the Prodigal Son, he tells us elsewhere,[56] there is one figure whose presence is seemingly absent from the story, namely the narrator, who is Jesus himself. He, Jesus, is the Father's love, the very one who "goes silently along the way into complete abandonment—suffering with us, truly representing all of us." Thus, comments von Balthasar,

> The father not only waits for the spontaneous or constrained return of the Prodigal, but (in the form of his son) sends out his love into his desolation. He allows his son to identify himself with his lost brother. And by this very power of identifying himself—without keeping a respectable distance—with his complete opposite, God the Father recognized the *consubstantiality*, the divinity of the one he has sent as his redeeming word into the world.[57]

God is determined, it would seem, to render absolutely, dramatically credible before his creation, the whole inner truth of the Word's enfleshment of human life and history. And so entering entirely into the brokenness of our condition, he evinces total and perfect passion for all human pain and loss. How apt, then, the metaphor of the *wounded surgeon* which the poet Eliot used to describe Christ in his *Four Quartets*:

> The wounded surgeon plies the steel
> That questions the distempered part;
> Beneath the bleeding hands we feel
> The sharp compassion of the healer's art
> Resolving the enigma of the fever chart.[58]

The Contribution of Origen and the Question of Patripassianism

Does it not follow, then, in light of the above analysis, that the Son of God, had he not from within the deepest precincts of eternal Triune life itself *felt* compassion for human wretchedness—indeed, if he were not *com-passion* itself—he would never have consented to become incarnate in a history covered with such pain and loss as ours routinely has been? Most certainly, for all his gracious descent into the human and the historical, he would have stopped short of subjecting himself to the ignominy of the Cross. Walter Kasper, in his exhaustive examination of *The God of Jesus Christ*, quotes Origen, who, in three telling sentences, has written:

> First he suffered, then he came down. What was the suffering he accepted for us? The suffering of love.

"Here," comments Kasper, "a solution is insinuated which has its basis in the innermost being of God himself, in his freedom in love."[59]

Here is an extraordinary theological breakthrough indeed. Von Balthasar, in his exposition of Christ as the very language of God, likewise credits Origen with having hit upon the exact solution; and reproducing the full text from Origen in which that solution is brilliantly proposed, he affirms the sense in which Origen, like Pascal after him, mystically understood the eternal duration of the Son's agony. We confront, no less, an eternal collision of the Christian Cross. Origen, says von Balthasar, by his sheer insistence on "seeing the inner, spiritual passion of the Word of God as antecedent to and the cause of the external fleshy passion," refused to consider the latter travail as the only genuine outpouring of Christ's pain, as though the Word's ordeal within the Trinity were merely a metaphorical suffering.[60] But let the text itself, in its entirety, reveal the profundity of the genius of Origen. "He came down to earth out of compassion with humanity," it begins, describing the motive of the Son's descent.

> He underwent our sufferings before he underwent the cross and before he took our flesh upon him, for if he had not already suffered he would not have entered on the course of human life. First he suffered, then he came down and became visible. What was that suffering that he went through for us? It was the suffering (*pathos*) of love. And the Father himself, the God of the universe, "slow to anger and abounding in steadfast love" (Ps. 102:8), does he not also suffer in a certain sense? Or do you not know that when he involves himself in human affairs in the shape of providence that he suffers the suffering of humanity with it? "The Lord your God bore you, as a man bears his son" (Dt. 1: 31). God supports our misdeeds, just as the Son of God takes our pain upon himself. The Father himself is not without compassion (*impassibilis*). If he is implored, he is merciful and shares in the suffering, he undergoes something through love and by it is transferred into those beings in which he cannot exist while seeing the sublimity of his own nature.[61]

In other words, compressing here the profound commentary of Origen, the suffering of the Son is ultimately a Trinitarian experience. And must it not at least be that much if our whole redemption wrought by the Son's Cross is likewise an event and work of the Blessed Trinity? The Persons of the Godhead do not operate in isolation, surely. In any case, it is thanks to one Alexandrian scholar of the third century that we see a depth previously unplumbed to the great mystery of our redemption; that same Origen who, to cite Joseph Cardinal Ratzinger's appreciative comment from his *Behold the Pierced One*, grasped most profoundly the idea of the suffering God and made bold to say that it could not be restricted to the suffering humanity of Jesus but also affected the Christian picture of God. The Father suffers in allowing the Son to suffer, and the Spirit shares in this suffering, for Paul says that he groans within us, yearning in us and on our behalf for full redemption (Rom. 8:26f.).[62]

To what extent, however, will the texts of Origen escape a *patripassian* reading? Is it entirely untenable to attribute such a reading here? Von Balthasar, for one, insists that the texts simply will not bear such a view, on the grounds that Origen is "only drawing the logical conclusion from the words of the Psalm, 'He who formed the eye, does he not see?' and, at the same time, denying a physical interpretation of the suffering of God." The essential point about Origen, says von Balthasar, is that, "like everything else in the human life of Christ, his suffering also is truly the Word of God."

> His suffering is an expression of the living, streaming love which—quite apart from the "occasion" offered by the sin of humanity which had to be borne—could find in all creation no better language in which to express itself than the passion. The Greek idea of *pathos* (which the philosophers kept carefully separate from God) unites splendidly the meaning and the expression.[63]

And likewise Ratzinger who, in his own study of the question, concludes that it was precisely Origen, "who gave the normative definition of the way in which the theme of the suffering God is to be interpreted: When you hear someone speak of God's passions, always apply what is said to love. So God is a sufferer because he is a lover; the entire theme of the suffering God flows from that of the loving God and always points back to it. The actual advance registered by the Christian idea of God over that of the ancient world lies in its recognition that God is love."[64]

On Kinship in Kenosis

Under such circumstances, does it not seem both appropriate and compelling to speak of the Cross in deep and intimate relation to the Holocaust? Indeed, to link its transcendent horror to all the horrors which endlessly beset a suffering humanity? Is it not true that here there exists that veritable kinship in kenosis which underlies the argument of the book?[65] Can it be much cause for wonder, therefore, that the present pope should so often refer to Auschwitz as "the Golgotha of the modern world"?[66] His point would seem to be that this Death Camp, which so perfectly emblematizes the evil of genocidal hatred in our time, is really the setting for this century's timeless re-enactment of the Christian drama of suffering and salvation. Why not, then, take up the theme of human redemption in Christ as the subject of one's first encyclical? "Can it be a surprise," he asked, on his visit to Auschwitz in 1979, "that the Pope who came to the See of Saint Peter from the diocese in whose territory is situated the Auschwitz camp, would have begun his first encyclical with the words *Redemptor Hominis,* and should have dedicated it to the cause of man...to his inalienable rights that can so easily be annihilated by his fellow-men?"[67]

Of all those who have come to Auschwitz since the closing of the camp, wave upon wave of silent visitors who pay their tribute to the dead, no doubt there were those who asked, "What is it to me?" Let them read the Pope's discourse on the suffering God's people endured, the very ones who gave to the world remembrance of that commandment forbidding murder; then watch the tears which signal their solidarity with the dead begin to flow. "I kneel on this Golgotha of the modern world," Pope John Paul II announced on his visit,

> on these tombs, largely nameless like the great tomb of the Unknown Soldier. I kneel before all the inscriptions that come one after another bearing the memory of the victims of Oswiecim in many languages.... In particular I pause before the inscription in Hebrew. This awakens the memory of the People whose sons and daughters were intended for total extermination. This People draws its origin from Abraham, our father in faith, as was expressed by Paul of Tarsus. The very People who received from God the commandment "Thou shalt not kill" itself experienced in a special way what is meant by killing. It is not permissible for anyone to pass by this inscription with indifference.[68]

Seeking the Ultimate Ground of Anti-Semitism

Lest anyone think the Pope's remarks mere rhetorical flourishes to mark that sadness which civilized decorum imposes in the presence of death, particularly victims of genocide, the historical record is frightfully clear. In other words, Adolf Hitler perfectly understood the theological significance of the Jewish People, and was accordingly disgusted and affronted in the face of the divine law, the sheer oppressive weight which international Jewry represented before the world. This is why they became the targeted victims of Nazi persecution; they were to be scapegoated for having borne for so many millennia a moral burden which other men had found too burdensome. The Jews' maintenance of that law inflamed the Nazi Third Reich because it painfully reminded men bent on wickedness of all that God had forbidden them to do. "In the days of Auschwitz," writes John M. Oesterreicher,

> Jews were defamed and killed because the Nazis had projected upon them the evil that possessed their own souls. The Jews are the people that heard—not once, but again and again—the words "You shall," "You shall not," words that are like thunder in man's rebellious ear.[69]

The rebellion of Adolf Hitler before the imperatives of the moral law was no trifling affair; yes, he well understood the peculiar significance of the Jews, those unwelcome men, women and children of the Book, the strictures of whose Law stood precisely athwart his ungovernable lust for conquest and destruction. Hence the real menace contained in Hitler's formal recognition of his Third Reich's intention, which consisted of "putting an end to the wrong path mankind had taken."

> The tablets of Mount Sinai have lost their validity.
> Conscience is a Jewish invention. Like circumcision, it mutilates man. ...
> One must distrust mind and conscience, one must place one's trust in one's instincts.[70]

Nevertheless, for all the fierce specificity of his hatred for the Jew, what Hitler's loathing amounted to at bottom was really an unmasking of his hatred and contempt for Christ and for his Church. Fr. Oesterreicher has noted that Nazi repugnance for the tablets of Sinai was, if it be possible, exceeded even by their hatred for Christ's Beatitudes, upon the teaching of which an unparalleled fury and hatred were heaped. And he adds: "That Nazi hatred of the Jews was, at its deepest layer, hatred of Christ is the conviction even of witnesses not necessarily friendly to the Church. In *The Black Book*, for instance, published by a group of organizations, prominent among which was the Jewish anti-Fascist Committee of Moscow, its authors declare:

> The war against Jewry and Judaism also served as the spearhead of the Nazi crusade against the Christian religion, diametrically opposed to the new gospel of the Fuehrer and the Fuehrer-state. Beginning with a vituperative attack on the Old Testament, the Nazis soon launched a crusade against the New Testament, "laden with the filth of Near Eastern Jewish and African life." They started by defiling and burning synagogues, but before they were through they nearly dominated the churches of Germany and the occupied countries. Anti-Semitism was the strategic weapon for the attack on "Jewish-tainted Christianity."[71]

How few have begun to understand, laments Oesterreicher, that for the leadership of the Third Reich, Synagogue and Church were always of a piece; and that pursuant to the "Final Solution of the Jewish Problem" both would have to go. Indeed the whole biblical legacy of gospel, grace, and mercy would have to be liquidated in order to secure the aims of the Master Race. As Oesterreicher observes, "the physical slaughter of the Jewish people was only a giant step toward this goal. To put it differently, Jews were made to 'pay' for having been the instruments of God's revelation."[72]

But is it finally possible to prevent God's revelation from its appointed goal of realization in the hearts of men? Particularly in the form of the pierced and crucified One who descends upon the Cross for the world's salvation? For the Nazi disciple, of course, whose anti-Semitic pathology derives from so much Nietzschean Superman mythology (in which Christ is only a contemptible "patron of the sick," "a spider," "a staff for the weary and a sheet anchor for the drowning"), certainly the message compounded of hate by which the Third Reich sought to rule the world would necessarily represent that sheer falsification of all that the Gospel Good News carried.[73] And though the despised God of the Gospels has overcome the world, to the author of *The Antichrist* and the generation of Nazi epigone it sired—men who could never bring themselves to identify with One whose invitation went out to "the poor, the crippled, the lame, and the blind" (Lk. 14:13) —God will always be just another Jew.

> He has remained a Jew, he has remained the god of back streets, the god of dark holes, of shacks, of all the unhealthy quarters of the world! His universal kingdom is, now as always, a domain of the underworld, a hospital, a basement realm, a ghetto kingdom.[74]

But for the Christian, this "spider god" is the very Lord of history, the *Kyrios* of the last days who can no more be kept from human history than those numberless millions of men and women who, as the Pope says, are living it, have lived it, or will ever live it. Not even such organized wickedness as the Nazis were able to mount and sustain for years and years is sufficient to abort the plan of Almighty God. "Your god must feel a bit disappointed when he looks at this world of his," confesses Graham Greene's Dr. Colin with deep bitterness of spirit before the old priest whose Order administers the Congo village where the lepers live and die. And surrounded as he is by a batch of sixty or so fresh cases, amid circumstances of devastating material futility, the irony of his observation does not go unnoticed. But, surely, on the basis of a God steeped in the sufferings of the very least and leprous, the ensuing exchange between priest and doctor as Greene imagines it is horribly, theologically false. It is sheer ungenerosity to God for Greene's priest to say, in answer to the doctor's atheist outburst, "When you were a boy they can't have taught you theology very well. God cannot feel disappointment or pain." (In which case, of course, the doctor's final riposte is absolutely right: "Perhaps that's why I don't care to believe in him.") Alas, it is all too, too facile; an unearned nihilism about life poisons the whole presentation.[75]

On Extending Frontiers of Kinship in Kenosis

Not only are we expected to be chivalrous towards God, we owe ourselves as much chivalrous deference as well. In fact, every attempt to exclude God from the stage of human history amounts to a fundamental act of aggression against man. What, after all, does Dostoevsky tell us in his profound and acute dramatizations of crime and punishment, sin and remorse, but that every humanism without Christ is bound to end in the inhuman. "Hitler and Stalin dwell in all men," writes Nathan Scott in an essay on Dostoevsky's work, "who venture really to live upon the premise either that God is dead or that he is hopelessly impotent."[76] In a world where belief in God is permitted to lapse, everything else will soon be permitted, except that comforting and sentimental illusion that what is ethically permissible will invariably be set by standards greater than what is technically possible. In other words, that humane ordering whereby just because a thing can be done is no reason why it ought to be done will, of necessity in a world without God, wither and disappear. Father de Lubac has shown us in his own brilliant dissection of the atheistic interpretation of Nietzsche's death of God, an eventuality which he deeply feared—the very corpse of man. "Atheist humanism," he writes, "was bound to end in bankruptcy. Man is himself only because his face is illumined by a divine ray."[77]

Only consider the myriad acts of blind anarchic aggression which serve already to characterize the quality of the century we live in. No survey of violence, it is being suggested, may exhaust itself amid the horrors of just this Holocaust; however distinctive and dreadful those horrors happened to be, any honest inventory of human iniquity, i.e., one which is adequate to the scale of human slaughter in our time, will not stop with this particular Final Solution. There were others as well.[78] In point of fact, as a result of such horrified attention paid exclusively to the subject of Jewish extermination, an entire historiography has tended to forget those other targeted victims of Hitler's hatred. For instance, the Poles, six million of whom perished by war's end, half of them Roman Catholic. In fact, the destruction of Polish Jewry began as late as 1942, by which time Christian Poland had been eviscerated. First, in the invasion which commenced in 1939, leaving hundreds of thousands of Poles dead; then the massive conscriptions involving, again, hundreds of thousands of free Polish citizenry sent off to Germany as slave labor; finally, the thousands executed across the land as reprisal measures against Poland's determination to remain free. And despite countless Nazi attempts to destroy it, Polish Christianity after 1942 when the ghettoes first came under fierce attack managed, in the teeth of the most brutal occupation in history, to provide continuing and heroic assistance to the Jews, some one hundred thousand of whom were saved thanks to the valor of their Christian countrymen.[79]

The point is, of course, holocausts of human beings—from aborted fetuses to Armenians to Biafrans to Cambodians to Ethiopians, and so on[80]—positively pockmark the century we live in with obscene and alphabetic regularity. The Great War alone succeeded very nicely in annihilating eight million or so human beings, only a handful of whom had most likely ever heard of Archduke Ferdinand and his consort, whose assassinations tipped over the bloody cauldron in the first place. "I have been reading my usual late-night fare," says the hero of Walker Percy's *Love in the Ruins*, "Stedmann's *History of World War I*. For weeks now I've been on the Battle of Verdun, which killed half a million men, lasted a year, and left the battle lines unchanged. Here began the hemorrhage and death by suicide of the old western world: white Christian Caucasian Europeans, sentimental music loving Germans and rational clear-minded Frenchmen, slaughtering each other without passion. 'The men in the trenches did not hate each other,' wrote Stedmann. 'As for the generals, they respected or condemned each other precisely as colleagues in the same profession.' "[81]

Yes, one has only to review the sad events of our time to know that aggression—massively, stupidly, demonically sustained—fairly reveals the central lineaments of modern life. "I think it would be very wicked indeed," concludes Evelyn Waugh's disillusioned classics professor, "to do anything to fit a boy for the modern world."[82] Ours, it seems, is a life which more and more assumes the surreal features of a Fellini film, with its numberless sunbathers blithe and insouciant beneath the Sign of their Salvation, i.e., an enormous Cross which, suspended from a helicopter, hovers high above the rooftops of *La Dolce Vita*. Not the least shadow of that Cross is permitted nowadays publicly to fall across the horizons of our world, a world that increasingly displays its hostility for all that is meant by the grammar and the poetry of the transcendent.[83]

All of this, it is now increasingly evident, forces the question: What has become the dominant reality of our moment in history? And the answer is certainly fraught with gloom, namely that the human person is in peril of extinction. Not, heaven knows, because of wholesale nuclear incineration of the race, however symptomatic of our common peril the specter of nuclear weaponry may appear to be. No, the present predicament is rather more fundamental, and far more menacing than mere atom bombs; it is a situation of virtual rejection, of *abolition* (to use a better word, and one which C.S. Lewis used in the title of a trenchant little work he wrote back in the '40s called *The Abolition of Man*) of all that heretofore had been the decisive understanding of man in the Christian West. The very understanding which the God-Man himself crafted from the materials of his own unspeakable agony upon the Cross.[84]

Conclusion: Prelude to Holy Saturday

Between the two—that is, the anguish and predicament of man whose apogee may have been reached in the Death Camps of our century *and* the cry of the Pierced One upon the Cross—profound analogical connections have been struck; which is exactly why, in the words of Julian Green,

> Jesus' torment goes on in this world, day and night. Having once been nailed to a Roman cross, He has been persecuted with inexorable cruelty in the person of His own people. One cannot strike a Jew without having the same blow fall on Him who is the Man par excellence and, at the same time, the Flower of Israel. It is Jesus who was struck in the concentration camps. It is always He. His suffering is never ended. Ah, to put an end to all this, and to begin anew! That we could only meet one another on the morning of the Resurrection, that we could embrace Israel, weep, and not say a word. After Auschwitz, tears alone have meaning. Christian, wipe the tears and the blood from the face of your Jewish brother, and the face of Christ will shine on both of you.[85]

And in wiping those tears we may come to understand a bit better, not just the historical event of the Cross, or the plight of God's People cast into gas ovens in our own century, but the deep mystery to all that the physical Cross is prelude, namely the mystery of Holy Saturday. Is it not here, finally, at this point of depth to the self-emptying of Almighty God—the event even of his seeming eclipse—that we touch something of ourselves, an experience shatteringly akin to our own blood-drenched century? "The participation in the experience of the *kenosis*," argues John S. Dunne, "the sense of being oneself forsaken by God, was perhaps in any case the fundamental spiritual experience of modern times."[86] It was Hegel who first uncovered, says Dunne, in the course of his reaching dialectically right into the heart of modernity, what he, Hegel, had called a "Golgotha of absolute spirit"; he attempted to understand the Cross of Christ which the old Lutheran hymn expressed in the words "O great distress, God himself is dead," and so came to describe the ineffable event of God's death as "a monstrous, dreadful spectacle which brings before the mind the deepest chasm of severance." Only later, of course, with the shrieking lunatic out of Nietzsche announcing a godless advent of his own, do we awaken to discover the face of that wilder despair which, in our post-modern sophistication, we have tried more or less to domesticate; so that, more and more, we need hardly think about it at all. Nevertheless, the world has grown weightless in its reeling from all that it now knows. What else is this, suggests Dunne, but "the human spirit's consciousness of being left to itself, of being altogether forsaken by God...abandoned to suffering and death"?[87]

What else, indeed, but the consciousness that we are all mysteriously implicated in the fate of the Jew? This is surely why, to quote Marcel Dubois, "the Calvary of the Jewish people whose summit is the Holocaust, can help us to understand a little better the mystery of the cross." And, to be sure, it may help us as well to rivet our minds and hearts on all that the Cross reveals of what is perhaps the deepest Christian mystery of all, i.e., Holy Saturday: the one day of the year which remains closest liturgically to the anguished cry of abandonment marking the Jewish experience of the Holocaust.

NOTES

1. Hans Urs von Balthasar, "The Last Five Stations of the Cross," *Theologians Today*, selected and edited by Martin Redfern, (London and New York: Sheed and Ward, 1972).

2. Elie Wiesel, *The Gates of the Forest*, (New York: Avon, 1967), p. 47.

3. Not the silence, as it were, of "the God of Abraham, the God of Isaac, the God of Jacob, the God of the Christians...a God of love and consolation," but the God of the philosophers who presume in their arrogance to know His name yet not to be in the least sensible to their own wretchedness as to ever call upon his help. See Pascal's *Pensées*, no. 449.

4. John 1:3.

5. T.S. Eliot, *Four Quartets*, (New York: Harcourt, Brace & World, 1943), p. 51.

6. On the strength of the Christology implied in the hymn, Paul attempts to inculcate among the Philippians certain sentiments of Jesus Christ. But what is the Christology here? The operative words would seem to be: *emptied himself* and *even death upon a cross*. Comments Joseph Fitzmyer: "Jesus, in becoming man, divested himself of the privilege of divine glory; he did not empty himself of divinity, but of the status of glory to which he had a right and which would be restored at his exaltation (cf. Jn 17:5; Mt 17:1-8). His voluntary giving up of *doxa* was the humiliation of the Incarnation." To which the nadir is reached in the phrase, *even death upon a cross*, concerning whose nature Fitzmyer writes: "The lowest depth of Jesus' humiliation is set forth in this phrase, added by Paul and

expressive of the point farthest removed from his celestial and glorious status. From this nadir the upward movement of the hymn begins." *The Jerome Biblical Commentary*, vol. II, (New Jersey: Prentice-Hall, 1968), p. 251. Fr. Galot, meanwhile, has hit upon the deeply sacrificial aspect to the hymn, which, by contrast he says, is only discreetly suggested in the hymn of John's Prologue: "The Word became flesh" (Jn 1:14). "The boldness of thought expressed in Paul's hymn consists in discerning a sacrifice in the very fact of the Incarnation." Which event, Galot suggests, could well have been infinitely and visibly glorious had God so chosen to manifest himself. "The flesh could have manifested the splendor of the divine state from the start. But kenosis implies the choice of a different kind of Incarnation, one that contrasts with Adam's sinful act. For the first man had wanted, in his human condition, to grasp at equality with God. Christ, on the other hand, although by nature divine, refused to grasp this equality. He preferred to assume 'the very nature of a servant.' " *Who is Christ: A Theology of the Incarnation*, (Rome: Gregorian University Press; Chicago: Franciscan Herald Press, 1980), pp. 183-184.

7. Hans Urs von Balthasar, *Convergences: To the Source of Christian Mystery*, (San Francisco: Ignatius, 1983). The German title of the text, *Einfaltungen*, is a word whose creative and flexible use, along with the verb *einfalten*, indicates—so the translator reports—"a movement of recentralization and convergence, a return of multiplicity into the unity that is its source—'in-folding' as the reverse of unfolding," p. 9.

8. *Convergences*, p. 12.

9. Hans Urs von Balthasar, *The Glory of the Lord: A Theological Aesthetics* in seven volumes, the first three of which have been translated into English by Ignatius Press. The work as a whole, however, is only the first part of a great trilogy in which all the transcendentals—truth, goodness and beauty—are penetrated from within the heart of Christian revelation. First beauty in *The Glory of the Lord*, then goodness in *Theodramatik* and finally truth in *Theologik*.

10. Michael Waldstein, "An Introduction to von Balthasar's *The Glory of the Lord*," *Communio* 14 (Spring, 1987), pp. 31-32. Elsewhere Waldstein quotes (i.e., in his unpublished doctoral dissertation) the following enlargement of the insight which appears in *Herrlichkeit*, II/1, pp. 9-10: "all that is beautiful in the world (and consequently also all that is true and good) is directed upward to the exceeding measure in which the living God of love glorifies Himself by lavishing His groundless love on His creatures kenotically unto His emptiness, yes, even unto what is strictly wholly-other than Himself, into the abyss of the guilty, godless darkness, unto being forsaken by God. By going to the outermost of not-being God, He establishes in a final way His lordship (*Herr-heit*) and lofty splendor (*Hehre*) in what is other than Himself, in man. From the glorified *kyrios* He glorifies also (*mitver-herrlicht*) mankind and the cosmos. Christ in His final prayer (John 17) states this glorification as an accomplished fact and calls for it as something to be achieved."

11. See Ignatius' Letter to the Ephesians 19.1 where he describes with rough eloquence the hiddenness of the divine strategy in disarming the devil for the

world's salvation: "Now Mary's virginity and her giving birth escaped the notice of the prince of this world, as did the Lord's death—those three secrets crying to be told, but wrought in God's silence," *Early Christian Fathers*, vol. I, The Library of Christian Classics, ed. by Cyril C. Richardson, (New York: Macmillan, 1970), p. 93.

12. It is, moreover, the deepest and final aspect of von Balthasar's particular trinitarian reading of the form of Jesus; an exposition which, as M. Waldstein observes in his essay, examines in turn each of the three features of the form, to wit, "claim, poverty and abandonment, as united by the central Johannine theme of the mission or obedience of Jesus," p. 27. But it is the unique abandonment of the God-Man, "his hour in final abandonment to the working of the Father," where "the whole weight and thrust (Hebrew, *kabod* = weight, glory) of God's rejection of sin is embraced by the far greater weight and thrust of God's love: It is embraced by the love of the Father who 'so loved the world that he gave his only Son' (John 3:16), and by the love of the Son who 'loved his own' in such a way that he 'loved them to the end' (John 13:1), to the end of 'bearing the sin of the world' (John 1:29)," p. 31. It is this which locates the deep center to all Christological thought, the paradoxical point where all perspectives converge.

13. Indeed, its very shape, transcendently vertical, suggests the sheer depth of redemption to which Christ's Cross extends in its reaching into the very soul of our wretchedness in order, finally, to set us free. The Cross, thus, represents the deepest and mightiest symbol of our solidarity.

14. Hans Urs von Balthasar, *A Theological Anthropology*, (New York: Sheed and Ward, 1967), p. 247.

15. The idea is not entirely my own, rather the germ of it I first came across in reading David Jones, an extraordinary Catholic poet, whose essays and verse have helped to shape a distinctive sacramental aesthetic for our time.

16. Karl Rahner, *Sacramentum Mundi II*, (London: Burns and Oates, 1969), p. 207.

17. Balthasar, *A Theological Anthropology*, pp. 275-276.

18. "For our sake he made him to be sin who knew no sin, so that in him we might become the righteousness of God" (2 Cor. 5:21). A much controverted text, the history of its varying interpretations reveals the much larger split in Christendom between Roman Catholics and those of Reformist persuasion, the latter breaking off from what had been the predominant understanding of Christ's redemptive sacrifice. See Stanislas Lyonnet and Leopold Sabarin, *Sin, Redemption, and Sacrifice* (Rome: Biblical Institute Press, 1970), pp. 187-244. The existing tradition, indeed, the one destined to achieve classical status around the thought of the Church Fathers, is ably expressed in Augustine who, say the authors, "clearly proposed for the first time the interpretation 'sin' as 'sacrifice for sin'.... In subsequent writings Augustine proposes again and again the same interpretation," p. 212. "Christ was made 'sin' means, then, for St. Augustine, that having come into a flesh similar to sinful flesh (Rom. 8:3) he offered it up on the cross and thus became sacrifice for sin," p. 215. St. Thomas Aquinas, too, shares

in the Augustinian understanding, as witness the following from the *Summa*, which the authors reproduce on p. 222:

> *God made Christ sin*—not, indeed, in such sort that he had sin, but that he made him a sacrifice for sin: even as it is written (Hos. 4:8): *They shall eat the sins of my people*—they—i.e., the priests, who by the law ate the sacrifices offered for sin. And in that way it is written (Is. 53:6) that *the Lord hath laid on him the iniquity of us all* (i.e., he gave him up to be a victim for the sins of all men); or *he made him sin* (i.e., made him to have *the likeness of sinful flesh*), as is written (Rom. 8:3), and this on account of the passible and mortal body he assumed. *Sum. Th.* 3a, 15,1, ad 4 (trans. Fathers of the English Dominican Province).

19. "Christ redeemed us from the curse of the law, having become a curse for us—for it is written, 'Cursed be everyone who hangs on a tree—' " (Gal. 3:13). Once again, Lyonnet and Sabarin, *Sin, Redemption, and Sacrifice*, draw our attention to the relevant distinctions, citing, among others, Aquinas, who reminds us of the two curses implicit in Paul's language, i.e., that of guilt and that of penalty. Comment our authors: "The first curse Jesus has incurred because, *in the eyes of men*, of the Jews mainly, he was reputed to be a sinner (see Jn. 18:30). Jesus took upon himself also the curse of penalty for our sake, when he assumed mortality which is the likeness of sin (see Rom. 8:3). And St. Thomas concludes: 'God made him to be "sin," that is, he made him suffer the penalty of sin, when he was offered up for our sins,' (*Super epist.* ad Gal. III,5)." They likewise quote Augustine, who writes in his *Sermo Guelferbytanus*, 31.1, in edit. G. Morin, 558, that "Christ came and found us lying in guilt and under a penalty; he took up the penalty only and thus removed both the guilt and the penalty." In addition, they refer to Hugh of St. Victor, who nicely summarizes the traditional view of Galatians 3:13 when he writes in the *Quaestiones et decisiones in epist. ad Gal.*, that of the two curses, "One is the curse of guilt, remote from Christ, another is that of penalty, which Christ voluntarily sustained, when he was made for our sake curse, or sin, that is, an offering for sin: in order to remove the curse of all, that of guilt and that of penalty." In other words, Jesus assumed the "necessity" of penalty so as to rid the world of guilt's "necessity." See Lyonnet and Sabarin's exhaustive discussion on pp. 222-223.

20. "For God has done what the law, weakened by the flesh, could not do: sending his own Son in the likeness of sinful flesh and for sin, he condemned sin in the flesh" (Rom. 8:3). Once again, the traditional view of Christ's expiation, robustly upheld from Irenaeus of Lyons through Augustine to Aquinas and, even beyond the Common Doctor, to Robert Bellarmine, insists that by the terms of our Lord's atoning sacrifice he voluntarily and out of a supreme love assumed our sinful flesh in order precisely by the strength and merit of his own divinely innocent life, so mysteriously inserted into the frame and flesh of sinful man, he might thereby undo the mortal damage wrought by sin. "When he became incarnate and was made man," writes Irenaeus (*Adv. Haer.* 3.18,1), "he recapitulated in himself the long history of man, summing up and giving us salvation in

order that we might receive again in Christ Jesus what we had lost in Adam, that is, the image and likeness of God." See Lyonnet and Sabarin, p. 190. Likewise Aquinas who, in his *Comp. Theol.*, 226, explains the cost of Christ's marvelous work of recapitulative mercy, namely Christ suffering all that we had merited to suffer because of our common link to the sin of Adam; inasmuch as all human sufferings are ordained to death—"For the wages of sin is death," Rom. 6:23— Christ willed to suffer and die. How otherwise is sin to be condemned in the flesh? "It can be said that Christ was in a way identified with sinners," report Lyonnet and Sabarin, "since by the incarnation he came 'in the likeness of sinful flesh' to be an offering for sin (Rom. 8:3). It would, however, be untrue to say that he ever was, like the condemned wicked, the object of God's vindictive justice (his wrath)," p. 234. It is this reading, nevertheless, which informs, among others of the Reformation legacy, Calvin's reading of the atonement. See his *Institutes* II, 16,5: CR 30, wherein he claims that the "Son of God has taken upon himself God's righteous vengeance." That Christ should be represented as victim -object of divine enmity and anger, enduring such wrath in order to allay its ferocity, is entirely repugnant to Paul's meaning. If Christ is to be called "sin," says Bellarmine in his *Controversies* (1586-89), it is surely not because sins are imputed to him but rather because he now chooses to atone for them. Thus, the truer title for Christ is not that of "sinner" but "righteous" insofar as one who satisfies for another is "most righteous." See pp. 234-235, 240 of *Sin, Redemption, and Sacrifice.*

   21.   "He had no form or comeliness that
            we should look at him,
         and no beauty that we should
            desire him." (Is. 53:2)

   22. "Having cancelled the bond which stood against us with its legal demands; this he set aside, nailing it to the cross," (Col. 2:14).

   23. Balthasar, *Does Jesus Know Us? Do We Know Him?* (San Francisco: Ignatius, 1983), p. 35.

   24. In *Two Say Why*, (Chicago: Franciscan Herald Press, 1971), p. 48, von Balthasar explains: "The Old Testament category of the '*pro nobis*' (Is. 53) comes immediately to mind as a pre-Pauline interpretation of the event upon the cross. But only reflection upon the Christ-event brings to light who he must have been who could effect this '*pro nobis*,' and how he was constituted. In the claim that isolates his 'I' from all the other 'I's lies the power of his supreme capacity to bear so much. This is what illumines the uniqueness of his abandonment by God."

   25. See *Translations from the Poetry of Rainer Maria Rilke*, by M.D. Herter Norton, (New York: W.W. Norton & Co., 1938), pp. 155-157.

   26. Philippe de la Trinité, O.C.D., *What is Redemption?* (New York: Hawthorn, 1961), pp. 34-35. This is immediately followed by a Father Pro, whose comment is reproduced approvingly, to wit, "Ultimately, all this retributive justice, this bargaining, this notion of a ferocious God seem to us to verge on blasphemy."

See his article (Fr. Pro, that is) "Vivre de Dieu" in *La Vie Spirituelle*, May 1959 (no. 450), p. 498.

27. Balthasar, *Theodramatik*, vol. III, (Einsiedeln: Johannes Verlag, 1980), pp. 312-313. Cited by M. Waldstein in his essay on von Balthasar. The essay goes on to quote Aquinas' assertion (*Summa Theol.*, III, qu. 46, art. 6,c) that Christ's passion necessarily exceeds in its horror all other pain: "First, on account of the cause of this pain.... For the cause of interior pain were the sins of the whole human race for which Christ atoned by suffering, which is why he ascribed these sins to himself, as it were (*quasi sibi adscribit*), as when he says in Psalm 21:2, 'My God, my God, why have you forsaken me?...' " and, to be sure, it is von Balthasar's point, ably brought out in the article by M. Waldstein, that the whole pivot on which the majesty of love turns, as shown in the sending of the Son, is precisely God himself. Indeed, says Waldstein, "the final root of the glory of the Lord lies in God himself. It lies in the fact that God is eternally Father, and thus a God who does not cling to his divinity, but exists only as the one from whom the Son proceeds. The complete relationality and fluidity of the Father is the ultimate foundation of the mission of Jesus. 'God's self-abandonment in the Incarnation has its ontic ground of possibility in God's eternal self-abandonment, his three-personal gift of self,' (von Balthasar, "Mysterium Paschale," in *Mysterium Salutis*, vol. III, 2 [Einsiedeln, Benziger, 1970], p. 133). The ultimate mystery, then, which is manifested and made present in the Cross of Christ is the Trinity, the fact that God is eternal and absolute love: God is God only as the Father who gives himself eternally and completely to the Son, as the Son, who eternally receives himself in this gift and returns himself to the glorification of the Father, and as the Spirit, who is the seal and witness of this unity of love," pp. 32-33.

This is the primordial drama which antedates even the mission of Jesus in the flesh inasmuch as it takes place eternally within the life of the Trinity. It is also the central thesis of von Balthasar's *Theodramatik* as the following makes clear: "It is meaningless," says von Balthasar, "to call this drama, which is superior to all time, 'static,' 'abstract,' or 'closed in itself,' in the opinion that it receives its movement and color only in the passage through sin, Cross, and hell. This is hubris and an excessive estimate of created freedom.... Rather, we must say that the 'emptying' of the Father's heart in generating the Son includes and surpasses every drama between God and a world, because a world can only have its place within the distinction between Father and Son which is held open and bridged by the Spirit," *Theodramatik*, vol. III, p. 304. Cited by Waldstein, p. 33.

28. Argues von Balthasar: "it is quite possible to speak of the Son of God suffering what the sinner deserved, i.e., separation from God, perhaps even complete and final separation," *Two Say Why*, p. 36. Provided, however, and the proviso here is absolutely crucial to the maintenance of right relations within the Trinity, that this separation *not* be taken ontologically as disrupting fundamentally that unity eternally perduring among the persons of the Trinity; rather the implied meaning must be in those mystical and psychological terms whereby Christ freely suffers himself to *feel*, and thus to endure even in that Divine Person to which the world's flesh is annealed, the effects of that very separation which

von Balthasar calls complete and final. In a more recent work, *Truth is Symphonic: Aspects of Christian Pluralism*, (San Francisco: Ignatius, 1987), von Balthasar enlarges upon the question: "According to Philippians, the same person appears now in the form of God, now in the form of a slave, and in the Gospel this same subject can say, 'The hour is coming…when you will leave me alone; yet I am not alone, for the Father is with me' (Jn. 16:32), and a little later, 'My God, my God, why have you forsaken me?' (Mk. 15:34). The experiences of the same subject are in contradictory modes, but they do not assail his identity. Prior to the Cross, Jesus can know that even in the coming experience of forsakenness he will not be forsaken by the Father; on the Cross itself, he experiences this forsakenness so deeply, for the sake of sinners, that he no longer feels or knows anything of the Father's presence. His relationship with the Father is indestructible; he says, 'My God'—but this God is hidden *sub contrario*. Indeed, the very profundity of his forsakenness is the sign of him who so profoundly conceals himself…His forsakenness affects his entire relationship with the Father; the mists envelop even the mountain peaks—but, walking through the valley of darkness, it does not cease being what it is, namely, sheer dependence, absolute obedience on the basis of boundless love…. All the same, since it is a question of encompassing the world in all its profanity—for its relation to God has been profaned—there can be no stopping halfway once the path of 'concealment in the opposite' has been taken up. It must be followed to the very end: 'He descended into hell,' " pp. 39-41.

29. Joseph Cardinal Ratzinger, *Behold the Pierced One: An Approach to a Spiritual Christology*, (San Francisco: Ignatius, 1986), p. 57. "For the heart is an expression for the human passion—i.e., not only man's passions but also the 'passion' of being human. Over against the Stoic ideal of *apatheia*, over against the Aristotelian God, who is Thought thinking itself, the heart is the epitome of the passions, without which there could have been no passion on the part of the Son," p. 56.

30. "And if a man has committed a crime punishable by death and he is put to death, and you hang him on a tree, his body shall not remain all night upon the tree, but you shall bury him the same day, for a hanged man is accursed by God; you shall not defile your land which the Lord your God gives you for an inheritance" (Deut. 21: 22-23). And, of course, Paul repeats the text in Gal 3:13.

31. Balthasar, *Two Say Why*, p. 36.

32. Balthasar, *A Theological Anthropology*, pp. 279-280. "The pitcher of the Word is empty because the source in heaven, the speaking mouth, the Father, has dried up. The Father has withdrawn. And the words of abandonment, shouted into the darkness, are, like standing water, condemned to evaporate, or are like the convulsions of amputated limbs," p. 280.

33. *A Theological Anthropology*, p. 242.

34. *A Theological Anthropology*: "Thus, he has passing time also in his grip, not through a poetic, legislative transcendence of time, but by dominating the inner time structure," p. 242.

35. Balthasar, *Two Say Why*, p. 38.

36. Franklin Sherman, "Speaking of God after Auschwitz," *Worldview* 17, no. 9, September 1974, p. 29. "We speak of God after Auschwitz," he insists in the same article, "only as the one who calls us to a new unity as between brothers—not only between Jews and Christians, but especially between Jews and Christians."

37. Abraham J. Heschel, *The Prophets,* (New York and Evanston: Harper & Row, 1962). To his dedication page Rabbi Heschel appends the following excerpt from Psalm 44, a cry of heart-rending poignancy and fidelity in the midst of sorrow and the silence of God:

> All this has come upon us,
> Though we have not forgotten Thee,
> Or been false to Thy covenant.
> Our heart has not turned back,
> Nor have our steps departed from Thy way...
> ...for Thy sake we are slain...
> Why dost Thou hide Thy face?

38. Heschel, p. 145.

39. *Ibid.*, p. 151.

40. Is. 63: 9.

41. Is. 40:11.

42. Abraham Heschel, *A Passion for Truth,* (New York: Farrar, Straus and Giroux, 1973), p. 273.

43 "The fourth song in Isaiah 52:13–53:12 expresses in moving language how God uses the undeserved violence against his servant to save other guilty people. This is the famous 'Suffering Servant' of Isaiah. It is a remarkable passage because it suggests more clearly than anywhere else in the Old Testament that God accepts one individual's suffering to atone for the sins of others," Lawrence Boadt, C.S.P., *Reading the Old Testament: An Introduction,* (New York: Paulist Press, 1984), p. 428. Or, again, from *The Jerome Biblical Commentary,* (New Jersey: Prentice-Hall, 1968), the following from Carroll Stuhlmueller on Deutero-Isaiah: "in the fourth song, the servant remains one with all people in sorrow and yet distinct from each of them in innocence of life and total service of God. The doctrine of expiatory suffering finds supreme expression in these lines. Style matches thought, for seldom does the Bible reach such extraordinary power of sound, balance, and contrast," vol. 1, p. 378.

44. Is. 53:4-6. On the basis of such sublime and kenotic language, is it any wonder that the Church should naturally attribute these words to the Word himself, who truly bore our sorrows and sins while being entirely innocent and full of the Spirit of endless joy? "The New Testament identifies Jesus as the Suffering Servant at his baptism (Mk. 1:11; Jn. 1:34), in his miracles (Mt. 8:17), and in his humility (Mt. 12:18ff.). John sums up Jesus' public ministry in the words of the Servant (Jn. 12:37-43). This attribution of the Servant theme to Jesus occurs in Acts (3:13-26; 4:27, 30; 8:32) and in the hymns of the early Church (Phil. 2:7; 1 Pet. 2:21-15)," Stuhlmueller, *The Jerome Biblical Commentary,* p. 378.

45. Jurgen Moltmann, *The Crucified God: The Cross of Christ as the Foundation and Criticism of Christian Theology*, (SCM Press Ltd, 1974), p. 222.

46. Isn't this, *mutatis mutandis*, the underlying meaning to that misery and belated remorse which finally overtakes the effete protagonist of Henry James' "The Beast in the Jungle," perhaps the most harrowing tale he ever wrote? A man is haunted almost unto damnation by his repeated failure to love the one person whom chance and circumstance—not to mention an all-seeing Providence—had thrown into the current of his life, and rather than rejoice in the delighted discovery of another's love, he elects to sink amid the backwash of his own paltry and passionless vanity. See *The Complete Tales of Henry James* edited and introduced by Leon Edel, vol. XI: 1900-1903, (London: Rupert Hart-Davis, 1964). "The tale has its autobiographical side," ventures Edel in his introduction. "James had known a woman and taken her friendship, and never allowed himself to know her feelings. She was kind and interested—and he had never imagined an interest beyond friendship. In the end she had taken her life, one winter's morning in Venice, in great loneliness and melancholy. All this had happened a decade earlier, and out of these sombre memories James seems to have distilled the essence of 'The Beast in the Jungle.' It is a story of an unlived life; and of a man who loses the love he might have had, through selfishness," p. 10.

47. Moltmann, p. 230. In other words, is God subject to change or isn't he? If yes, are we left then with a God as mutable as men. To admit as much would, concedes Moltmann, cancel at once the Church's rejection of Arius at Nicaea, which rightly insisted upon the unchangeableness of God. "However," he argues, "the conclusion should not be drawn from this that God is unchangeable in every respect, for this negative definition merely says that God is under no constraint from that which is not of God," p. 229. But is not suffering among those "constraints" to which the condition of not being God subjects the rest of us? And if so, does God then not suffer? "The mainstream church," he continues, "maintains against the Syrian monophysites that it was impossible for God to suffer. God cannot suffer like creatures who are exposed to illness, pain and death. But must God therefore be thought of as being incapable of suffering in any respect?" Only if the one alternative to suffering is that condition of inherent and necessary incapacity to suffer which the ancient world understood as *apatheia*. "But there are other forms of suffering," Moltmann reminds us, "between unwilling suffering as a result of an alien cause and being essentially unable to suffer, namely active suffering, the suffering of love, in which one voluntarily opens himself to the possibility of being affected by another," pp. 229-230. Deny God the right to suffer in this sense, i.e., the absolute incapacity for suffering, and he is at once reduced to lovelessness. It is this understanding of God—as a being for others, as sheer relational existence, as love—which snapped the Aristotelian spell.

48. Dante, *The Divine Comedy*, Book Three, Paradiso XXXIII, line 127 to the end.

49. "Dentro da se del suo colore istesso / Mi parve pinta della nostra effige / Per che il mio viso in lei tutto era messo." The translation reads: "Within itself, and in its own color, / Seemed to be painted with our effigy; / And so absorbed my attention altogether." From a new verse translation by C. H. Sisson, (Chicago: Regnery Gateway, 1980).

50. Joseph Ratzinger, *Introduction to Christianity*, (New York: Seabury Press, 1969), p. 142.

51. *Ibid.*, p. 141.

52. "When I see the blind and wretched state of man," says Pascal in number 198 of his *Pensées*, "when I survey the whole universe in its dumbness and man left to himself with no light, as though lost in this corner of the universe, without knowing who put him there, what he has come to do, what will become of him when he dies, incapable of knowing anything, I am moved to terror, like a man transported in his sleep to some terrifying desert island, who wakes up quite lost and with no means of escape. Then I marvel that so wretched a state does not drive people to despair." In Blaise Pascal, *Pensées*, translated and with an introduction by A. J. Krailsheimer, (Middlesex, England: Penguin, 1966), p. 88.

53. Balthasar, *Convergences*, p. 136.

54. See, for example, Frederick Wilhelmsen, *The Metaphysics of Love*, (New York: Sheed and Ward, 1962), pp. 145ff. for his discussion of the primacy of love within a Catholic metaphysics of being.

55. Balthasar, *Convergences*, pp. 136-137. Professor Wilhelmsen's conclusion from the text cited above is worth quoting in the context of von Balthasar's "only if": "Paul Tillich reminds us that the word *trotz*—'in spite of'—recurs constantly in the writings of Martin Luther. The Protestant of tomorrow will meet the new world in spite of the anxieties it brings, in spite of the heroism that it demands.... But we Catholics have an inheritance all our own—the inheritance of folly. All love is folly because all love is based on the impossible paradox that a man will gain his soul only by throwing it away. But the more we are dwarfed by the stars beyond, the more we shall love them as creatures of the Triune God. And the more we love them, the more will they be brought low and the more will we be exalted above them. We shall know all these things, but we shall not love because of this knowledge. And this love will be our Catholic courage—the courage of fools," p. 155.

56. Balthasar, *Two Say Why*, pp. 51-52.

57. *Ibid.* The recognition, again, as von Balthasar has been at some length trying to make clear, is the Trinitarian one: "He (the Father) recognizes that this word, become man, has been able to do what the Father intended when he generated and uttered this word; to make himself audible and intelligible to anyone who does not want to hear any more about God. In other words: that Jesus could become the brother of the very least and of the lost; that he could reveal, more by deed than by word; that God, as all-powerful, is love, and, as love, is all-powerful; that he is this intrinsically, in the mystery of his Trinity, which can be explained only by the total opposition—between being with God and being abandoned by God—within God himself.

"As the three in one, God is so intensely everlasting love, that within his life temporal death and the hellish desolation of the creature, accepted out of love, can become transmuted into an expression of love. (The necessary concealment of a vicarious accompanying into abandonment also results in a certain concealment of the resurrection in the eyes of the world; an event which can be accepted only by an act of receptive faith could not become a neutral datum of world-historical publicity)," pp. 52-53.

58. Eliot, *Four Quartets*, p. 29. The imagery owes much of its inspiration to both Sir Thomas Browne, who wrote "For this world I count it not an inn but an Hospital; a place not to live, but to dye in," and St. John of the Cross, who speaks of the soul as "under treatment for recovery of its health, which is God Himself." Eliot himself often acknowledged such august sources as necessary stimulants for his own creative poetry.

59. Walter Kasper, *The God of Jesus Christ,* (SCM Press, 1983), p. 191.

60. Balthasar, *A Theological Anthropology*, p. 277.

61. *Ibid.*, p. 278. The text from Origen is: *Homiliae in Ezechielem* 6, 6 (GCS Orig. 8, 383ff.), cf. *Commentarium in Epistulam ad Romanos* VII, 9 (PG 16, 1127C-1130A).

62. *Behold the Pierced One*, p. 58. Ratzinger reproduces the following from Origen in a footnote which is worth passing on: "...The Father himself is not without feeling (*impassibilis*). When we cry to him, he has mercy and shares in the experience of suffering; because of love he tastes something which, from the point of view of his sublimity, he cannot experience," cf. Origen, *Ezech*. h. 6, 6 (Baehr. VIII, 384f.). St. Gregory Nazianzen writes similarly in his poem on human nature, Ratzinger notes; see V. 121f. (PG 37.765) for confirmation of his point.

63. Balthasar, *A Theological Anthropology*, p. 278.

64. *Behold the Pierced One*, p. 58. See also Jean Galot, *Il Mistero Della Sofferenza Di Dio*, (Assisi: Cittadella Editrice, 1975), p. 95. "Per la descrizione del gesto redentore del Padre, amore e sofferenza sono inseparabili. Ora tale gesto redentore e la verita capitale di tutta la rivelazione e, per conseguenza, l'amore sofferente appare come disposizione essenziale del Padre, disposizione nella quale egli si fa conoscere piu profondamente da noi come Padre." A rough translation of the foregoing would be: "To describe the redeeming gesture of the Father, we can say that love and suffering cannot be separated. Now this redeeming gesture is the capital truth of all revelation and, as a consequence, the suffering love appears as an essential disposition in the Father, a disposition in which he makes himself known as a Father to us more profoundly." This necessary conjunction of divine suffering love would seem to follow also from Scripture, and doubtless a fair number of proof-texts might be summoned to show that God suffers in virtue of the immensity of his love for us. (See, for example, the tears of Christ recorded in Lk. 19:41 as he wept over the city he had come down to earth to save.) Nor may we assign suffering here merely to, say, Christ's humanity, as if the instrumentality of his redemption—i.e., the *what* he had assumed in becoming one of us—were somehow the subject itself of Christ's redemption and not the Word, the Son, *who* effected that very redemption. Here the lesson of

Ephesus is most instructive: that Council taught (cfr. the Letter of St. Cyril to Nestorius, COD[3], 42) that the Son appropriated to himself all the sufferings inflicted upon his human nature.

Nevertheless, the Church's teaching is clear, namely that God remains both immutable and impassible. According to the Commission *Theologique Internationale: Textes et Documents* (1969-1985), Preface du Cardinal Ratzinger (Cerf), pp. 257-261, a number of distinctions need to be kept firmly in view. One, the inexhaustibility of the divine life is to be affirmed in order that God not be construed as somehow needing creatures to complete himself. "No created event could bring to Him something *new*, or actuate in Him any potentiality whatsoever...it is His property to be absolutely immutable." Thus God does not require, as Hegel would have it, the travail of the world to evince the fullness of who God is; that the idea of God needs its own negation—the "hardness of abandonment"—to achieve itself. Two, the immutability of the living God may in no way be opposed to his supreme freedom, as witness that divine liberty exercised in the Incarnation. Three, the truth of God's immutability is not tantamount to establishing his essential indifference to human misery, as though God's changelessness were meant to imply an inability to love. "Divine immutability and divine love in total freedom mutually complete one another; neglecting the one, or the other, would not respect the concept of God as He has revealed this to us." Four, what God fundamentally is—yes, even in his very immutability—is compassion, an attribute which he possesses to an infinite and perfect degree. "His compassion is the inclination of commiseration...and is not the lack of power. Such compassion is compatible with eternal beatitude itself." Thus, for example, when the poet Charles Péguy, in his incomparable poem, "Night," attributes the following to God the Father, who in speaking of the Son's crucifixion, exhorts us, "Let us not mention it anymore. It hurts me." It is one of those admissible anthropomorphisms behind which stands an immense truth about God, to wit, that he is full of compassionate love.

> "All was over," says God, "that unbelievable adventure
> By which I, God, have tied my arms for my eternity,
> That adventure by which my Son tied my arms,
> For eternally tying the arms of my justice, for
>   eternally untying the arms of my mercy,
> And against my justice inventing a new justice,
> A justice of love, a justice of Hope. All was over."

See his *Men and Saints: Prose and Poetry*, (New York: Pantheon Books, 1944), pp. 271-299. Finally, from Galot, *Il Mistero Della Sofferenza Di Dio*, p. 98: "If the Father has suffered in this decision (i.e., to send the Son to redeem us) which only an immense love for humanity could have moved him to assume, he must have suffered profoundly in the realization of this sacrifice. With his decision he had freely exposed himself to suffer in his Fatherly heart the sufferings inflicted on Jesus. He had deliberately entered in the way of compassion."

65. Because the implied equation is so essential to the argument of the chapter, see John M. Oesterreicher's *Auschwitz, The Christian, and The Council,* (Montreal: A Palm Book, 1965), which marshals a great many illustrations pursuant to that thesis. For instance, he writes: "Eyewitnesses also tell of many who, the very instant they realized their doom, prayed aloud. Often the Jewish profession of faith: *Shema Yisra'el,* 'Hear, O Israel, the Lord our God, the Lord is One' rent the air, thereby turning defeat into victory. That men, about to breathe the deadly gas, could proclaim the living God; that at the moment of agony, they could call upon Him who is love, foretold the ultimate ruin of the would-be masters of destruction," p. 15.

But far and away the finest example he cites is from Sholem Asch's *In the Valley of Death,* where, referring to a proclamation by the underground forces of Warsaw on the mass murder of Polish Jewry, he notes: "There is one sentence in the proclamation which is characteristic: 'Catholics dying with the name of Christ and their Holy Mother on their lips, together with orthodox Jews calling their last prayer, *Hear O Israel...*' I do not believe that since Nero those two calls have been mingled together in one arena of martyrdom." Quote on p. 15.

66. See Paul Johnson, *Pope John Paul II and the Catholic Restoration,* (London: Weidenfeld and Nicolson, 1982), p. 4. The comparison, suggests Johnson, has become a dominant theme of the Pope's pontificate.

67. See Diana Dewar, *The Saint of Auschwitz: The Story of Maximilian Kolbe,* (San Francisco: Harper and Row, 1982), p. 131. The title of the Pope's homily which he delivered at Auschwitz—June 7, 1979—was "The Love That Casts Out Hatred," and it refers, to begin with, to John's First Letter where the power of love is enshrined above all else as God's chosen instrument in his conquest of the world (1 Jn. 5:4); and, in the second place, to the stunning example of Maximilian Kolbe, who offered "final and definitive witness," said the Pope, against Auschwitz, "a place built on the *denial of faith*—faith in God and faith in man— and on a *radical vilification* not only of love but of any and every manifestation of human dignity and of humanity itself. It is a place built on hatred and contempt for human beings in the name of an insane ideology. It is a place that was built on cruelty." But—and here is the whole point of the homily—thanks to "the power that has conquered the world," through the faith and the love of one man, Jesus Christ, and all those to whom he is *anagogically* wedded, even the hatred and contempt and cruelty embodied in this place of negation cannot remain the last word. Christ's negation of the negation as expressed, for example, in the kenosis of Kolbe, remains the truly last and only definitive word.

68. *Ibid.,* pp. 131-132.

69. Oesterreicher, p. 19.

70. Quoted by Oesterreicher, p. 19.

71. *Ibid.,* p. 21. The text he quotes is: *The Black Book: The Nazi Crime Against the Jewish People,* (New York: Duell, Sloan and Pearce, 1946), pp. 12-13. The words which the authors cite in their text belong to Alfred Rosenberg, a virulent anti-Semite who achieved great prominence in the Nazi hierarchy.

Father Oesterreicher reproduces in his study a marching song of the storm troopers called "Out with the Jews! Out with the Pope!" It is illustrative, in its sheer hate-filled vulgarity, of the thesis which I am anxious to press in these pages. He cites four of the stanzas whose theme is endlessly repeated, to wit, "Out with the Jews! Out with the Pope! Turn them out of Germany's house!" I reproduce them as follows:

> Defiantly, we struggled for fifteen years to win abiding power.
> We stormed, we won, even though Rome and Judah mocked.
> We did not shed our blood, without name or glory,
> So that Christianity keep Jew-ridden the German way...
> Let the Christian offer Palestine his years, his heart, his hand;
> We are free of Mount Sinai, Germany is our Holy Land...
> Pope and rabbi, both must go. Heathens we will be again,
> No longer crawl to Church. Ours is the sun wheel's lead. (pp. 21-22)

72. Oesterreicher, p. 22. To this end he reproduces a remarkable testimony from Maurice Samuel, who writes:

> Anti-Semitism is the expression of the concealed hatred of Christ and Christianity, rising to a new and catastrophic level in the western world....
>
> We shall never understand the maniacal, worldwide seizure of anti-Semitism unless we transpose the terms. It is of Christ that the Nazi Fascists are afraid; it is in *his* omnipotence that they believe; it is *him* that they are determined madly to obliterate. But the names of Christ and Christianity are too overwhelming, and the habit of submission to them is too deeply ingrained after centuries of teaching. Therefore they must, I repeat, make their assault on those who were responsible for the birth and spread of Christianity. They must spit on the Jews as "the Christ-killers" because they long to spit on the Jews as the Christ-givers.
>
> The fury of anti-Semitism is universal and inevitable because to destroy Christ and Christianity is the most important single objective of the force-philosophy. It is, in fact, *the* objective. (Cited on pp. 23-24. See Maurice Samuel's *The Great Hatred* [New York: Knopf, 1940], pp. 36, 56, 128-129, 142.)

73. Oesterreicher, p. 26. See Nietzsche's *The Anti-Christ*, which he wrote in 1888 and which reveals an obsessive and deranged hatred of the Christian religion. For example, as Oesterreicher notes on p. 26, the book teems with venom directed at the Gospels, a book Nietzsche said one must put on gloves before reading, it was simply unclean. "One would as little choose 'early Christians' for companions as Polish Jews.... Neither has a pleasant smell." Or that Pontius Pilate remains the only gentleman in the New Testament. Is it any wonder such poisonous views came to bloom amid the Third Reich?

74. Oesterreicher, p. 28: "Christianity, sprung from Jewish roots and understandable only as a growth of that soil, is the counter-movement against every morality of breeding, race, and privilege: It is the anti-Aryan religion par excellence. Christianity is the transposition of all Aryan values." And so it goes, the

Nietzschean tocsin whose shrill cry of nihilism will ignite the world within a few short years of his death. The text is from his *The Twilight of the Idols,* VII, 4.

75. See Graham Greene, *A Burnt-Out Case,*(New York: Penguin, 1960), p. 199.

76. Nathan Scott, Jr., *Craters of the Spirit,* (New York: Random House, 1968), p. 43. "If you will not have God," says Eliot, "who is a jealous God, then you can pay your respects to Hitler and Stalin."

77. Henri de Lubac, S.J., *The Drama of Atheist Humanism,* (New York: Meridian Books, 1963), p. 31.

78. See, for example, the remarks made by Czeslaw Milosz, winner of the 1980 Nobel Prize for Literature, in his acceptance speech. While expressing alarm that even the existence of the Holocaust was being questioned in books and pamphlets published across Europe and America, he went on to say: "[The poet] feels anxiety, though, when the meaning of the word Holocaust undergoes gradual modification, so that the word begins to belong to the history of the Jews exclusively, as if among the victims there were not also millions of Poles, Russians, Ukrainians, and prisoners of other nationalities. He feels anxiety, for he senses in this foreboding of a not distant future when history will be reduced to what appears on television, while the truth, because it is too complicated, will be buried in the archives, if not totally annihilated." Quoted in William Styron, *This Quiet Dust: And Other Writings,* (New York: Random House, 1982), pp. 105-106.

79. For confirmation see Richard C. Lukas, *The Forgotten Holocaust: The Poles under German Occupation, 1939-1944,* (Kentucky, 1986).

80. Under "so on" put the continuing Communist persecution of Christianity which, to quote Joseph Sobran's review of *Where Christ Still Suffers,* by Richard Wurmbrand (Bridge Publications, 1968), "is the greatest scandal in the world today. It has been going on since 1917 and has ceased to be a serious topic of interest even in most of the free churches of the West." Wurmbrand's book, he suggests, is a good place to begin researching the forms and places of torture, practiced wherever Communist regimes—from Cuba to Poland to Vietnam—have set up their godless tyranny. "By torture," he writes, "I mean beating, gouging out eyes, sexual mutilation, and forcing people to watch their children tortured and murdered. Sometimes Christians have been forced to torture and kill each other, producing agonies of betrayal and destruction of self-respect in addition to the physical pain." Wurmbrand, a Lutheran pastor from Rumania, spent fourteen years behind Communist bars for his beliefs, the strength and persistence of which his book eloquently and copiously documents, despite countless degrading conditions calculated to break body and soul. "It is not too much to say that these things are diabolical," comments Sobran. "If Aquinas has five proofs for God's existence, Communism offers mountains of evidence for Satan's." It ought to be, in other words, as lively a concern for Christians to heighten attention to the iniquities of Communism as it has been for Jews to fix the world's attention—and deservedly so—on the iniquities of Nazism. See Sobran's piece in the *National Review,* August 15, 1986, pp. 42-43.

See also Paul Johnson, *Modern Times: The World from the Twenties to the Eighties*, (New York: Harper and Row, 1983), which, in its meticulous documentation of the horrors of our century, places particular emphasis upon the record of Soviet Communist cruelty. So vast was the Stalinist concentration camp system, argues Johnson, an apparatus in place long before the outbreak of war, that it both rivaled the Nazi model and served as its prototype. At all stages, he writes, "even at the height of the SS extermination programme in 1942-5, there were many more Soviet camps, most of them much larger than the Nazi ones, and containing many more people. Indeed, the Soviet camps, as Solzhenitsyn and others have shown, constituted a vast series of substantial territorial islands within the Soviet Union, covering many thousands of square miles.... In these circumstances, the death-rate was almost beyond the imagining of civilized men...the scale of Stalin's mass atrocities encouraged Hitler in his wartime schemes to change the entire demography of Eastern Europe. In social engineering, mass murder on an industrial scale is always the ultimate weapon: Hitler's 'final solution' for the Jews had its origins not only in his own fevered mind but in the collectivization of the Soviet peasantry," pp. 304-305.

81. Walker Percy, *Love in the Ruins: The Adventures of a Bad Catholic at a Time Near the End of the World*, (New York: Farrar, Straus & Giroux, 1971), pp. 44-45. The theme would seem to be persisting for Percy, as witness the following from his latest novel, *The Thanatos Syndrome*, (New York: Farrar, Straus & Giroux, 1987), p. 86: "I was reading a new history of the Battle of the Somme, a battle which, with the concurrent Battle of Verdun, seemed to me to be events marking the beginning of a new age, an age not yet named. In the course of these two battles two million young men were killed toward no discernible end. As Dr. Freud might have said, the age of thanatos had begun." Or, to quote Ezra Pound's oft-repeated comment on the war, "There died a myriad, / And of the best, among them, / For an old bitch gone in the teeth, / For a botched civilization," *Modern Poetry*, vol. VII, p. 12.

82. The reference, of course, is to his long short story about a gentle and hapless professor of classics awakening in the midst of a nightmare world of the totalitarian state, called *Scott-King's Modern Europe*, written in 1947.

83. See, for example, Eliot's early essay, "Thoughts After Lambeth," published in 1931, in which he looks out upon a "world which will obviously divide itself more and more sharply into Christians and non-Christians. The Universal Church is today, it seems to me, more definitely set against the World than at any time since pagan Rome. I do not mean that our times are particularly corrupt; all times are corrupt. I mean that Christianity, in spite of certain local appearances, is not, and cannot be within measurable time, 'official.' The World is trying the experiment of attempting to form a civilized but non-Christian mentality. The experiment will fail; but we must be very patient in awaiting its collapse; meanwhile redeeming the time: so that the faith may be preserved alive through the dark ages before us; to renew and rebuild civilization, and save the world from suicide," *Selected Essays*, (London: Faber, 1931), p. 377.

84. See Lewis' *The Abolition of Man*, (New York: Macmillan, 1947).

85. Oesterreicher, *Auschwitz, The Christian, and The Council*, pp. 36-37.

86. John S. Dunne, *The City of the Gods: A Study in Myth and Mortality*, (London: Sheldon Press, 1965), p. 188.

87. *Ibid.*, pp. 188-189.

88. Marcel Dubois, "Christian Reflections on the Holocaust," *Sidic* 7, no. 2, 1974, p. 15.

III
THE MYSTERY OF HOLY SATURDAY

THE FOURTEENTH STATION
Jesus Is Laid In The Tomb

This is what is known as a first-class funeral.
The solicitous ones seem to be chiefly intellectuals.
With solemn gestures they flourish gravecloths,
making a liturgy,
absorbing themselves in its dignity.
Nothing indicates they expect a resurrection.

The corpse is swathed according to custom.
Only the face cannot be subdued.
All suffering stares from that head.
Impossible to wrap it in a great and festive forgetting.

So already his unquiet image haunts heads and hearts.
Already the spirit is freed.
Already the Easter question takes shape...

But silently.
For tomorrow is only Holy Saturday.
The day when God is dead,
and the Church holds her breath.
The strange day that separates life and death
in order to join them in a marriage beyond all human thought.
The day which leads through hell,
and, after all the paths of the world,
into a pathless existence.

Hans Urs von Balthasar[1]

Crucifixion: The Shame and Significance

On Good Friday the faithful do well to devote their most worshipful attention to the slow torture and death of God. This was certainly no ordinary end of a man's life. The obscenity of crucifixion was not like the last hours of Socrates, with the fastidious philosopher sipping his hemlock among friends before taking civilized leave of a world too surly to suit his taste. There was nothing civilized about Roman crucifixion. Nor could there be when the whole point of the thing was no ordinary death at all; rather the point of it was a death in which the most protracted, unimaginable pain and humiliation were first visited upon the hapless victim before mercifully delivering him. For instance, the nails routinely driven through the hollows of the wrist striking the median nerve were calculated to cause immediate, overwhelming, and prolonged agony. Likewise the feet, which, fastened by one or more spikes, sent waves of pain continually rushing to the head. And, of course, neither wound was meant to be fatal; the major blood vessels were spared in order that, again, maximum suffering be sustained for the longest time. What usually brought on death was asphyxiation, the result of diminishing attempts by the victim to breathe. The legs which had been left deliberately bent to allow the feet to push the tortured body upward could not do so indefinitely. Hence, the pre-crucifixion ritual of scourging, designed to weaken the condemned through trauma and blood loss; plus the frequent breaking of legs near the end to hasten death. Without these added touches, a man might live for days on the cross; and even when scourged and broken, it was not unusual for victims to survive as long as thirty-six hours. Is it therefore any wonder that not until the fifth century at the Church of Santa Sabina in Rome, no depiction of the Christian Cross in paint or stone was done which included the corpus?[2]

Regarding Roman crucifixion in particular—although, to be sure, the origins are not Roman at all, rather Persian, the obvious merits of whose discovery soon spread across the Mediterranean to Rome where it was carried to a high level of perfection—Walter Kasper quotes Cicero, who thought the practice so unspeakably cruel and degrading that, he declared, "The very idea of the Cross should never pass through their thoughts, eyes, or ears." Indeed, so shameful a death was not even to be talked about among decent people (decent people meaning free Roman citizenry who, in any case, were spared the ignominy of the cross even for capital and heinous crimes).[3]

And when the putative victim of such protracted pain and hideousness is the Son of God himself, what then? The story is told of the sculptor and craftsman Eric Gill, who, while working on Stations of the Cross in Westminster Cathedral, found himself one afternoon accosted by a smartly dressed woman wanting to know who had been carving them. When he told her that he had she announced primly, "Then I don't think they are at all nice." She was not prepared for his reply: "Neither do I, Madam." To scourge and spit upon and revile a man, to strip naked and nail him onto a couple of planks, and then to raise him up between earth and sky for men to jeer at while he is left slowly to die, is not something which is meant to be nice.[4]

How remarkably sanitized, under the circumstances, are the accounts of Christ's crucifixion which appear in the Gospels! "And so they took him to a place called Golgotha," reports Mark, "...and then crucified him" (15:22-24). Matthew and John, meanwhile, record much the same thing. Even Luke, for all his close attention to somatic detail, says simply, "they crucified him there" (23:33). Was it pious reticence which so reduced the narrative to stark and succinct form? Or rather long familiarity with the form of execution itself, which thereupon made description unnecessary? The latter presumably, crucifixion having been a fairly widespread practice of the time; which, for Rome, lasted from around the year 600 BC until its formal prohibition under Constantine in 337 AD, the Christian emperor having already found the practice of branding slaves a repugnant infliction of the flesh which bore God's image. Do Christians, one wonders, think often enough of what Christ's Cross delivered the world from? "When St. Paul preached in Athens," writes Charles Williams, "the world was thronged with crosses, rooted outside cities, bearing all of them the bodies of slowly dying men. When Augustine preached in Carthage, the world was also thronged with crosses, but now in the very centre of cities, lifted in processions and above altars, decorated and jewelled, and bearing all of them the image of the Identity of dying Man." Everywhere, says Williams, there was offered *the clean sacrifice*. "Men were no longer to die, for Man had died...."[5]

Thus Christians are to venerate the Cross because they believe the Son of God himself bore the curse of the world upon its wood, thereupon ridding the world of its mortal burden. Christianity believes, that is to say, on the strength of its faith, that by the defilement of Christ we, his members, are miraculously made whole. "He himself," St. Peter tells us, "bore our sins in his body on the tree. By his wounds you have been healed" (1 Peter 2:24).[6] That is what Christ's crucifixion means, understood in terms of a straightforward soteriology of Christian belief. It means he was accursed, rejected, handed over to men eager to inflict every possible pain and ignominy upon him; again, to cite the Old Testament text, repeated by St. Paul in the Letter to the Galatians (3:13), "Cursed be everyone who hangs on a tree."[7] And, finally, it means he did it for us, for thee and me: the very Lamb of God who was without sin, is made sin, in order that in his body he might bear it all painfully away.[8]

Descending Lower: Lesson of the Mystics

Yet, we do not stop here, here at the foot of the Cross gazing up at the torn and bloodied Body of the Son of God; we must, to quote Eliot, descend lower,

> Into the world of perpetual solitude,
> World not world but that which is not world...[9]

We do not stop here because in dying things happen to Christ which will, if it be thought possible, surpass in their pain and sorrow and loss even that Cross the sum total of whose physical torments will soon enough conspire to kill him. It is an experience of anguish no living person could possibly endure, although among the saints there have been certain vicariously granted visions. St. Teresa of Avila, for example, despite paragraphs filled with the most harrowing detail, will repeatedly confess her complete incapacity to do adequate justice to the experience, so inexpressibly awful was her vision of it. "I felt a fire," she writes, "within my soul the nature of which I am utterly incapable of describing." It was, she allows, infinitely more painful than even those bodily sufferings she endured whose intensity exceeded anything she bore on earth; "even these are nothing by comparison with the agony of my soul...." It was, she insists,

> an oppression, a suffocation and an affliction so deeply felt, and accompanied by such hopeless and distressing misery, that I cannot too forcibly describe it. To say that it is as if the soul were continually being torn from the body is very little, for that would mean that one's life was being taken by another; whereas in this case it is the soul itself that is tearing itself to pieces. The fact is that I cannot find words to describe that interior fire and that despair, which is greater than the most grievous tortures and pains. I could not see who was the cause of them, but I felt, I think, as if I were being both burned and dismembered; and I repeat that that interior fire and despair are the worst things of all.[10]

Or St. John of the Cross. In his descriptions of the soul's *dark night*, one is literally reminded, as with Teresa, Spain's kindred mystic par excellence, of the blackest pains of hell. Concerning these, Fr. von Balthasar has noted how the experience essentially consists of God having left the soul and the soul knowing this leave-taking to last forever. "Being truly forsaken by God always has this definitive quality: there can be no forsakenness 'for a time' or involving room for hope. Other mystics in this situation have felt, not only that 'it will always be like this,' but 'it has always been like this': they experience a kind of eternity of this 'hell' from which no one can deliver them but God himself. And he has disappeared.[11]

Yes, but what of the saint's own prior conviction of innocence, his fixed consciousness that God in fact loves him and is only suspending, for a time as it were, all sensible consolation of the fact? Surely this state of forsakenness cannot be perceived by men and women already steeped in holiness of life as something meant to go on forever? And, *a fortiori*, what of Christ's own infinite innocence and integrity? Will not Our Lord's necessarily greater and surer conviction of his being the very righteousness of Almighty God, generate all the more heroic resolution in facing the torments of his Passion? But, says Newman, in a striking paragraph of his Sermon,

> This being the case, you will see at once, my brethren, that it is nothing to the purpose to say that He would be supported under His trial by the consciousness of innocence and the anticipation of triumph; for His trial consisted in the withdrawal, as of other causes of consolation, so of that very consciousness and anticipation. The same act of the will which admitted the influence upon His soul of any distress at all, admitted all distresses at once.... As men of self-command can turn from one thought to another at their will, so much more did He deliberately deny Himself the comfort, and satiate Himself with the woe. In that moment His soul thought not of the future, He thought only of the present burden which was upon Him, and which He had come upon earth to sustain.[12]

And precisely in His sustaining of that burden on which all the force of Christ's consciousness is fastened, there must remain that timeless and eternal sense of his having been forsaken by God.[13]

In our own time, too, the mystical transport to hell is not unknown. In his *First Glance at Adrienne von Speyr*,[14] von Balthasar discusses an extraordinary woman's legacy to the Church, namely the record of her share in the sufferings of Christ. "A landscape of pain of undreamt-of variety was disclosed to me," he begins, who was permitted to assist her:

> how many and diverse were the kinds of fear, at the Mount of Olives and at the Cross, how many kinds of shame, outrage and humiliation, how many forms of God-forsakenness, of Christ's relation to the sin of the world, quite

apart from the inexhaustible abundance of physical pain. ...While she was experiencing the weight of sins upon herself, she knew herself to be an inveterate sinner, separated by an abyss from the purity of the Lamb of God, and yet in an inconceivable proximity to him.[15]

Every year, apparently, from 1941 on, just as soon as the Good Friday Passion would end at about three o'clock in the afternoon, "with a death-like trance into which flashed the thrust of the lance," she commenced her mysterious *descent into hell*.[16] "What Adrienne experienced is actually more horrible," insists von Balthasar, "than the hell depicted for us by medieval imagination; it is the knowledge of having lost God forever; it is being engulfed in the chaotic mire of the anti-divine; the absence of faith, hope and love; the loss as well, therefore, of any human communication." So utterly real was her experience of hell, he adds, that for one to persist in the disbelief of it would be both ludicrous and blasphemous.[17]

KENOSIS

Extremity of Christ's Self-Emptying

It is perforce unthinkable that anyone following in the footsteps of Christ could possibly leave deeper tracks of pain than his own. Hence the appropriateness of the following passage from St. Thomas More's meditation on the Passion which he composed in the Tower where he awaited his own passion. In it he attributes these words to Christ, addressed to those timorous souls who, unlike the legendary martyrs of long ago who rush headlong into the jaws of beasts, hang back out of fear and terror:

> Pluck up thy courage, faint heart; what though thou be fearful, sorry and weary and standest in great dread of most painful torments, be of good comfort; for I myself have vanquished the whole world and yet felt I far more fear, sorrow, weariness and much more inward anguish too, when I consider my most bitter, painful Passion to press so fast upon me.[18]

The meditation concludes with Christ entreating the timorous soul not to set out in heroic emulation of so many glorious, valiant martyrs, but "think it sufficient for thee only to walk after me which am thy Shepherd and Governor, and to mistrust thyself and put thy trust in Me. Take hold of the hem of my garment therefore; from hence shalt thou perceive strength and relief to proceed."[19]

No, it is neither right nor seemly that we predicate of others a pain in excess of his own; the river can never aspire to something greater than its source. Thus Adrienne von Speyr's experience of hell, for all its ghastly detail, remains (mercifully!) vicarious; it can only be, as von Balthasar has noted elsewhere, "a muted echo of the unique and incomparable burden which the God-Man endured."[20]

Nevertheless, on the strength of von Speyr's own description of the experience, one cannot but come away convinced that Christ's unique descent into that state of bitter privation most surely marked his deepest, most definitive expression of pure obedient love before the Father. Why? Because hell is all that God is not, and for the Son of the Father willingly to go there—never mind for the moment that there is no *there* to go to, hell being a state of spiritual everlasting loss—must have testified to an intensity and depth of love for the Father which is wholly incomprehensible for mere human beings to imagine. And, most assuredly, he knew whereof he spoke. In fact, he uses in the New Testament three symbols to express the nature of that state of ultimate pain and forlornness.[21] Hell is, to begin with, understood as a place of punishment, "everlasting punishment," he calls it in Matthew (25:46). Secondly, it is referred to as a place of destruction ("fear him who is able to destroy both body and soul in hell," Mt. 10:28). And, finally, a place of ultimate privation, exclusion or banishment into 'the darkness outside,' as in the parables of the man without a wedding garment or of the wise and foolish virgins. And through his use of the recurrent image of fire, something of hell's ineffable torment and destruction is certainly suggested. "You will remember," says Lewis, recalling Matthew 25:34, 41,

> the saved go to a place prepared for *them*, while the damned go to a place never made for men at all. To enter heaven is to become more human than you ever succeeded in being in earth; to enter hell, is to be banished from humanity. What is cast (or casts itself) into hell is not a man: it is "remains." To be a complete man means to have the passions obedient to the will and the will offered to God: to *have been* a man—to be an ex-man or "damned ghost"—would presumably mean to consist of a will utterly centred in its self and passions utterly uncontrolled by the will. It is, of course, impossible to imagine what the consciousness of such a creature—already a loose congeries of mutually antagonistic sins rather than a sinner—would be like.[22]

Again, what is hell but the place or state of soul where God is not present at all; it is where the lights of faith, hope and love have all gone out. "If there is damnation," muses the narrator of A. Dubos' short story *Rose*,

> and a place for the damned, it must be a quiet place, where spirits turn away from each other and stand in solitude and gaze haplessly at eternity. For it must be crowded with the passive: those people whose presence in life was a paradox;...(who) witnessed evil and lifted neither an arm nor a voice to stop it, as they witnessed joy and neither sang nor clapped their hands.[23]

The conclusion would seem to be inescapably exact; von Balthasar, not surprisingly, has drawn it with all the rigor and trenchancy it requires. "Hell," he says, "is what the judging God condemned and cast

out of his creation; it is filled with all that is irreconcilable with God, from which he turns away for all eternity. It is filled with the reality of all the world's godlessness, with the sum of the world's sin; therefore, with precisely all of that from which the Crucified has freed the world."[24] And in some mysterious and ultimately inexpressible way, Christ has gone *there*, to that state or place of which the Creed speaks, thus constituting belief in its truth as fundamental to Catholic faith.[25] Here Christ "encounters his own work of salvation, not in Easter triumph, but in the uttermost night of obedience, truly the 'obedience of a corpse.' " Von Balthasar continues:

> He encounters the horror of sin separated from men. He "walks" through sin (without leaving a trace, since, in hell and in death, there is neither time nor direction); and, traversing its formlessness, he experiences the second chaos. While bereft of any spiritual light emanating from the Father, in sheer obedience, he must seek the Father where he cannot find him under any circumstances.[26]

This is the terrifying descent which Christ, moved by an impossible extravagance of love for the Father (who, meanwhile, has been moved by the same love for the world, upon which he freely lavishes the Son), elects to make into Sheol, into the grave of silence and shadow, of which the saints and the mystics have vicariously spoken. Wherein the experience of abandonment, both of God from God and from ourselves, becomes almost, as it were, absolute. God's Son is truly dead in that place, and the fact of it, of his sheer absence from himself and from others, has never been rendered more plain, nor more poignant. That the grave should conceal, leaving thoroughly and shamefully mute, what had so recently borne aloft all our hopes! In emptying all the tabernacles of the world, the Church fittingly commemorates this most deep and dolorous humiliation of her Lord. It remains, paradoxically, the sublimest symbol of Christ's kenosis.[27] Well might the Christian be tempted to say with the pagan Homer who, speaking of Hades, fearful god of the underworld, "Men hate him most of all the gods."[28] And who has not, on seeing the Holbein depiction of the dead Christ awaiting entombment, pronounced it oppressive in the extreme. Death-Deposition-Descent: the most terrible trinity of all.[29]

Towards a Soteriology of Solidarity

Has not this trinity been transposed to our own time, to the Godforsaken Death Camps of our century where, alongside numberless others, the death of the "sad-eyed angel" re-presents once again the unique and unrepeatable death of God's Son? "Immeasurable emptiness streams forth from the hanging body," says von Balthasar, in a sentence which might have been written to describe the child strung from a makeshift gallows at Auschwitz.

> Nothing but this fantastic emptiness is any longer at work here…. There is nothing more but nothingness itself. The world is dead. Love is dead. God is dead.[30]

Then does not Wiesel's *Night*, setting aside for now what *his* theology makes of it, really provide the most vividly riveting account one can conceive of this deeply mysterious linkage between the Cross and human suffering, particularly the suffering of the innocent? Here is the theological basis for that soteriology of human solidarity which situates the Cross of Christ at the crossroads of the suffering human community. Because of Auschwitz we now see more clearly the centrality of the Cross in the work of the Incarnation; only the Cross truly fashions a convincing link between God and man, especially the man who suffers without apparent meaning or hope. Thus, as Douglas Hall writes, Israel's faith is only comprehensible because one "sees at its heart a suffering God whose solidarity with humanity is so abysmal that the 'cross in the heart of God' (H. Wheeler Robinson) must always be incarnating itself in history. Reading the works of Elie Wiesel, one knows, as a Christian, that he bears this indelible resemblance to the people of Israel."[31]

It cannot be a question of compensating the tortured child for all the hideousness of his life with glib promises of bliss when he dies. For that whole ethic of pie in the sky when you die, there can only be contempt.[32] No, truth to tell, there can be nothing more important than the suffering of innocent children, the horror and revulsion we feel for it, and the terrible urgency of finding reasons to account for it. As Camus' Fr. Paneloux pleads before his plague-stricken parish, he tells them how,

> In other manifestations of life God made things easy for us and, thus far, our religion had no merit. But in this respect He put us, so to speak, with our backs to the wall. Indeed, we were all up against the wall that plague had built around us, and in its lethal shadow we must work out our salvation. He, Father Paneloux, refused to have recourse to simple devices enabling him to scale that wall….
>
> No, he, Father Paneloux, would keep faith with that great symbol of all suffering, the tortured body on the Cross; he would stand fast, his back to the wall, and face honestly the terrible problem of a child's agony. And he would boldly say to those who listened to his words today: "My brothers, a time of testing has come for us all. We must believe everything or deny everything. And who among you, I ask, would dare to deny everything?"[33]

Yes, suffering doubtless exists, here, in these tortured and maimed bodies of little children; it exists in the most insupportable of circumstances amid all the horrors of the Death Camps, here at the infernal center of our century. But the deepest meaning and significance of all these sufferings, indeed their only significance, is necessarily to be found in Christ, in the Eternal Word made literally and historically flesh. "There is only one physician," as Ignatius reminded the Ephesians en route to Rome to die, who alone confers healing for those who suffer; and in his compact credal expression, he conjoins the elements of his identity: "of flesh yet spiritual, born yet unbegotten, God incarnate, genuine life in the midst of death, sprung from Mary as well as God, first subject to suffering then beyond it—Jesus Christ our Lord."[34] The self-same Christ whose flesh has become a curse and is cruelly delivered up to the frightful desolation of Good Friday's Cross and all the hellish torment surrounding it. And why, one asks? Because the God-Man really chooses to "take upon himself" the sin of the world (Jn. 1:29) and represents it in its entirety (2 Cor. 5:14; Gal. 3:13; Eph. 2:14-16) before that same world whose redemption he will win at the cost of his life. In other words, Christ has freely chosen to remain in agony until the end of the world, in order that from the vantage of his own singular and unrepeatable anguish and abandonment—his willed descent into the wordless, lifeless dark of Sheol—every single experience of human extremity and loss might then derive its deepest, most ultimate and salvific meaning. "Only in the brokenness and pain of life am I with him where he continues to live in agony," writes Louis Dupré in a searching meditation on the Negro Spiritual which begins, "Were you there when they crucified my Lord?"

> That very suffering of mine, however despicable and even sinful in its origins, *is* Jesus' agony in me. I find a comparison with Jesus' Passion almost blasphemous. But I forget that all suffering is lowly and humiliating, that it all began with a curse.... Suffering means always failure to him who suffers. Jesus' words on the cross—My God, my God, why have you forsaken me?—...say what suffering has said from the beginning of the world and what it says in me now: In this I am hopelessly alone.[35]

Alone, yet in some extraordinarily mysterious way, not alone at all, for Jesus' agony is precisely my own, and I am what I suffer, neither more nor less. "Whatever the undignified causes of my suffering—and they are all undignified in a cursed world, for Jesus as well as for me— my suffering is all I am in my very existence—dignified or not!

> It is isolation with no past to comfort and no future to hope for, the empty desert of a bleak, unending present. Nor is there peace in this desert,

infested as it is with the howling, barking, roaring animals of frustrated desires, broken expectations, tormenting visions of an impossible future. Its blank nothingness means not peace but absence, the lack of fulfillment which I need to be whole. "Were you there when they laid him in the tomb?" Yes, Lord, I was there in the tomb of my loneliness.[36]

But while it is a tomb of apparent and unrelieved bleakness—an eternal, trackless loneliness—it is in fact fraught with all the grace of ultimate deliverance, too, because its source is always the Cross onto which Jesus hammers his own and the world's pain. "Were you *there* when they nailed him to the tree?" asks the Negro Spiritual; and from the elements of an old plaintive hymn Professor Dupré weaves his meditation on its meaning. "Was I *there* in my suffering?" he asks. "For that is where he is being crucified—in me, not in Jerusalem." (Though it is because of that prior crucifixion in Jerusalem that my own pain derives meaning insofar as it roots itself deep within the *anagogue* of Christ's unique Passion.)

> There stands the tree from which grace flows. For grace is not a pipeline from which each taps according to his needs. Grace is my individual election, my being called by my name. It is as personal as my suffering. Indeed, it is my suffering. For in this world there can be no grace but through redemptive suffering, through Jesus' death—in me. This then was God's election: the utter rejection of Gethsemane and of Calvary.[37]

And so it remains, from top to bottom, the most redeeming tree in the universe. Here, tied helpless and alone to the tree of an endless seeming pain, stands the triumphant tree of Christ:

> that degradation unredeemable has become the sign of God's grace, that rejection has become the call of election and that hopelessness itself henceforth witnesses to the presence of redemption. It has been written: "A curse comes to being as a child is formed...." Over the beginning of all life stands the sign of failure. How it will fail, we do not know—as a murderer or a saint—but it will fail enough to make its mother weep. The joyous mystery of Good Friday is that the failure itself has become redemptive. Jesus fails in me. That is the mystical union, the only one, between God and me: Jesus in agony in me.[38]

Horror of Abandonment:
Univocal Despair Versus Christic Descent

The temptation, however, and here the peculiar and accelerating horrors of our century conspire to intensify its fatal attraction, has been to see only the failures, each mounted upon the other to form a veritable mosaic of despair; and when sensitive and thoughtful men theologize only on that univocal basis (that is, an evil is only an evil and forever unresistant to utilization by grace[39]), seeing in the apparent horror and degradation an absolute and final meaning, then despair is all that matters. Suicide, as Camus would have it in his "Myth of Sysiphus," becomes the only philosophical problem. Putting the matter another way: "It is true," as Fr. Lynch puts it in his seminal work on the dimensions of the imagination, "that a fact is a fact is a fact, and a rose is a rose is a rose." But the true debate is:

> What is the fact and what is its true dimension? We have insisted that the mysteries of Christianity are a penetration deep into the fact of man, all the way into his Christic center.... It is not at all a matter of constructing levels outside of the fact. The levels are proposed as deeper borings into actuality.[40]

Citing the self-confessed atheist Camus, who will not abide a God who is powerless to prevent the sufferings of little children, and who plainly announces in both *The Plague* and *The Fall* that Christ himself must feel guilt because of so many children murdered in his name, Fr. Lynch replies, with all the force and analogical resilience of the Christian imagination that, yes, of course, "the children cried, within this history, [but] because they suffered, as much as children can, within the cries of Christ. A man can only *cause* pain to somebody outside of himself. Christ's cries are wider than we think and grow more actual through the body of our own."[41]

Cries wider than one's own. What manner of misery must first exist in God before it can contain so universal a weight as other men's misery? "He was not like us," writes Charles Williams, "and yet he became us...in the last reaches of that living death to which we are exposed he substituted himself for us. He submitted in our stead to the full results of the Law which is he."[42] Let him then die for us, for at least the life which courses divinely through him is not sundered from our own, though it appear to be sundered from his. But how was it sundered? To what hideous lengths did he go in woeful conformity to the wood of the Cross? In other words, what were those last reaches of that living death which, in substituting himself for us, he freely surrendered himself, body and soul, into Sheol?

There are passages in Chesterton, I would suggest, which give hint of an answer; or, at best, they help sharpen the edges of the question. In *Orthodoxy*, he sets out the case for Christ's divinity, arguing in effect that if it be true, it must certainly then be revolutionary, inasmuch as Christianity would then seem to be the only religion in the world which thought the attribute of divine omnipotence left the divinity of its God strangely impotent. And remember: for men of Camus' philosophic cast, it was the apparent absence of omnipotence which for them stripped the Godhead of its believability, and here is Chesterton intimating the exact opposite, that in precisely what appears to have been withheld from God, namely that power which would perhaps have commended him to Camus, there is a more wondrous exercise thereof. I reproduce the text in its entirety. "Christianity alone," it begins,

> has felt that God, to be wholly God, must have been a rebel as well as a king. Alone of all creeds, Christianity has added courage to the virtues of the Creator. For the only courage worth calling courage must necessarily mean that the soul passes a breaking point—and does not break.
>
> In this indeed I approach a matter more dark and awful than it is easy to discuss.... But in that terrific tale of the Passion there is a distinct emotional suggestion that the author of all things (in some unthinkable way) went not only through agony, but through doubt. It is written, "Thou shalt not tempt the Lord thy God." No; but the Lord thy God may tempt himself; and it seems as if this was what happened in Gethsemane. In a garden Satan tempted man; and in a garden God tempted God. He passed in some super-human manner through our human horror of pessimism. When the world shook and the sun was wiped out of heaven, it was not at the crucifixion, but at the cry from the cross: the cry which confessed that God was forsaken of God.

Let the revolutionaries choose their own creed and a god to give it force, they will not, says Chesterton, find one who was himself in revolt. But were the atheists themselves to choose a god, he concludes, they would "find only one divinity who ever uttered their isolation, only one religion in which God seemed for an instant to be an atheist."[43]

Some years later, following Chesterton's reception into the Church, he wrote his masterpiece, *The Everlasting Man*, as stirring an example of Catholic apologetics as ever graced the page; and in which the following luminous and piercing insight into the Passion may be read:

> There were solitudes beyond where none shall follow. There were secrets in the inmost and invisible part of that drama that have no symbol in speech; or in any severance of a man from men. Nor is it easy for any words less stark and single-minded than those of the naked narrative even to hint at the horror of exaltation that lifted itself above the hill. Endless expositions have not come to the end of it, or even to the beginning. And if there be any sound that can produce a silence, we may surely be silent about the end and the extremity; when a cry was driven out of that darkness in words dreadfully distinct and dreadfully unintelligible; which man shall never understand in all the eternity they have purchased for him; and for one

annihilating instant an abyss that is not for our thoughts had opened even in the unity of the absolute; and God had been forsaken of God.[44]

We did not do this to God, he willed rather to do it to himself. Here then is the essential distinction to be grasped, that in sorting out the true proportions of pain borne by God's Son, it is necessary to know that while Christ suffers in his physical passion those torments which others have inflicted upon him, in his unique agony of loss he wills to suffer what he had inflicted upon himself. "At certain hours of life," writes François Mauriac in his moving account of the last hours in Jesus' life, "in the silence of the night, every man has experienced the indifference of matter which is blind and deaf." But in the case of Christ, says Mauriac, this matter proved altogether crushing: "in his flesh he felt the horror of an infinite absence. The Creator had withdrawn, and creation was but the bottom of an empty sea; the dead stars were scattered in space; in the darkness he could hear the cries of beasts being devoured." It is, you see, the night of Gethsemane, the evening before the bloody Cross; but in its own way Gethsemane contains more anguish and loss than the world will ever hold.

> Then this Jew, blotted against the earth, crushed to the ground, arose. The Son of God was abased so low that he had need of human consolation. His turn had come, he thought, to rest his bloody head upon a friendly bosom. He therefore rose and approached the three sleeping men ("sleeping for sorrow" says St. Luke).[45]

Hour of Infinite Silence: Salvation's Secret

It is, in other words, the sinner's abandonment by God, his eternal exclusion from every precinct of felicity, which is that very state of God-forsakenness implied by sin, that Christ permits freely to happen to him when, out of obedient love for the Father's will, he is delivered up to the Cross. This is why there can be no comfort in Gethsemane, though a legion of angels await the Word and a handful of sleeping disciples would, on command, spring to his beleaguered side. Only Christ knows what it means to remain in agony until the world's end.

And only the Son can suffer this in a final way since none other than he *knows* the Father, and thus feels the extremity of that loss to which the evangelist points in the cry of absolute and hellish "thirst" from the Cross (Jn. 19:28). What, after all, had been the Son's center of gravity as testified to in the holy Scriptures but the sheer constancy and warmth of his communication with the Father? The Church's designation of Jesus as Son in fact constitutes the most comprehensive title of all, for it furnishes the key to everything else. Indeed, nothing in Christ's life was allowed to happen without that profound interior dialogue with the Father; lacking that intimate, unceasing converse with his Father, in whose very will consisted the Son's peace, the whole life of Christ reduces to a heap of unrecollected ruins.[46]

What follows from all of the foregoing, it seems to me, is this: that what the Church desires above all to teach through her own unbending insistence upon Christ's real descent into hell, a descent affirmed and expressly defined by two ecumenical councils,[47] is the truth, at once applicable to the evils of the crematoria—through which so many went, in silence, their voices stilled forever—that silence too can be salvific. That the very Word, after speech, wills to plunge himself headlong into the abyss of silence, bespeaking there his presence, his solidarity, with numberless silent victims. The silence of the Word, no less than his speech, shares in the mysterious efficacy of the Cross. In fact, the Cross is precisely efficacious in winning salvation through the consent of the one who silently lets it happen to him. Revelation, we need remind ourselves, consists not simply in the pure articulated intelligibility of God's Word, fully armed, as it were, with an eternity of super-abundant meaning. Revelation comes also to unravel itself in silence, in order that it might stand in complete vulnerability—fully dis-armed!—before the gaze and the ridicule, the organized beastliness of wicked men. What else is Christ's Cross but the Father's strategy of pure paradox, of sheer unending collision among opposites: life found in death, holiness amid humiliation, strength in weakness, speech in silence, redemption in hell? Joseph Ratzinger has put it very well in the following superb un-packing of the Creed:

> Thus the article about the Lord's descent into hell reminds us that not only God's death but also his silence is part of the Christian revelation. God is not only the comprehensible word that comes to us; he is also the silent, inaccessible, uncomprehended ground that eludes us. To be sure, in Christianity there is a primacy of the *logos*, of the word, over silence; God *has* spoken. God *is* word. But this does not entitle us to forget the truth of God's abiding concealment. Only when we have experienced him as silence may we hope to hear his speech too, which proceeds in silence. Christology reaches out beyond the cross, the moment when the divine love is tangible, into the death, the silence and the eclipse of God. Can we wonder that the Church and the life of the individual are led again and again into this hour of silence, into the forgotten and almost discarded article, "Descended into hell"?[48]

"Where did I triumph," asks Christ in von Balthasar's *Heart of the World*, "if not on the Cross? Are you so blind...to think that Golgotha was my downfall and my failure? Do you believe it was only later—that I recovered from my death and climbed up laboriously from the pit of Hades to appear among you once again?"

> Look: this is my secret, and there is no other in heaven or on earth: My Cross is salvation, my Death is victory, my Darkness is light.[49]

And later on, from the same lyric-strewn chapter:

> This was my victory. In the Cross was Easter. In death the grave of the world was burst open. In the leap into the void was the ascension to heaven. Now I fill the world, and at last every soul lives from my dying.[50]

The whole point of Revelation absolutely requires this dimension of perfect, paradoxical unspeakability; this depthless place of silence and shame into which the Word freely wills himself to go in search of the least and the lost. It is a realm of Godforsakenness, moreover, of absolute desolation, about which we can have no access of understanding. Such a strange divinity of rhythms at work here! Clearly it would seem that the Word's triumphant re-ascent into speech, even unto the glory of the Father in heaven, altogether and mysteriously depends upon this deep prior descent into silence, into Sheol.

Christology: To the Ultimate of the Finite

"My own position," writes Fr. Lynch, "pictures the imagination," of which the great and fruitful paradigm is Christ himself (a thesis Lynch sustains brilliantly throughout his book), "as following a narrow, direct path through the finite. With every plunge through, or down into, the real contours of being, the imagination also shoots up into insight, but in such a way that the plunge down *causally generates* the plunge up."[51] Does not St. Paul in his Letter to the Ephesians exactly endorse such causality?

> Therefore it is said, "When he ascended on high he led a host of captives, and he gave gifts to men." (In saying, "He ascended," what does it mean but that he had also descended into the lower parts of the earth? He who descended is he who also ascended far above all the heavens, that he might fill all things.)[52]

Under the circumstances, how otherwise are we to imagine Christology if not as a series of descents, each progressively deeper into the dust, into the human and historical bedrock, the sheer actuality of being?[53] Above all else, it seems, it is necessary to attend to what Lynch rightly calls "the great fact of Christology, that Christ moved down into all the realities of man to get to his Father."[54] Yes, even to the very seat of ultimate human wretchedness, whence to pry men loose from its hellish hold. "How little we understand the Passion of Christ," the Dominican Father Gerald Vann observed,

> unless we understand at least that! Perhaps the deepest mystery of redemption and divine love is precisely that we can be redeemed not merely from our squalors but, in a sense, in our squalors. If holiness did mean possessing God we might well despair; but holiness means being possessed by God, and so in spite of our frailties and betrayals we can continue to hope: the Word is long since descended into us: there is nothing there that can frighten him now.[55]

There can be no gnostic and effortless leaps into infinity for Christ. The entire scandalous particularity of his life, so deeply shocking to people of docetist sensibility, should once and for all disabuse us of the mythic notion that Christ came to earth dispensing magic. Whether it be the episode in the desert where he evinces supreme contempt for the devil's tawdry enticements to an immediate and painless glory, or his sorrow over Jerusalem, for which beloved city he will weep rather than rush messianically forward to lead to glory; or his own Passion, Death, and Descent, the whole wearily protracted business of which Christ will not hasten to an end, no, not even the ultimate end of his own long-deferred glory. All of this painstaking finitude points unassailably to Christ's complete abandonment before the human, the historical, his unhesitating plunge into the icy currents of time and space, right down to the hermetic horror and bleakness of the tomb. "Ay, but to die, and go we know not where," to quote the anguished cry of Shakespeare's Claudio,

> to lie in cold obstruction and to rot.
> This sensible warm motion to become
> A kneaded clod and the delighted spirit
> To bathe in fiery floods, or to reside
> In thrilling region of thick-ribbed ice—
> To be imprisoned in the viewless winds,
> And blown with restless violence round about
> The pendent world....
> The weariest and most loathed worldly life
> That age, ache, penury, and imprisonment
> Can lay on nature is a paradise
> To what we fear of death.[56]

"There is no other," Lynch reminds us, "who could say as authentically, of human time, as he: 'It is consummated.' It is not accurate to say

that Christ redeemed tim   ed redeeming; it only
needed someone to expl   fully, and add even
further resources to it, as h   and new is the exploration, in his case, that it i   n insight but with the
Resurrection."[57]

And, thus, concludes L   ist's having faithfully
bored right down into the basest mire of the human, his willingness to
endure the human lot, even unto the cold obstruction of the grave,
imprisoned amid the viewless winds,

> His victory over Satan is internal and complete, not a victory that is extrinsic
> and Manichaean. His Son is the Sun, but the course of this sun is through
> man. Above all he is a bridegroom and an athlete running the whole length
> and breadth of the human adventure. He marches to the ultimate of the
> finite. Wherefore he has been exalted and every knee shall bow to him, of all
> the things that are in heaven or on earth or under the earth. And this is not
> merely a mark of an external reward for suffering and obedience; it is the
> perfect sign and accomplishment of the mysteries or stages of human life,
> that they are, on a level much more intense than ever before, an intrinsic
> path to the infinite. We miss the point if we only say that Christ is the gate
> and do not also add that man is the gate. It is our recurring mystery of more
> than one level in the one act and in the one fact.[58]

Sheol—The Dark Model of Death

The ultimate of the finite. How far, one asks, must Christ's march
through time and man be before reaching that end, that finality to which
finitude itself tends? Through death, certainly, and, as I have tried to
show, to whatever horror of loneliness and dereliction surround the
soul's passage through that gate. Christ's coming into this world, then,
both to live and to die on its harsh terms, left nothing human out of
account; but the last, most harrowing descent of all had to have been into
that silence, the hellish solitude of Sheol. There, says the prophet, praise
of God is impossible; there all remembrance of Yahweh will be wiped
clean away.[59] And what is Sheol anyway? We know the word to be
Hebrew certainly, and doubtless many an exegete has counted up the
sixty or so times the word recurs in the Old Testament.[60] But what does
it really mean? To call it the Abode of the Dead settles very little since the
real question—What does it mean to die, to be in the condition of one
who is dead?— remains unanswered. Apropos of the skull which smirks
at one from beneath the skin ("Webster was much possessed by death /
and saw the skull beneath the skin; / And breastless creatures under
ground / Leaned backward with a lipless grin"[61]), to get at its message

one must peel away the flesh. In other words, what does happen at the point of death? At the point of Christ's death, which, in going before us to face, he has quite divested of its power to harm?

Rather, one should say, its power to confer ultimate harm. In what Bartholomew J. Collopy, S.J. has called "the dark model of death," one sees at once the most horrible human and temporal harm indeed. "From beginning to end, a dark model would present death as relentless and implacable, a breaking of the whole human person, an unacceptable and repugnant event, disintegration rather than achievement, a final fall into the weakness of being human—a fall even for religious faith and theological articulation. With such a model, theology would be called into grievous and desperate struggle."[62] This is because, surely, death represents the harrowing of all that we have, all that we know; it is no less, after all, than the complete sundering of body from soul, a prospect which, in even the best of humours, must fill a man with deep horror and dismay. And so the theological effort to understand death (and only theology can ultimately do so) must stand somewhat silent and unassuming before this last emptiness and horror; it may not, that is to say, stand any differently than Christ himself, who went in muteness and humility to the Cross.

Literature, too, in its imaginative arrangement of the data of death—art's encounter with all the concrete ineluctability of death—is able to render and renew, and thus make the reader *see*, which is always preferable to merely stating, the shape and form of this dark model. "The weapons of art," Fr. Lynch reminds us, "are terrible and not merely ornamental. They are the cognitive allies of the Holy Ghost...."[63] Let the following two examples serve to illustrate the imaginative reach and precision of art in the presence of death. In a popular novel by P.D. James, a still beautiful actress shortly to be murdered, though she does not know it yet, is asked, "What is it that you're really afraid of?"

> Oh, don't you know...Death. That's what I'm afraid of. Just death. Stupid, isn't it? I always have been, even when I was a child. I don't remember when it began, but I knew the facts of death before I knew the facts of life. There never was a time when I didn't see the skull beneath the skin.... It isn't the death of other people. It isn't the fact of death. It's my death I'm afraid of. Not all the time. Not every moment. Sometimes I can go for weeks without thinking about it. And then it comes, usually at night, the dread and the horror and the knowledge that the fear is real.... It comes in a rhythm, wave after wave of panic sweeping over me, a kind of pain. It must be like giving birth, except that I'm not delivering life.... Sometimes I hold up my hand, like this, and look at it and think, Here it is, part of me. I can feel it with my other hand, and move it and warm it and smell it and paint its

nails. And one day it will hang white and cold and unfeeling and useless, and so shall I be all those things. And then it will rot. And I shall rot. I can't even drink to forget.... And it's no good saying that I ought to believe in God. I can't. And even if I could, it wouldn't help.[64]

And, finally, from François Mauriac, that self-styled "metaphysician in the concrete,"[65] whose works early on won for him literature's Nobel Prize; it is a scene in which a young man is about to enter a room where his father, freshly dead, awaits entombment. Mauriac at once intensifies and enlarges his treatment of death, which makes this excerpt a better example of death as a dark model might envision it. *DEATH*

He began to tremble all over like a sapling. What did it matter whether this was his father or someone else? It was an emblem of death, of the death that lies deep down in all of us, ready to take charge, the one indubitable truth, the only certainty. How was it that the trams could run so heedlessly? Ought they not rather to have stopped, and the passengers been made to get out. "Don't you know that you have got to die?" What was the point of reading newspapers? How could anything in the world matter when death was the sentence under which it lay? *That* news emptied all other news of meaning. Why strive to learn, when tomorrow one would be cast forth as refuse, rotting and decayed? The only truth...If there exists anything beyond, we do not know it. We can be sure only of death. Religion? Systems of philosophy?—so many columns raised to front the void, a seeming solidity in the mists that veil an utter emptiness.

He began to moan, not for a father lost, but because the sight of death was evidence of death's unalterable law. The sound was like the howl of an animal feeling its fate at hand. The calf rears with terror in the slaughterhouse, the lamb smells the odour of spilled blood, and man, the eternal child, must gaze with open eyes upon the inevitable lot of humankind. How can people of flesh and blood act as they do, how busy themselves with trivial tasks, worrying of this and that, forming attachments for others less dedicated than themselves to nothingness, going through the movements that will give birth to future corpses and swell the ranks of death?... They may, perhaps, believe, have faith.... But death is not a matter of belief. We see it at each moment of the day, rub shoulders with it, salute it in the streets....

He was conscious of his sister's arm about his shoulders and pressed his tear-stained face against her frail and tender breast. He clung to this living sister—living, yet but another destined victim of eventual death. Only stones are free from the necessity of dying.[66]

Elements of a dark model of death may not blink before the stark reality of this apparent final cancellation; to do so diminishes, among other things, the truth of that Easter Mystery which, finally, delivers a man from all that appears definitively to crush him at the hour of his death.

And so, with the poet Webster, we need to understand the attitude of those who say, "On pain of death, let no man name death to me: It is a word infinitely terrible."[67] This is why John Donne, another of those Elizabethans who habitually saw the skull beneath the skin, remains ever so grateful in his "Good Friday Meditation," that he cannot see,

> That spectacle of too much weight for mee.
> Who sees Gods face, that is selfe life, must dye;

But then screws his courage sufficiently to ask,

> What a death were it then to see God dye?[68]

Christ in Sheol: The Presence of Love
Amid the Loneliness of the Lost

Here is one of those questions which, to paraphrase Pascal, takes a man by the throat. We are not, as it were, at liberty not to ask it and then go blithely about pretending we had left undisturbed the deposit of Christian faith. Refuse to ask that question, or ask it without the slightest intention of giving real, as opposed to notional, assent to the answer and, in a flash, one has left all of one's faith in ruins. This is because, to the degree Christ's tomb contains the last measure of that which, from the womb of the Woman to the wood of the Cross, he willed to empty out of himself, it remains completely integral to the Incarnation itself. Faced thus with this climactic gesture of kenotic outpouring, Christ's self-emptying carried to the very last extremity of suffering, what else can the believing Christian do but stoutly believe that it happened? However much the implications may fill some with pious dismay, or for others simply that the effort at understanding appears all too daunting to mount,[69] we are nevertheless constrained to ask, again, what must it have meant for God to die? And I do believe that in the death cry itself, uttered in unspeakable agony from the Cross, we have the beginning of an answer.

"My God, my God, why have you forsaken me?" Here is the decisive datum concerning Christ's death, and its meaning bespeaks the mysterious descent into the silence, the terrifying silence of Sheol. "It is a brief, questioning cry," says Adrienne von Speyr, "an accusation. And the Father is not addressed in his divine personal relationship with the Son; here it is the *man*, the creature, who cries out to *God*. Father-to-Son here has become God-versus-human being. As Father he has disappeared. The 'Father' has forsaken him: he calls to 'God'—this is all that remains of their relationship."[70] And so a deadly silence has ensued, for the

Father does not answer the Son; and thus in this silence, as in the sorrow of Gethsemane, Christ, our brother, enters into full communion with man, into the most deeply imagined solidarity of all, that of apparent final human separation from God. "Into this finality (of death) the dead Son descends," says von Balthasar, "no longer active in any way, but stripped by the cross of every power and initiative of his own, as something purely to be disposed of, as someone lowered to pure matter, absolutely indifferent in obedience, incapable of any active entering into solidarity—that is how he first comes to that 'sermon' to the dead. He is (out of a final love, however) dead together with them." And here von Balthasar's analysis builds to an extraordinary exegetical tension:

> And in this he disturbs the absolute loneliness sought after by sinners. Sinners, separated from God, wanting to be damned, in their loneliness find God again, but God in the absolute powerlessness of love who, unfathomably, makes himself one in the place-without-time with the self-damning. The words of the psalm, "If I make my bed in Sheol, thou art there" (139:8), thereby take on an entirely new meaning. And even "God is dead" as the autocratic decree of the sinners for whom God is something done away with, receives an entirely new, objective meaning provided by God himself.[71]

What can one conclude from all this? To begin with, that it is not mythology tricked out in theological language *and* that the idea expressed by von Balthasar can be construed in a way harmonious with the mind of the Church. Which is to say, in his disturbing presence among the damned, in the form which Christ's passive solidarity takes, there can be no attempt to force a salvation which, by definition it would appear, the damned have themselves already spurned and rejected. They must perforce remain free to say no to God. What C.S. Lewis, in answering the objection that the ultimate loss of even one soul means the defeat of God, has called "the most astonishing and unimaginable of all the feats we attribute to the deity"—i.e., his having created beings endowed with a liberty to refuse even that summons which Love himself went to the Cross to show—is doubtless correct; and so, in Lewis' own image, "the doors of hell are locked on the *inside*," these rebels against God having barred them shut forever.[72] Under the circumstances, Christ's entry therein cannot overturn in an absolute way the fate of souls whom the Church would fairly adjudge to be theologically dead, i.e., souls in whom the life of charity has run definitively dry and who evince an absolute unwillingness to replenish the supply. But, on the other hand, is not God equally free to send his Son to languish in sorrow and in silent solidarity in their midst? This is not that *apokatastasis* according to which an eschatological reconciliation of everything takes place, including even the most obdurate sinner's decision of eternal defiance before God; "the freedom of the human being and his or her responsibility before God may not be devalued," comments Medard Kehl. "Human decisions cannot be degraded to an ultimate insignificant child's game which God in his paternal goodness and wisdom can simply annul any time he wants."[73] And, in any case, Mother Church in her wisdom has never countenanced such a position though we are permitted to hope, indeed we are commanded to do so, that all might be saved and none lost at the very last, and this despite the apparent fixed refusal of men to respond to God's invitation to grace.

And yet, notwithstanding this essential freedom which Christ in his descent among the dead may not undo, "do human decisions have so much power that they—in the form of their no—can make God's love for the sinner ultimately ineffective for them?"[74] In other words, asks Kehl, how are the two truths to be con-joined without doing fundamental violence to the integrity of Christian faith? That is, "How does the universal, liberating love of the Son of God dying on the cross go together with the abiding freedom of the human person to say no to this love? This ultimate mystery of faith," insists Kehl, "is simply not capable of being 'dissolved' by theological reasoning."[75]

All that von Balthasar has attempted to do, galvanized by the example of von Speyr, the woman in whom he saw the whole outline of Catholic faith "hollowed out in her like the interior of a mold" even before he received her in 1940 into the Church—she whose subsequent "ecclesial mission" would consist of "continual and complete movement away from oneself, in self-forgetfulness and virginal readiness for the word of God," yes, even unto that final depth where Christ plunges her into vicarious communion with him in hell[76]—has simply been to try and understand something of what Christ's "night of the Cross" might possibly mean, both for Christ and for men. And his answer, the result of long meditation on this mystery of Christ's descent, precisely allows, says Kehl, "the universal power of the love of God, with full respect for human freedom, to hold its full validity—exactly as power of love, which does not overpower sinners and 'force them to salvation' against their will, but rather which accompanies them, in the wordless gesture of just being there, into their final loneliness. It must remain open," he concludes, "just how human beings experience in themselves such 'companionship' (somewhat like beatifying 'salvation')." For the universal hope of faith, this alone is all-important:

Only in absolute weakness (writes von Balthasar) does God mediate to the freedom he has created the gift of love which shatters every prison and loosens every confinement: in entering into solidarity from within with those who refuse all solidarity. *Mors et vita duello....*[77]

So Christ, in this paradoxical form of the wordless Word, mysteriously comes to those who, in their apparent choice to be always alone, refuse the gift of another's love, and offering his own passive witness of silent solidarity, he encamps alongside these lost souls. For to be is always to be in relation to another; but in the abandonment of Sheol there is no other, there is only the radically, fearfully solitary self; there is only the self destined from birth to be with the other, yet self-condemned, now, to an abyss everlastingly lonely. As Chesterton has masterfully reminded us in *Orthodoxy*, "It is not well for God to be alone."[78] But here amid the stark desolation of those lacking all otherness, the true horror of Christ's descent into that same loneliness, the condition of those who seemingly have refused every gesture of relation, is startlingly evident: Christ too is alone, the Blessed Company of God having freely consented to allow the Son to endure this apparent eclipse of all *relatio* with God.[79]

In short, Sartre was dead wrong: hell is not other people, as depicted in *No Exit*.[80] Hell is being alone, absolutely and forever. Hell is when the soul, having long habituated itself to a life of absolute self-enclosure, announces forever before God: "I don't want to love. I don't want to be loved. Just leave me to myself."[81] It is, suggests Josef Pieper, the radical posture of those who literally insist on never "giving a damn": that attitude of mind, fixated forever upon itself, is precisely an invitation to be damned. He adds: "In Dostoevsky's novel *The Brothers Karamazov* Father Zossima says: 'Fathers and teachers, I ponder, What is hell? I maintain that it is the suffering of being unable to love. Once in infinite existence, immeasurable in time and space, a spiritual creature was given, on his coming to earth, the power of saying: I am and I love.' "[82] Not to exercise this capacity to love the other, to anchor all one's *eros* to one's own self, this is the philosophy on which hell rests. And, to be sure, God, taking us finally at our word—that terrifying compliment paid to creatures on whom from the very start the liberty to refuse felicity had been conferred—will not stop us. Thus we are horrifyingly free, at the last, to declare before God, in words which recur throughout C.S. Lewis' fantasy *The Great Divorce*, "not Thy will, but *mine* be done."[83] And so it is done, forever; and from that weight of sheer self-will the soul sinks into everlasting hell. "There was a door," cries the loveless, self-tormenting husband to his unloving wife in Eliot's *Cocktail Party*,

And I could not open it. I could not touch the handle.
Why could I not walk out of my prison?
What is hell? Hell is oneself,
Hell is alone, the other figures in it
Merely projections. There is nothing to escape from
And nothing to escape to. One is always alone.[84]

It is this prison of the self, a place insupportably bleak, that Christ willed to enter in that last self-surrender we call the Mystery of Holy Saturday. Could any physical torment exist, either whose intensity or duration might equal the pain of that loss? What possible violence to the human person—to one whose whole being remains profoundly, irreducibly even, relational, and whose very completion as a person depends on communion with others and with God—what violence to such a being could possibly exceed a state of loneliness so starkly absolute? Is it not to force a man out into a circumstance of solitude he simply was not created to endure?

Imagery of Hell—Four Examples

Four images come to mind which may help to crystallize the idea. The first two are from the cinema and, perhaps significantly, they do not come from Hollywood. There was, some twenty or so years ago, an Ingmar Bergman film of disturbing resonance called *Cries and Whispers.* Set in a manor house at the turn of the century, the story concerns the last hours of a young woman dying of cancer. Two indifferent sisters have come to attend her final agony, joined by a third woman, a stolid servant who, unlike the two worldly and cynical sisters, remains mutely, selflessly devoted to her stricken mistress. In due course, the woman dies. Here, however, the movie begins to build to a sublime, unbearable climax. For following the death of this young woman, in the very midst of her disintegration, as it were, she undergoes an experience of abandonment so acute that, crying out—her dead hands extended in a gesture fraught with the most terrible eloquence for the living—she commences to plead, voicelessly, with those others (the living!) to join and comfort her among the dead. Both sisters at once refuse, rushing in horror and disgust from the room, in sensible flight from the unspeakable otherness of death, of its laying hold of what once was alive, no rigored thing then but verily alive, their sister, who, likewise, has become a horror to herself. The servant alone agrees to cradle the corpse, assuming therein the very likeness of Our Blessed Lady, whose own dead Son once lay draped across her arms. There can be no mistaking Bergman's intent here, which is to give mute testimony to that other, paradigmatic *Pieta*.

The other cinematic image is that of the character Zampano, the circus strongman in the 1956 Fellini film *La Strada*, whom we see at the very end, broken and alone on a deserted beach, his fists pounding the sand as he remembers the dead, dim-witted girl he had lived with, all of whose dreams he'd smashed along the way. She had only wanted someone to love and he'd answered her with brutal insistence: "I don't need anyone. I want to be left alone." He had gone on to murder her one friend, the circus Fool, who alone had given her a reason to believe the world was good and had need of her. All that Zampano had destroyed in his willful and terrible betrayal and desertion of her, leaving her soul prey to the torments of metaphysical loneliness. The whole harrowing realization of all that he'd done and lost in a lifetime's treachery suddenly illumines the face of this ravaged man at the last, and the viewer is overwhelmed by the sight. "Never are we less protected against suffering than when we love," says Sigmund Freud, whom Pieper quotes approvingly in his study *About Love*.[85] Who can doubt but that Zampano, in the midst of his heart-wrenching loss, is experiencing for the first time man's genuine need for another, his unwillingness indefinitely to be left alone. "Love anything," says Lewis, "and your heart will certainly be wrung and possibly be broken. If you want to make sure of keeping it intact, you must give your heart to no one, not even to an animal."[86] Even Zampano, for all his brutishness, is no animal; he too hungers for that love which, in order to receive, you must first give recklessly away to another. Failing that test of love's true mettle, he flails away at the sand in desperate, damnable sorrow.

The third image is drawn from a short story by Flannery O'Connor called "The Artificial Nigger,"[87] in which an old man and his grandson journey into the dark city where the boy undergoes an unspeakable ordeal of abandonment at the hands of his own grandfather. The latter, in considering what he had done to his own flesh and blood, undergoes a searing experience of shame and loss, of a loneliness whose proportions must be very near to what the pain of eternal loss means to those condemned everlastingly to hell. And although certain distinctions need to be observed (for instance, that the old man's sin is even now, within the story's own rhythm of loss and gain, being expiated; and that, of course, there is *time* in which to expiate it), notwithstanding all that, before genuine forgiveness can begin the sinner must know something of what O'Connor has called the *depth of his denial*. This depth awaits exploration and, in fact, to the degree that its depths are plumbed, so too the soul's correlative ascent. This particular sinner, in any case, is forced to feel the full depth of his denial in the most salutary way; the story thus is a dramatization of sin and suffering and grace to redeem. He experiences a state of abandonment, of sheer estrangement and enmity from the one living relation God had given him to love, which thrusts him out into a world of such privation and loss as to be, *mutatis mutandis*, indistinguishable from hell. O'Connor's description is worth quoting in full for it is frightfully lucid: "When Mr. Head realized this"—realized, that is, what he had done and the child's refusal to forgive what he had done—

> he lost all hope. His face in the waning afternoon light looked ravaged and abandoned.... He knew that now he was wandering into a black strange place where nothing was like it had ever been before, a long old age without respect and an end that would be welcome because it would be the end.... He felt he knew now what time would be like without seasons and what heat would be like without light and what man would be like without salvation.[88]

Finally, there is the image of the selfish giant, whose garden is perpetually bleak and wintry because he has never allowed himself to love another. But one morning he awakens to the loveliest of sounds (it is really only a linnet singing but so starved has he been for love that its music is splendid); rushing to his window he sees a little boy out in the garden struggling to climb onto the branches of a tree. "And the giant's heart melted as he looked out. 'How selfish I have been!' he said: 'Now I know why the Spring would not come here. I will put that poor little boy on the top of the tree, and then I will knock down the wall, and my garden shall be the children's playground for ever and ever.' "

So he steals quietly behind the boy lest the sight of him distress the child, and gently places him high up into its branches, which at once burst into blossom. And the boy thereupon kisses the giant, at the sight of which all the other children return excitedly into his garden. There they play for many years though the mysterious boy never returns and when asked, the others confess that they have never seen him.

One day, however, when the giant is very old he sees him and rushes out to him in joy and gladness. And when he came quite close his face grew red with anger, and he said, "Who hath dared to wound thee?" For on the palms of the child's hands were the prints of two nails, and the prints of two nails were on the little feet.

> "Who hath dared to wound thee?" cried the Giant. "Tell me, that I may take my big sword and slay him."
>
> "Nay," answered the child, "but these are the wounds of Love."
>
> "Who art thou?" said the Giant, and a strange awe fell on him, and he knelt before the little child.

And the child smiled on the Giant, and said to him, "You let me play once in your garden, today you shall come with me to my garden, which is Paradise."

And when the children ran into the garden that afternoon, they found the Giant lying dead under the tree, all covered with white blossoms.[89]

The Final Question and Answering Faith

What if there really were a loneliness so complete and final that nothing in this world could remedy the sorrow of it? A state of abandonment so definitive that neither word nor gesture could deliver us from it? Would not that frightful condition find its precise and formal theological equivalent in what we call hell? Isn't hell that very depth of loneliness where no love, no relation of real communion, can reach one in order to set free the soul of one's solitude? A life bereft of hope or home, a life lacking all sense of community or sanctuary or escape? The Prodigal Son fated never to find his father's love but, like the Flying Dutchman, left aimless and alone forever; an eternity of grief no less, who could endure it? In her memoir of the short story writer John Cheever, his daughter Susan explains the origin of the book's title, *Home Before Dark;* her explanation includes this remarkably moving vignette on the theme of what life would be like were any of us unable finally to get home before dark:

> My father liked to tell a story about my younger brother Fred. ...Once, at twilight after a long summer day, my father was standing outside the house under the big elm tree that shaded the flagstones in front of the door. Fred came back from playing with some friends, worn out and tired too, and when he saw Daddy standing there he ran across the grass and threw his little boy's body into his father's arms.
>
> "I want to go home, Daddy," he said, "I want to go home." Of course, he *was* home, just a few feet from the front door, in fact. But that didn't make any difference, as my father well understood. We all want to go home, he would say when he told this story. We all do.[90]

And what if there were no home to go to, no one to welcome the child when he got there (when it comes to going home we are all children); indeed, our own father telling us in words so final that nothing more will ever be said to soften the sentence: "I do not know you"? Is there not such a state of soul as I have described already awaiting us? Death doubtless awaits us all, that nightfall through the silence of which we must someday pass and will, ineluctably, pass alone. Death's door will admit only one at a time, and all have been scheduled to enter through it at different times. "Someday," Karl Barth has written, "a company of men will process out to a churchyard and lower a coffin and everyone will go home; but one will not come back, and that will be me. The seal of death will be that they will bury me as a thing that is superfluous and disturbing in the land of the living."[91] Here is the central augury of that ultimate ruin which, as Newman describes it in "The Dream of Gerontius," is far worse than pain:

> That masterful negation and collapse
> Of all that makes me man; as though I bent
> Over the dizzy brink
> Of some sheer infinite descent....[92]

Asked once by an interviewer what bothered him most about life, the late American poet Robert Lowell answered simply, "That people die."

"It is the blight man was born for," says the narrator of Hopkins' "Spring and Fall," to the young child who has wandered innocently into the autumn woods where, weeping but not knowing why, she watches all the fallen leaves die. "Margaret," he asks, "are you grieving / Over Goldengrove unleaving?" Alas, he tells her, "it is Margaret you mourn for."[93]

We must all die, and so, like young Margaret, we are given over to grief at the loss even of the leaves; since in nature's passing we glimpse the clearest prefiguring of our own. But we are not resigned to die—neither are we resigned to suffer, or to remain always alone—and so we rage, some of us, against the dying light.[94] These things are a problem to us, an outrage even, against the heart of what it means to be human, which is the yearning to live always and in communion with others, and without pain.

Is the problem even soluble? Or is it perhaps one of those mysteries whose understanding awaits the revelation of still other and deeper mysteries?[95] I believe the latter but, in any case, death remains, on the face of things, the one fact or eventuality which most conspires to keep us from getting home before dark. "We are, of all our miseries," wrote Hilaire Belloc in a moving letter to Katherine Asquith (who, like himself, suffered early on the tragic ending of a marriage with the death of a much loved spouse), "much the most afflicted by Mortality: and that means not mere Death...but the impermanence of all things, even of love: the good-byes and the changes that never halt their damning succession: the unceasing tale of loss which wears down all at last. *That* is mortality. *That* is the contradiction between our native joy and our present realities, which contrast is the curse of the Fall."[96]

Belloc is right of course, humanly speaking, and the pathos of his implied contrast grows painfully evident in the face of every lost love.

But what of Christ's descent into this hell, indeed, into all the places where love seems lost forever? Does not the whole inner dimension of that descent, the salvific meaning no less of the mystery of Holy Saturday, consist in the ultimate unleashing of Easter light and joy? Surely this is the meaning of that faith and hope which, in confronting the vastness of modern suffering of which the Holocaust remains a pre-eminent example, assist grace in raising a fallen world to the dignity of a Christian sacrament. The gap, in other words, between Belloc's own native joy and our present realities, is precisely spanned by the Spirit; the very One who, as Hopkins already reminds us,

> over the bent
> World broods with warm breast and with ah! bright wings.

Meanwhile, what remains characteristic of most Old Testament thought, and something of the Bellocian mood belongs to that moment, is that it should use one word only to describe two things: Sheol understood as both death and hell. This is because, under the aspect of the Old Testament vision of the Last Things, the Abode of the Dead—Sheol—came to represent that state of darkness and silence and solitude to which all would be sent simply in virtue of having lived.[97] Add to that the certainty of never getting out, God having washed away all memory of men who go there, and one begins to see the screw of human suffering as it tightens in ways increasingly awful. And what is such unrelieved pessimism anchored to but the clear, oppressive evidence of human sin, tracing finally back to Adam, who first cast the long shadow of sorrow across the world. Thus, for example, Pope John Paul II, in giving homiletic effect to his "Meditation on the Fourteenth Station," describes a world steeped in that state of sin: "From the moment when man, because of sin, was banished from the tree of life, the whole earth became a burial ground. For every human being there is a tomb. A vast planet of tombs."[98] But since we live now amid the bright shadows of the Cross, whose beacon of light reaches into every corner and abyss of human grief and loss, there remains sufficient hope for all who suffer. It is here, therefore, that the real cornerstone of Christian teaching emerges, on the truth of which this book depends for its reflection of hope amid such horrors as the Holocaust of the Jews, an evil which plainly strikes at the root of all hope. And what is that teaching but the Suffering of Love who wills to descend even to that state of final human loneliness and loss where death appears definitively to triumph; and there Love imparts the message of absolute consolation on the basis of Christ's having substituted himself for us in shouldering the weight of man's terror before the everlasting night. Thus, in Christ's free assumption out of a depth of love altogether

Trinitarian, of all the absurd futility and fear, the hopeless unending losses sustained by men who must suffer, the abandonment and grief of sin and sorrow, the Son of God himself succeeds forever in ridding us of all the hell of being human. Gerontius, faced with that which he had never felt before, may well cry out,

> Be with me, Lord, in my extremity!
> That I am going, that I am no more.
> 'Tis this strange innermost abandonment.
> As though my very being had given way,
> As though I was no more a substance now,
> And could fall back on nought to be my stay.[99]

But an answer has been given to Gerontius' grief: Jesus the Christ will be his mainstay, having first plunged headlong into that hellish night of pure negation for the world's salvation. Here, then, are the theses which drive the discourse toward those seemingly bereft of hope: One, that because there inheres in God himself such infinite and mysterious sensitivity to human suffering, we are justified in speaking of a kind of wound of love at the heart of Triune reality. Not, heaven knows, as defect or shortcoming which would only serve to weaken or contract the reach of God's sovereign love; rather, God's being is so purely and eternally determined by love that it does not shrink even from that intimate embrace with human sorrow and pain which, while not limiting his own nature, perfectly dramatizes his involvement with ours. And, two, the sheer extent of Christ's involvement in love's embrace of human grief and failure is to be found in the truth of the Church's solemn affirmation of the Descent. "Death was dead when Life was dead on the tree," to cite the Office of Vespers on the Feast of the Holy Cross. In other words, but for Christ's descent into all the horror of human desolation, there would yet remain one, continuous, eternal Kingdom of Death, in whose folds all men would fit simply for having ceased to be. But having willed to enter into that nether world, Christ has broken its tyranny for all time and eternity; only those who obdurately refuse salvation's gift, preferring an eternity of the self-centered self, only they may not profit from his pain. "In one of the innumerable tombs," says the Pope, now shifting from Jehovah to Jesus, "scattered all over the continents of this planet of ours, the Son of God, the man Jesus Christ, conquered death with death."[100] That spiritual iron curtain which no living man can breach—"a gulf impassable, an impenetrable darkness, and a distance as it were limitless, infinite," as Belloc described death in his letter to the widow of Lt. Asquith, in which a new mood of hope is struck—was in fact once breached by One whose assault upon it has since set free the souls of all creatures subject to sin and death. "The miracle whereby such an enormity coming upon immortal souls does not breed despair," notes Belloc,

> is the chief miracle of the Incarnation...and to work that miracle, the Incarnate One—with what a supreme energy—accepted our pain, almost refused it, but accepted it; and it was greater than any pain of ours: physically beyond endurance and in the spirit a descent into Hell.[101]

Death and hell, then, are the twin realities which, in complete faith, we believe the Lord actually and mysteriously suffered: the reality of the one representing sheer terrified helplessness in the face of vacant extinction; the other representing that state of lasting, radical loneliness without love which, on any human reckoning surely, is infinitely worse: both, however, supremely vanquished at the very moment when Christ entered fully into the depths of each, squeezing the last measure of horror and futility and pain from whatever abyss they contained. Therefore, it follows, the Article in the Christian Creeds which declares both the truth and the necessity of Jesus Christ's descent into hell, does so in order to signal the most profound gesture of kenotic kinship with all whom sin has divested of self and other. (But, again, the whole prior and ontic ground of which is the Suffering Love of a God whose being remains eternally relational, fixed on and for the other.) Yes, Christ died and went to hell: not the hell where the alleged wrath of an irate Father inflicts its sting of revenge forever; nor that state of fixed enmity for God which defines the fate of men who turn their faces to the wall forever. Rather, it is the Son's acceptance, his freely taking on all that cries out to God in sorrow and loneliness and pain; all that is summed up in the hell of being human Jesus Christ freely submits to in this blackest night of obedient love. "He loved them to the last," confesses the Church in the words of St. John's Gospel.[102] What does this mean but that he so emptied himself in loving obedience to the Father of all power and outward glory (attributes precisely his own by dint of shared divinity with the Father) in order to effect in the most fundamental and dramatic way total affinity with all the tragic finitude of human life. Moving thus not only through human life and time, but human death as well—the six million deaths, say, of those whom his Father had long ago chosen to be his own—indeed, moving all the way down through even that final extremity of solitude and fear and Godforsaken abandonment where there can be neither speech nor love. And there he planted his Father's Word which is himself, its obedient expression having reached right to the limit of filial love. *Death*, says he, speechlessness now giving way to speech—descent opening once more onto ascent—*Thou shalt die!* Then death, which heretofore had meant hell, is thrown into the lake of fire which, in the Book of

Revelation, becomes the Second Death, reserved only for those who persist in the refusal to share in love's exchange. For the blessed rest (it is one's deepest prayer that it include such as us) the door of death no longer stands shut, love having quite unhinged it by first going straight through it. With the poet George Herbert, we do well then to announce,

> Death, thou wast once an uncouth hideous thing
> > Nothing but bones,
> > The sad effect of sadder groans:
> Thy mouth was open, but thou couldst not sing. ...
>
> But since our Saviour's death did put some blood
> > Into thy face,
> > Thou are grown fair and full of grace,
> Much in request, much sought for as good.
>
> For we do not behold thee gay and glad,
> > As at Doomsday;
> > When souls shall wear their new array,
> And all thy bones with beauty shall be clad.
>
> Therefore we can go die as sleep, and trust
> > Half that we have
> > Unto an honest faithful grave;
> Making our pillows either down, or dust.[103]

NOTES

1. Hans Urs von Balthasar, "The Last Five Stations of the Cross," *Theologians Today*, selected and edited by Martin Redfern, (London and New York: Sheed and Ward, 1972).

2. Indeed, as an instrument of torture and death, crucifixion had the manifest advantage of inflicting the greatest concentration of pain over the longest period of time; and, in addition, it was a torture so horrifying to witness that even the most barbaric of sensibilities would naturally shrink before committing whatever crimes led to it. See Ian Wilson, *The Turin Shroud*, (London: Victor Gollanz, 1968), especially Chapter III, "The Shroud and Medical Opinion," for additional information on the subject.

3. Walter Kasper, *Jesus The Christ*, (London: Burns and Oates, 1976), p. 113.

4. Apropos of von Balthasar's meditations on Christ's Way of the Cross, in which he submits his imagination to the full reality of that drama which Gill tried to capture in stone and in which all humanity stands implicated, see Donald MacKinnon's essay from *The Analogy of Beauty: The Theology of Hans Urs von Balthasar*, edited by John Riches, (Edinburgh: T&T Clark, 1986), pp. 164-174.

"It is not that he allows his commitment to faith in Christ's Resurrection to be undermined; it is rather that he would insist that where this *ultimate* victory is concerned, we should not forget the profound lessons to be learnt from the reply of the Duke of Wellington to a gushing woman, who had spoken to him of the supremely exhilarating experience of a victory: 'Madam,' the Duke replied, 'a victory is the most terrible thing in the world, only excepting a defeat,' " pp. 166-167.

5. Charles Williams, *The Descent of the Dove*, (London: Longmans, 1939), p. 76. In other words, here is a variant note on that which recurs throughout the Fathers. See, for instance, Athanasius' statement, "The Logos was made man that we might be made God." *The Incarnation of the Word*, 54: PG 25.192. Or the saying of Irenaeus: "On account of his immense love for us, the Word of God, our Lord Jesus Christ, made himself what we are, in order that we might become what he is himself," *Adv. Haer.* V, prologue: PG 7.1120. Ambrose expressed the same idea: "The Word was made flesh in order that flesh might become God," *De Virg.* 1.3. Or, finally, Augustine: "He was made to have share in our mortality; he made us to have share in his divinity," *De Trin.* IV.1,2-3; 2,4. Concerning the above statements, see the judgment of Stanislas Lyonnet and Leopold Sabarin, *Sin, Redemption, and Sacrifice: A Biblical and Patristic Study*, (Rome: Biblical Institute Press, 1970), p. 203: "An impartial study of the history of dogma reveals that substantial agreement characterizes the development of the doctrine of redemption in the two great Christian traditions, the Greek and the Latin. They share the same basic doctrine: the Word became flesh so that man might participate in divine life."

6. "Him who knew nothing of sin God made to be 'sin' for our sakes (2 Cor. 5:21). He who was to condemn sin in the flesh (Rom. 8:3), he the sinless One, was himself made 'sin': by the flesh he condemned sin in the flesh, for he who was without flesh was made flesh for our sakes; thus for our iniquities he was wounded (Is. 53:5)." So wrote St. Hilary, the fourth-century bishop of Poitiers, in his *De Trinitate*, X, 47: PL 10, 381. Cited by Lyonnet and Sabarin, p. 204. In other words, by Christ's work of substitution, his vicarious surrender of life for the many, we reach the sublime center of the New Testament witness of salvation. "A fundamental law of the whole history of salvation," stands revealed, i.e., that solidarity of sin and grace which, like a golden thread, stitches the whole of salvation history together. In Adam's fall we sinned all. But in Christ's assumption of that fall into sin and death, "the foundation for a new solidarity" is laid and hereafter Christ's death promises life for all who stand under sentence of death. "The interpretation of the death of Jesus as vicarious suffering entered into the oldest tradition of the community (1 Cor. 15:3) and was taken up and deepened in the New Testament in many places (Jn. 10:15; 1 Jn. 4:10; 1 Pet. 2:21-25; 1 Tim. 2:6, among others)." See *The Church's Confession of Faith: A Catholic Catechism for Adults*, (San Francisco: Ignatius Press; Communio Books, 1987), pp. 157-158.

7. "What hanged on the tree," asks Augustine, "if not the sin of the old man, which the Lord for our sake received in the mortality of the flesh? The Apostle then had no shame and no fear in saying that God made him 'sin' for our sake,

adding 'in order that by sin he might condemn sin.' Our old self would not have been at the same time crucified, the Apostle says elsewhere, if in this death of the Lord, had not hanged the image (*figura*) of our sin, that the sinful body might be destroyed, and we might no longer be enslaved to sin (Rom. 6:6)." *Expos. in Gal.* 3.13: PL 35,2120; cf. *Contra Adimantum* 21: CSEL (25), Aug. 6, p. 180. Cited by Lyonnet and Sabarin, p. 213.

"And although he himself committed no sin, yet because of 'the likeness of sinful flesh' (Rom. 8:3) in which he came, he was himself called 'sin' and was made a sacrifice for the washing away of sins. Indeed, under the old law, sacrifices for sins were often called 'sins' (Hos. 4:8).... He himself is therefore sin as we ourselves are righteousness—not our own but God's, not in ourselves but in him. Just as he was sin—not his own but ours, rooted not in himself but in us...." Augustine, *On Faith, Hope and Love*, 13.41 (PL 40: c. 253), trans. A.C. Outler in *Library of Christian Classics*, vol. VII, (London, 1955), p. 365.

8. John Henry Newman, "Mental Sufferings of our Lord in His Passion," Discourse XVI, p. 335. Newman, in effect, asks the question, "what was it He had to bear, when He thus opened upon His soul the torrent of this predestined pain? Alas! He had to bear what is well known to us, but what to Him was woe unutterable...the scent and the poison of death—He had, my dear brethren, to bear the weight of sin; He had to bear your sins; He had to bear the sins of the whole world. Sin is an easy thing to us; we think little of it...we cannot bring our imagination to believe that it deserves retribution.... But consider what sin is in itself; it is that, if I may use a strong expression, which, could the Divine Governor of the world cease to be, would be sufficient to bring it about. Sin is the mortal enemy of the All-holy, so that He and it cannot be together; and as the All-holy drives it from His presence into the outer darkness, so, if God could be less than God, it is sin that would have power to make him less."

9. Eliot, *Four Quartets*, p. 18. Another poet, Paul Claudel, in attempting to render justice to the fullest extent of Our Lord's descent into hell, reminds us in his lyric meditation on The Fourteenth Station of that which, mysteriously bound to the Son of God himself, truly entered into the dreaded sepulcher on Good Friday eve; it was, he says, "my own flesh.... It is man—Thy creature, O God!—more profound than earth."

> Now that His heart is opened and His hands with wounds are lit,
> There is no cross of our living where His body will not fit,
> There is no sin of ours for which He has not a wound.
> Oh, then, from Thine altar, Saviour, come where Thy sheep are found!
> See how Thy creature is pierced to depths profound!

See his *Coronal*, (New York: Pantheon Books, 1943), p. 257. Nevertheless—the argument of the book rests upon this point—one may not presume here to deduce from the lyric, particularly its image of the Son "pierced to depths profound," a state of real and absolute Godforsakenness which, as in the case of Calvin, follows upon the Son's appeasing the Father's wrath and thus enduring the full penalty of the damned. Writes Calvin: "It was expedient...for him

(Christ) to undergo the severity of God's vengeance, to appease his wrath and satisfy his just judgment. For this reason, he must grapple hand to hand with the armies of hell and the dread of everlasting death...submitting himself, ever as the accursed, to bear and suffer all the punishments that they ought to have sustained. ...No wonder then, if he is said to have descended into hell, for he suffered the death that God in his wrath had inflicted upon the wicked! ...He paid a greater and more excellent price in suffering in his soul the terrible torments of a condemned and forsaken man." See his *Institutes of the Christian Religion*, II, 16,10: CR 30 (Calv. 2), c. 376f. Cited by Lyonnet and Sabarin, p. 233. Calvin is surely wrong on this issue, a) because neither the Father's wrath nor the Son's appeasement thereof does fundamental justice to that limitless suffering love which moves in tandem the Father and Son in their joint work of salvation. And, b) because whatever torments Christ endures amidst the apparent absence of the Father, i.e., the strangled cry of the Godforsaken Son, it is not the suffering of the damned which the Son undergoes since those sufferings precisely trace to the sinner's obdurate refusal to love God by keeping his commandments. In other words, sin represents a state of fixed enmity for God which is entirely at variance with the Person and Mission of the Son, the One whose entire existence remains in necessary and complete rhythmic relation to the Father and for the world. Even unto that final stage of descent where the Son seems to move in anguished silence, neither seeing nor hearing the Father's presence? Yes, but always in obedient love to that presence whose absence alone is felt. See *The Church's Confession of Faith: A Catholic Catechism for Adults*, p. 163. "The extreme passion, the extreme night of obedience, the ultimate solidarity of Jesus with the dead in their abandonment and loneliness, his entering into the entire hell of being human—all these are the *victory of God over death and over the powers of darkness and death*" (emphases in the original).

10. *The Complete Works of Saint Teresa of Jesus*, translated and edited by E. Allison Peers, (London and New York: Sheed and Ward, 1957), p. 216.

11. Balthasar, *Does Jesus Know Us? Do We Know Him?* pp. 37-38.

12. Newman, pp. 334-335.

13. For a profound and stirring artistic illustration of the theme, see Gertrud von Le Fort's *The Song at the Scaffold*, (New York: Image Books, 1961), in which a young and timorous postulant, Blanche, aspires to full membership in the Carmelite Order amid the menace of persecution in France during the Revolution; she is given the name of Jesus au Jardin de l'Agonie, inasmuch as Christ himself may be said to be in the garden of Gethsemane at this supreme moment of crisis in the life of France, eldest daughter of the Church. The whole point of the name, of course, is that, according to Carmelite practice, the name confers special access to the mystery which it enshrines. Some time later, her Prioress having adjudged Blanche unsuitable for religious life on the grounds that her timidity in the face of the impending Terror reveals a fatal want of courage, Blanche expostulates with her in the following terms: "...yes, you are doing me an injustice." And when asked if she still hopes then to overcome her weakness, Blanche replies,

"No, Reverend Mother." There was something quite hopeless in her voice and at the same time a strange note of peace.

The Prioress felt as though suddenly all her standards were collapsing. "Look at me," she commanded. Blanche dropped her hands from her small tortured face that held only a single expression of endless depths. The Prioress hardly recognized her. A series of quite unconnected images suddenly floated before her: little dying birds, wounded soldiers on the battlefield, criminals at the gallows. She seemed to see not Blanche's fear alone but all the fear in the world.

"My child," she said brokenly, "you cannot possibly harbor within yourself the fear of the whole universe—" She stopped.

There was a brief silence. Then Madame Lidoine said almost shyly: "You believe then that your fear—is religious?"

Blanche sighed deeply: "Oh Reverend Mother," she breathed, "consider the secret of my name!" (pp. 64-65)

14. Hans Urs von Balthasar, *First Glance at Adrienne von Speyr*, (San Francisco: Ignatius, 1981).

15. *Ibid.*, pp. 64-65.

16. *Ibid.*, p. 65. "Not just the Cross (which for all the renunciation it symbolizes, retains something of a positive valence), but the hiatus between Cross and Resurrection, the absurd emptiness of Holy Saturday, lies at the center of Adrienne's life and mission. To the blinding brilliance of God's self-revelation to which Adrienne responds with Marian transparency, one must add the utter darkness and incomprehensibility of Love's descent into the abandonment of Hell. Wherever this dark ray pierces the prayer of Adrienne—and it is rarely long absent—only the answering hiatus of awed and awful silence will suffice. One cannot simply read on." Fr. Joseph Fessio, "How to Read Adrienne von Speyr," *La Mission Ecclesiale d'Adrienne von Speyr*, an International Colloquy held in Rome, September 27-29, 1985, p. 5.

17. *First Glance*, pp. 66-67.

18. Cited in Bernard Basset, *Born For Friendship: The Spirit of Sir Thomas More*, (London: Burns & Oates, 1964), p. 205.

19. *Ibid.*, pp. 205-206.

20. See von Balthasar's *Does Jesus Know Us? Do We Know Him?*, where the question is asked, "Could the Redeemer of humanity let himself be surpassed by men in the knowledge of human suffering? Should the poet's 'nothing human is foreign to me' not apply to him? Could he have had only a moderate, average knowledge of human guilt and human pain, leaving others to go to the extremes? But then, how could he say that he is 'the first and the last,' that he has 'the keys of death and hell' (Rev. 1:18)?" p. 38.

21. C.S. Lewis, *The Problem of Pain*, (Glasgow: Collins, 1940), pp. 112ff.

22. *Ibid.*, pp. 113-114.

23. A. Dubos, *The Last Worthless Evening*, (Boston: Godine, 1968), p. 194. There are three kinds of people, it has been proverbially remarked: those who make things happen, those who watch things happen, and those who wonder what

happened. Of these, the latter surely go to hell, the sheer weight of their indifference drawing them gravitationally down into doom.

24. *First Glance at Adrienne von Speyr*, p. 66.

25. For a historical chronology of the doctrine's emergence in fixed credal form, see J.N.D. Kelly, *Early Christian Creeds*, (London, 1960), pp. 378-383. "The belief that Christ spent the interval between His expiry on the cross and His resurrection in the underworld was a commonplace of Christian teaching from the earliest times," p. 379. Kelly mentions a number of early Church Fathers, among them Ignatius, Polycarp, Irenaeus and Tertullian, whose writings testify to this belief; the upshot of it would seem to be the Church's necessity of establishing the fact that Jesus Christ really died and was buried, thus ensuring that God's share in the human lot was fully complete. "To say that Jesus Christ had died, or that He had been buried, was equivalent to saying that He had passed to Sheol," says Kelly on p. 380. But what exactly is *meant* by the claim that Christ underwent this descent into Sheol? The effort of this chapter in particular aims to unearth an answer to that very question.

26. *First Glance*, p. 66.

27. "Here," declares Kasper, having in mind the Christ-hymn of Phil. 2:5-11, "the whole Christology is one great drama of debasement and exaltation. He who was obediently reduced to the state of a servant is exalted by God as the *Pantocrator*," Walter Kasper, *Jesus The Christ*, (London: Burns & Oates, 1976), p. 36. Or, elsewhere, Paul's reference to Christ having descended "into the abyss" (Rom. 10:7) before his return from the abode of the dead. Likewise Eph. 4:9-10, to continue the idea, although some divergence of opinion exists among exegetes concerning its precise meaning. "Some think," writes Fr. Galot, "that the lower parts of the earth refer simply to the earth itself, lower than the heavens. The descent into the lower regions would then designate the Incarnation," hardly the sublimest possible symbol of Christ's kenosis. "However, it is more probable that these lower regions signify hell, the abode of the dead conceived as a place situated underground. This was its meaning given by the Jews. For them, this lower region was Sheol: cf. Ps. 63:9; Ps. 86:13; Ps. 88:6; Si. 51:6; Lam. 3:55." And, he adds, it was this descent into the abyss, i.e., into hell, that St. Paul had in mind when writing Rom. 10:7. "The context also suggests this interpretation, for Paul deliberately contrasts Christ's extreme humiliation and his supreme exaltation. Now, this extreme humiliation consists in the descent into hell, which continues the descending movement of the Incarnation to its lowest point. Likewise, in Philippians 2:8-11 the contrast is stressed between the death of Christ which is the utmost emptying of the Incarnation and the glorification that follows it," Jean Galot, S.J., *Jesus Our Liberator, A Theology of Redemption*, (Chicago: Franciscan Herald Press, 1982), pp. 333-334.

28. Though they knew the gods took a keen interest in all that men do, the Greeks were never so naive as to assign blessed motives to their countless ministrations. They expected perfect justice from none of them. "In such a universe, one must proceed warily and avoid extremes. Piety consisted in doing nothing to anger the gods, and in pleasing, or appeasing, them through offerings...a

Greek's fondest wish was that the gods would leave him alone," Richard B. Sewall, *The Vision of Tragedy*, (New Haven and London: Yale University Press, 1959), p. 26. Especially Hades, chief deity of death and that reign of misery without end; his governance of the underworld left no man alone, and both hero and villain were powerless to escape the vast encompassing darkness of his kingdom. "Hateful darkness seizes him, and his soul goes down to Hades bewailing its fate, leaving behind its youth and strength. After the horror of such a death nothing remains for the soul but a dark and comfortless world, the mouldering house of Hades, and a shadowy and senseless existence, forever banished from the light and warmth and activity of life. For the poet has abolished from the world any form of posthumous reward or blessedness, insisting that death is the end of everything sweet," Jasper Griffin, *Homer*, (Oxford-Toronto-Melbourne: Oxford University Press, 1980), p. 34. No wonder Achilles says, "We men are wretched things, and the gods who have no cares themselves have woven sorrow into the very pattern of our lives," *The Iliad*, Bk. 24.

29. "The descent into hell is our guarantee that Christ really experienced death. Had there not been this intermediary period, and if the Resurrection had immediately followed Jesus' last breath, there could have been doubt as to the reality of his death. The descent into hell attests that the end of Jesus' life was not a kind of fleeting passage in which he merely brushed death. Christ really entered this lower region of human death, and this was the extreme limit of his humiliation," Galot, *Jesus Our Liberator, A Theology of Redemption*, p. 334. See also Galot's comment on the status of the hypostatic unity, which death, in its violent wrenching of soul from body, would appear to have perhaps disturbed. Not so, says Galot: "The immensity of the mystery consists precisely in that a change as radical as the separation of the soul from the body could occur in spite of the hypostatic unity. The Son of God assumed not only human nature but the whole of human destiny, which includes death.... The Word became flesh so completely as to accept that his flesh should become a corpse," p. 336.

And the divinity, what of its eternal and absolute nature which Father and Son equally share, the mutuality of whose love being the very Spirit? Here, John J. O'Donnell commenting on the merit of von Balthasar's distinctive contribution to the question, a *separation* indeed occurs but one which remains entirely and mysteriously sustained by that Spirit who is the very bond of love among the members of the Trinity. "Balthasar wants to stress that the cross is a separation of Father and Son but the dramatic caesura that rends the heart of God on Calvary has already been embraced from all eternity by the divine Trinity. For from eternity the Father has given himself away to the Son, has risked his being on the Son, and from eternity the Son has been a yes to the Father, a surrender of obedience. Thus the Father's risk of himself on the Son creates a space for the Son. The Father separates himself from himself, so that the Son can be. But this separation is also bridged over in eternity by the Holy Spirit, the communion of the love of the Father and the Son." See Fr. O'Donnell's *The Mystery of the Triune God*, (London: Sheed and Ward, 1987), p. 65.

30. Balthasar, *Heart of the World*, (San Francisco: Ignatius Press, 1979), p. 150.

31. "Rethinking Christ," in *Anti-Semitism and the Foundations of Christianity*, ed. by Alan T. Davies, (New York: Paulist Press, 1979), p.183. See also Jurgen Moltmann's insistence that theology after Auschwitz would reduce to obscene futility "were not the *Sch'ma Israel* and the Lord's Prayer prayed in Auschwitz itself, were not God himself in Auschwitz, suffering with the martyred and murdered. Every other answer would be blasphemy. An absolute God would make us indifferent. The God of action and success would let us forget the dead, which we still cannot forget. God as nothingness would make the entire world into a concentration camp." See his essay on "The Crucified God," in *Theology Today* 31, 1 (April, 1974), p. 9. However, despite Moltmann's intention, which clearly aims at maximizing the presence of God amid the horrors of human suffering, one must be careful not to purchase it at too high a price, namely that Patripassianism which, at least since the fourth century, has stood condemned by the Church. See, for example, the "Tome of Damasus," issued by Pope Damasus I at the Council of Rome in 382, in which the errors of those who attribute the passion of the cross to God himself—God as God—and not the flesh perfectly assumed by the Son, the Suffering Servant, is adjudged false. (*The Christian Faith in the Doctrinal Documents of the Catholic Church*, ed. by Neuner and Dupuis, [New York: Alba House, 1981], p. 147.) In other words, the "cross in the heart of God" may not be other than an image of that absolute and Trinitarian love lavished freely and kenotically upon a bleeding world; it mustn't be construed as so many wounds within the Godhead as such, the existence of which somehow contingently comes about as a result of the world's own pain. Then God is no longer God and the wound of love which he bears can do us no good. Far better, it would seem, to work out the details along those Trinitarian lines laid down, for instance, by von Balthasar, which O'Donnell nicely summarizes as his own conclusion: "that the most profound hermeneutic of the cross is a properly theological one, that the cross can only be grasped adequately if it is seen as an event between God and God, between the Father and the Son, an event which is the working out in history of a primordial drama between the Father and the Son who from eternity risk their being on one another, who are thus distinct but yet one in the Holy Spirit who is their bond of communion," *The Mystery of the Triune God*, p. 66.

32. And contempt also from the standpoint of a comprehensive exegesis of the text as understood by the medieval Schoolmen who practiced its fourfold analysis. See, for example, Fr. Walter Burghardt's description of the method in his essay "On Early Christian Exegesis" in *Theological Studies*, XI (1950), pp. 104-106. The four levels, he says, "are not just parts of a whole; it is always the selfsame reality seen under its successive parts." In other words, the conferral of eternal life is not recompense, not compensatory at all, but the fullness of the literal itself, when at last the facts of history are given eternal flesh and we see the glory therein. Fr. William Lynch reproduces the essay in *Christ and Apollo*, pp. 229-232. However, for an interesting if slightly oblique discussion of the problem of evil, in which the matter of compensation is brought in, see E.L. Mascall, *The Christian Universe*, (London: Darton, Longman & Todd, 1966), pp. 150-

153. What fundamentally besets us in facing evil, he reports, is that "we cannot imagine anything that would ultimately compensate for it.... I can imagine what will make my toothache ultimately not matter.... But I cannot *imagine* how even God could produce a situation in which I could say, 'I now see that even Belsen doesn't really matter.' " To overcome the despair induced at this point, he says, requires an immense faith in God's resources, "inexpressibly ampler than anything I am able to conceive," which is taken fundamentally for granted in the fourfold method. God can draw meaning and finality from even this "poor potsherd of a man," who, thanks to God's infinite resources, becomes—to conclude Hopkins' lyric—"immortal diamond." With God there is simply no problem of scarcity of resource, as witness his own broken body becoming the manifest Glory of the Triune Lord.

33. Camus, *The Plague*, pp. 201-204.

34. *Early Christian Fathers*, ed. by Cyril C. Richardson, p. 90.

35. Louis Dupré, "Jesus Still in Agony?" *Word and Spirit, A Monastic Review* (Massachusetts: St. Bede's Publications, 1979), pp. 191-195. "A great deal has been written about the purifying, strengthening qualities of suffering. These qualities may be known to him who has suffered, but not to him who suffers. Within my actual suffering I detect no meaning. I experience it as absurdly gratuitous.... To suffer is to be alone. No one can follow the sufferer into this most private world.... It is like nothing else and, in it, I am like no one else. Indeed, it is the only part of myself that is exclusively me, that bears my name. No one enters this most intimate dwelling. 'Were you there when they crucified my Lord?' Yes, Lord, I was there in the only way I could be present to your suffering: in the solitude of my own pain," pp. 192-193.

36. "Jesus Still in Agony?" p. 193.

37. *Ibid.*, p. 194.

38. *Ibid.*, p. 195. For an interesting treatment of the same theme, see John Navone, S.J., *A Theology of Failure*, (New York: Paulist Press, 1974), wherein the very universality of our common human experience becomes, as it were, the ironic foothold for Christ, who comes to establish that invincible hope which alone may uphold a man in the midst of terrible trials and sufferings. This same Christ who, Navone shows, is the proto-typical failure of the New Testament. "Jesus, like man in everything but sin, experienced human failure. He wept over Jerusalem which had not known the day of its visitation. His preaching failed to convert his people. His crucifixion was an act of rejection and public disgrace. The hatred vented upon him during his passion and death gave him a profound experience of moral evil. His last moments of life were filled with the consciousness of his failure to communicate his Father's message to his people. And when it was all over, his disciples realized that Jesus' acceptance of failure and death was the divinely appointed way for effectively communicating all that the Father wanted to communicate, even if Jesus himself might not have realized this in his final moments of consciousness," p. 1.

39. The hero of Camus' *The Plague*, for example, would fashion a new priesthood univocally bent upon the eternal exclusion of pain in all its particulars from

the universe of men. As parable, the novel mounts the most rigorous and uncompromising of assaults upon suffering; and its author, in summoning us to so univocal a crusade, would even level the entire universe in order to rid it of all unpleasantness. That such a remedy would perforce eliminate all need of the Son's complete assumption of our pain, the whole incredibly ironic strategy of the Father, who seeks less the perfection of the universe than its redemption, is the point of the narrative. See Fr. Lynch's brilliant dissection of the univocal mind and imagination in *Christ and Apollo*, pp. 120-133.

40. *Christ and Apollo*, p. 165.

41. *Ibid.*, p. 186. Here is the seed of that Christological humanism which, at the Second Vatican Council, achieved its fullest bloom in the Pastoral Constitution, *Gaudium et Spes*. See Article 22 where the root of the human is struck deep within Christ. "In reality it is only in the mystery of the Word made flesh that the mystery of man truly becomes clear...Christ the Word, Christ the new Adam, in the very revelation of the mystery of the Father and of his love, fully reveals man to himself and brings to light his most high calling. ...Human nature, by the very fact that it was assumed, not absorbed, in him, has been raised in us also to a dignity beyond compare. For, by his incarnation, he, the son of God, has in a certain way united himself with each man. He worked with human hands, he thought with a human mind. He acted with a human will, and with a human heart he loved. ...The Christian is certainly bound both by need and by duty to struggle with evil through many afflictions and to suffer death; but, as one who has been made a partner in the paschal mystery, and as one who has been configured to the death of Christ, he will go forward, strengthened by hope, to the resurrection," *Vatican Council II: The Conciliar and Post Conciliar Documents*, General Editor: Austin Flannery, O.P., (Northport, New York: Costello Publishing Co., 1981), pp. 922-924.

42. Charles Williams, "The Cross," *Selected Writings*, ed. by Anne Ridler, (London: Oxford University Press, 1961), p. 102.

43. G.K. Chesterton, *Orthodoxy*, (New York: John Lane Co., 1908), pp. 255-257.

44. *The Everlasting Man*, (New York: Image Books, 1925), p. 216.

45. *Life of Jesus*, (New York: David McKay Co., 1937), p. 218.

46. Joseph Ratzinger, *Behold the Pierced One: An Approach to a Spiritual Christology*, (San Francisco: Ignatius Press, 1986), pp. 15-18. "The title 'Son' comes in the end to be the only, comprehensive designation for Jesus. It both comprises and interprets everything else.... Calling Jesus the 'Son'...corresponds most strictly to the center of the historical figure of Jesus. For the entire gospel testimony is unanimous that Jesus' words and deeds flowed from his most intimate communion with the Father; that he continually went 'into the hills' to pray in solitude after the burden of the day (e.g., Mk. 1:35; 6:46; 14:35, 39). Luke, of all the Evangelists, lays stress on this feature. He shows that the essential events of Jesus' activity proceeded from the core of his personality and that this core was his dialogue with the Father."

47. To wit, the Fourth Lateran Council in 1215, at which the Albigensian denial of his descent among the dead, his rescue of the just who had died before

the Incarnation, is rejected. And the Second Council of Lyons in 1274. See Galot, *Jesus Our Liberator, A Theology of Redemption*, p. 329.

48. *Introduction to Christianity*, (New York: Seabury Press, 1969), pp. 225-226.

49. Balthasar, *Heart of the World*, p. 175.

50. *Heart of the World*, p. 181. "The Christian East," he writes elsewhere, "has preserved a certain tradition of the Redemption which has been lost to the West at an early stage. The Western image is Golgotha: the crucified Christ between the two thieves...the image of the suffering Man (while the Divinity remains invisible) and of the earthly fruit of this suffering.... For the East the image of Redemption is the descent into Hades: the bursting open of the eternally-closed gate, when Christ stretches out his hand to the first Adam who, hardly trusting his eyes, sees the Easter light in the darkness of death. Thus the Greek Fathers have always preached, thus the Byzantines and the Russians have made visible the other-worldly event of the Redemption," *The God Question and Modern Man*, (New York: Seabury Press, 1967), pp. 129-130.

See also Joseph Ratzinger, who confirms this view when he writes of the joyful colors which illumine the end of the Paschal spectrum in the Eastern Church: "She does not show the Lord having burst from the grave, suspended in a brilliant, divine glory above the world, as in Grunewald's impressive and masterful painting. Since Scripture itself does not portray the Resurrection event, Eastern believers too refrained from depicting it. The icon, by contrast, represents as it were the mysterious inner dimension of the event...which we profess in the Creed when we say, 'He descended into hell.' In the perspective of the icon, this is an affirmation concerning Jesus' victory. The icon shows him having shattered the bolt of this world, having torn its gates from their hinges. It depicts him as the 'stronger man' who has opened and penetrated the domain of the 'strong man.' It portrays him as the Victor, having burst through the supposedly impregnable fortress of death, such that death is now no longer a place of no return; its doors lie open. Christ, in the aura of his wounded love, stands in this doorway, addresses the still somnolent Adam and takes him by the hand to lead him forth. The liturgy of Holy Saturday circles around this event," *Behold the Pierced One*, p. 123.

51. Lynch, *Christ and Apollo*, p. 27.

52. Eph. 4:8-10. See also Karl Rahner, *On the Theology of Death*, (New York: Herder and Herder, 1961), p. 66. "When the vessel of his body was shattered in death, Christ was poured out over all the cosmos; he became actually, in his very humanity, what he had always been by his divinity, the heart of the universe, the innermost centre of creation." We should, he adds, always be attentive to "this ultimate depth of the world which was occupied by Christ when, in death, he descended into the lower world." Eph. 4:8-10 remains, to be sure, a much controverted text. But can its meaning be less than that which Rahner, among others, adverts to in speaking of the Lord's shattered vessel poured out upon the world, its effects penetrating all creation both before and after? In a word, can it be interpreted as less than that which Job longed to be delivered from? He asks only for a little joy before being delivered over to the silence and solitude of

Sheol (Jb. 10:20-22). And if Christ, as Paul makes clear, had really descended into that place of infernal gloom, whose darkness and silence so filled Job with terror, would it not precisely have brought such deliverance as Job, here representing all human beings, longed to experience? See, for example, the image of liberation which finds so lapidary an expression in Irenaeus' *Adv. Haer.* IV,33,1: "...Christ was led as a sheep to the slaughter, and by the stretching forth of his hands destroyed Amalek; while He gathered into his Father's fold the children who were scattered abroad, and remembered his own dead ones who had formerly fallen asleep, and came down to them that he might deliver them...."

55. Or, for that matter, Christ's Church, understood as the real, albeit sacramental insertion of himself into all that is human and historical. See Jean Daniélou, S.J., *Prayer as a Political Problem*, (New York: Sheed and Ward, 1967), in which he argues that since Christ came to take up and consecrate *all* that pertains to men, nothing human or historical can be a matter of the least indifference to the Incarnate Word or that Body he intended to act as his very extension in the world. Thus Daniélou concludes with this paean: "I love best of all that Church which is mud-splashed from history because it has played its part in history, that Church of the poor which is denounced for its weaknesses by pharisees whose hands are clean but who can point to no single person they have saved," p. 55.

"Our alternative to Marxism is not a Christian civilization, even as an ideal, which operates on the same level as itself, but an affirmation of Christianity in all its fullness. It is not in the order of civilization that we have first to look for the superiority of Christianity, but in the fact that Christianity reaches to where civilization cannot reach, to the root of man's wretchedness, to the darkest places of his being—and that it alone brings with it grace to heal," p. 46.

54. Lynch, *Christ and Apollo*, p. 28.

55. Gerald Vann, O.P., *The Water and the Fire*, (New York: Sheed and Ward, 1954), p 40.

56. Shakespeare, *Measure for Measure*.

57. Lynch, *Christ and Apollo*, p. 63. A distinction is in order here, lest the reader imagine that time, as *saeculum*, is not subject to the redeeming work of Christ and his Cross. In fact, because both time and space (the latter being *mundus*) comprise the whole created world, neither one is lacking in that fundamental need of transforming grace which the fall of Adam made necessary and the blood of Christ made available. However, in fairness to Lynch, it does not seem that his intended meaning here is that of time in the precise moral sense, i.e., as part of a fallen world awaiting the Word to speak redemption upon it, but rather in the looser sense of that medium or setting in which Christ moved and exercised his human being. "Christian belief," writes Lynch, "is in its essence belief in a person who, having created time, could not possibly be hostile to it; who had directed it from the beginning by way of His providence and His having substantially and inwardly shaped it (so that He is the master of both history and psychiatry), who finally entered it and grew into it with such subtlety and power that He is not the enemy of but the model for the imagination and the intelligence," p. 62. And further on in his analysis of time: "Catholic

doctrine is the very reverse of this magical idea; rather it is a divine command of the mind and the will to enter, on the divine and the human planes, into a historical, actual and *eventful* set of facts which penetrate reality to the hilt," p. 69. He then cites two pieces of evidence to justify the view. "The first is the liturgy of the Church which in its changing year reviews the events in the life of Christ. The second is the Apostles' Creed itself, that central statement of belief which has no magic whatsoever in it. It is a sort of summary of the *actions* of God in three forms, in the form of His eternal majesty, in the form of Christ, and in the form of that Church which claims no warrant with men unless it be itself Christ as His larger and growing Body. The Creed begins with God and ends with eternal life for men, but in between is time, that time through which Christ passed and that time through which doctrine implicitly commands us to pass," pp. 69-70.

58. *Christ and Apollo*, pp. 174-175. See also Karl Rahner, "The Eternal Significance of the Humanity of Jesus for our Relationship with God," *Theological Investigations* III, (London: Darton, Longman and Todd, 1961), p. 43: "...according to the testimony of Faith, Christ's created human nature is the indispensable and permanent gateway through which everything created must pass if it is to find the perfection of its eternal validity before God.... He who sees him, sees the Father...."

59. Isaiah 38:18.

60. Not to mention the fifty-five or so references to the phrase, whose meaning may be rendered as "among the dead," in the New Testament.

61. T.S. Eliot, "Whispers of Immortality."

62. "Theology and the Darkness of Death," *Theological Studies* (Vol. 39, No. 1) March, 1978, pp. 22-54.

63. "...and, as Aristotle said, they are indeed more philosophical than history; they are superior to history and superior to pure concepts. The mind that has descended into the real has shot up into insights that would have been inaccessible to pure concepts," Lynch, *Christ and Apollo*, pp. 37-38.

64. P.D. James, *The Skull Beneath the Skin*, (New York: Charles Scribner, 1982), pp. 109-110.

65. "From the very beginning, his stories set out to tell the truth about human beings, to lay bare both the grandeur and the sorrow of the human soul. Like his great mentor Pascal, that giant of the French moralist tradition, in whom the critic Sainte-Beuve observed the highest intensity of feeling for the human person, there exists throughout the work of Mauriac an enormous, brooding sensitivity to the human condition as it is actually lived. A self-confessed 'metaphysician working in the concrete,' Mauriac fashioned a narrative art both imaginative and prophetic," Regis Martin, "Remembering Mauriac," *Communio: International Catholic Review* (Summer, 1982), pp. 183-185.

66. François Mauriac, *The Unknown Sea*, (Penguin Modern Classics, 1962), pp. 43-44.

67. See his *The White Devil*, Act V, Scene III; the speaker is Brachiano, destined himself for a most horrible end.

68. John Donne, "Good Friday, 1613. Riding Westward," *Metaphysical Poets*, ed. by Helen Gardner, (London: Penguin Books, 1972), pp. 86-89.

69. See, for example, John J. Strynkowski's *The Descent of Christ Among the Dead*, (Rome: Gregorian Univ., 1972), the opening pages of which concede that, while belief in the descent is confessed in the Apostles' Creed, its importance is neglected by many theologians. He cites, among others, J. Crehan in his article "Descent into Hell," *A Catholic Dictionary of Theology II*, (London, 1967), p. 163, as an example of this widespread neglect.

70. *The Cross: Word and Sacrament*, (San Francisco: Ignatius Press, 1985), p. 39. Adrienne continues: "The Son knows that he is forsaken. He *knows*; it is not merely his imagination. But he does not know *why*...." The cry of abandonment, she says in this chapter in which that word is applied to the sacrament of Ordination, "is the complete expression of a man stretched beyond endurance, who can go no further. This is the end of the road. The notion of a guiding providence has disappeared. Yet one thing remains...his mission. Tenacious, indomitable, vast, his mission erupts right through the suffering.... The only thing that matters now is that his task shall be carried out, involving precisely this experience of dereliction. The Son shall be forsaken; he shall be aware that it is God who has forsaken him; but he will not know why. ...And so this 'why?' becomes the 'why?' of every Christian mission. The priest utters this 'why?' when at last he fails to join heaven and earth together in his work, when he can see no way forward...and there is nothing left but his priestly service which has become meaningless and impotent.... But in this dark night the priest (with St. John of the Cross) need no longer proclaim his forsakenness publicly: the Son has done it for him on the Cross. He carries not only every sin, but also the wages of sin, this forsakenness of those who follow him. The Son's cry is a prophecy, an anticipation, bearing *in advance* all that will happen to those who are his...," pp. 39-40.

Nevertheless, von Speyr's point must not be pressed so far that an ontological disjunction opens in the heart of God itself, and the very identity of Christ as the Word whom the Father perpetually speaks, and hence the Word's perpetual mission of answering response, were suddenly to cease amid the enveloping silence of Calvary, and Christ were truly, absolutely forsaken by God. To sunder the Son of God in such a way (that is, to so disjoin the divine and human within the Word, indeed to shatter the Godhead itself which the Word fully possesses) is really an affront to that divine dignity and status which is Christ's by dint of participation in the Trinity itself; it is always the Second Person who acts through the chosen instrument of a human nature perfectly assumed, and thus the abandonment expressed in Christ's cry of dereliction—while fully evincing the most terrible pain of loss in his human soul—bespeaks no final ontological separation within the Godhead. Besides, for all of its anguish-seeming finality, the cry is ultimately one of victory; moreover, to be understood rightly, i.e., in the full context of the Passion and its implicit trajectory towards Easter triumph, it must be balanced by all the other words spoken from the Cross since each is equally fraught with all the fullness of the Eternal Word himself. "We will probably never be able to determine exactly which words Christ pronounced on the cross. But if we hold that the entire historic reality of the cross is expressed in the cry: 'My God, why have you abandoned me?' (Mk. 15:34; Mt. 27:44), while the sentences, 'Father, into your hands I commend my spirit' (Lk. 23:44) and 'All is fulfilled' (Jn. 19:30), are legendary accretions not corresponding to the historic reality, we fail to see what value the Johannine soteriology still has. If instead we accept all three...as true interpretations of historical reality (Jesus, although feeling himself abandoned, gave himself faithfully and courageously to the Father and with that fulfilled his mission), we find the basis for a full participation in the Church's doxology: 'We adore you, O Christ, and we bless you because by your holy cross you have redeemed the world,' " Maurizio Flick, "The Birth of a Theology of the Cross," from *The Cross Today*, by Gerald O'Collins, Robert Faricy and Maurizio Flick, (Rome and Sydney: E.J. Dwyer, 1977), pp. 5-6. See also Karl Rahner, *On the Theology of Death*, (New York: Herder and Herder, 1961), p. 70: "The real miracle of Christ's death resides precisely in this: death which in itself can only be experienced as the advent of emptiness, as the impasse of sin, as the darkness of eternal night, and which 'in itself' could be suffered, even by Christ himself, only as such a state of abandonment by God, now, through being embraced by the obedient 'yes' of the Son, and while losing nothing of the horror of the divine abandonment that belongs to it, is transformed into something completely different, into the advent of God in the midst of that empty loneliness, and the manifestation of a complete, obedient surrender of the whole man to the holy God at the very moment when man seems lost and far removed from him."

71. *The Von Balthasar Reader*, ed. by Medard Kehl and Werner Loser, (New York: Crossroad, 1982), p. 44.

72. C.S. Lewis, *The Problem of Pain*, p. 115.

73. *The Von Balthasar Reader*, p. 45.

74. *Ibid.*

75. *Ibid.*

76. See his *First Glance at Adrienne von Speyr*, especially the chapter on "The Theological Task," pp. 50-94.

77. *The Von Balthasar Reader*, p. 45. See, too, his remarks under the heading "Purgatory and Hell," no. 110, pp. 420-422, in which von Balthasar has written: "It is only permissible to say so much: God even as redeemer respects the freedom which God has bestowed upon his creature and with which it is capable of resisting his love.... It remains however to consider whether God is not free to encounter the sinner turned away from him in the form of weakness of the crucified brother abandoned by God, and indeed in such a way that it becomes clear to the one turned away: this (like me) God-forsaken one is so for my sake. In this situation one can no longer speak of any overpowering if, to the one who has chosen (maybe one should say: thinks he has chosen) the complete loneliness of being-only-for-oneself, God himself enters into his very loneliness as someone who is even more lonely. To get an insight into this, one must recall what was said at the start according to which the world with all its destinies of freedom has been founded anticipatorily in the mystery of the sacrificed Son of God: this

descent is *a priori* deeper than that to which one lost in the world can attain. Even what we call 'hell' is, although it is the place of desolation, always still a christological place," p. 422.

78. "Chesterton once wrote in an awful illumination whose light lifts the darkness of hell, 'that it is not well for God to be alone,' " Frederick Wilhelmsen, *The Metaphysics of Love*, (New York: Sheed and Ward, 1962), p. 154.

79. For a precise theological analysis of the concept *relatio*, i.e., the phenomenon of *dia-logos*, as it applies to God, see J. Ratzinger, *The Introduction to Christianity*, pp. 114-137. "Inasmuch as Christian faith acknowledges God, the creative meaning, as person, it acknowledges him as knowledge, word and love. But the confession of faith in God as person necessarily includes the acknowledgment of God as relatedness, as communicability, as fruitfulness. The unrelated, unrelatable, absolutely one could not be a person. There is no such thing as person in the categorical singular," p. 128.

80. "In his play *No Exit*, Jean Paul Sartre portrays man as a being who is hopelessly trapped. He sums up his gloomy picture of man in the words, 'Hell is other people.' This being so, hell is everywhere, and there is no exit, the doors are everywhere closed," J. Ratzinger, *Behold the Pierced One*, p. 128. In fact, says Ratzinger, heaven *is* other people, and through Christ, who opens the doors of human solitude—having himself plunged more deeply than anyone into that hell—we obtain the grace to see the beatific possibilities of our neighbors. "Christ summons us to find heaven in him, to discover him in others and thus to be heaven to each other. He calls us to let heaven shine into this world, to build heaven here...so that Easter may be now," p. 128.

81. I owe this formulation to Fr. Herbert Alphonso, S.J., who used it in my presence when conducting "An Intensive Initiation into the Study of the Text of the Spiritual Exercises," held in Rome in May of 1987. Fr. Alphonso is Director of the Ignatian Spirituality Center in Rome.

82. Cited by Pieper in his book, *About Love*, (Chicago: Franciscan Herald Press, 1974), p. 75.

83. C.S. Lewis, *The Great Divorce*, (London: G. Bles, 1945).

84. T.S. Eliot, *The Cocktail Party: A Comedy*, (London: Faber and Faber, 1949), p. 87.

85. Cited by Pieper in *About Love*, p. 75.

86. *About Love*, p. 76.

87. Flannery O'Connor, from *A Good Man Is Hard To Find*, (New York: New American Library, 1975).

88. O'Connor, p. 212.

89. "The Selfish Giant," *The Complete Fairy Tales of Oscar Wilde*, (New York: Franklin Watts, 1960).

90. Susan Cheever, *Home Before Dark: A Biographical Memoir of John Cheever*, (Boston: Houghton Mifflin, 1984), pp. 10-11.

91. Karl Barth, *Dogmatics in Outline*, (London: SCM Press, 1949), pp. 117-118. One is also reminded of the Jewish writer Saul Bellow's wry account of a story he had sent to the *New Yorker*, a magazine of stylish fashion and progressive

opinion, which they promptly returned, on the grounds, said Bellow, of having "violated one of their tenets: it ended with a funeral." *New York Times Book Review,* July 21, 1985, p. 29.

92. John Henry Newman, "The Dream of Gerontius," published in 1865 and re-issued: (Oxford and London: Mowbray, 1986), p. 15.

93. *Poems and Prose of Gerard Manley Hopkins*, p. 50.

94. The reference is to the Welsh poet Dylan Thomas, whose poem, "Do Not Go Gentle into that Good Night," is movingly addressed to his dying father.

95. Gabriel Marcel, among others, has drawn the important distinction between problems, which are inherently soluble because we stand outside and above their texture, and mysteries, which can never be solved inasmuch as they enclose us. That a man should succumb, say, to a tumor, is a problem which the medical experts can theoretically solve; but that a man should have to die at all is quite beyond the reach of medical science.

96. See A.N. Wilson's biography *Hilaire Belloc,* (New York: Atheneum, 1984), pp. 338-339. Belloc's piety, reports Wilson, considerably deepened following a visit to the Holy Land in May of 1935; he was particularly affected by the sight of Gethsemane. "He did not brag about it in his books," says Wilson. "But there can be no doubt of it if we read his letters on this journey to Katherine Asquith, who was perhaps his closest confidante in religious matters," p. 338.

97. "The Old Testament description of Sheol presents it as a place of darkness, silence, being forgotten, solitude, inactivity—a state of impossibility of receiving the rewards of God himself," Fr. Joseph Henchey, CSS, unpublished class notes on "The Mystery of Redemption," 1984. If such is the state of the dead, to which all will be sent simply in virtue of having lived (this being the Old Testament understanding), then the prospect of one's going there must remain, strictly speaking, hellish in the extreme; and the added certainty of never getting out tightens the screw of human suffering in ways infinitely awful.

98. Pope John Paul II, *Way of the Cross,* (New York: The Catholic Near East Welfare Association, 1982).

99. Newman, pp. 7-8.

100. John Paul II, *Way of the Cross,* "The Fourteenth Station."

101. Wilson, *Belloc,* pp. 338-339.

102. "Perhaps we may say," writes Pieper, "that true love makes us realize, more directly than any theorizing can, that the beloved as a person cannot simply drop out of reality, and even—though this to be sure will be evident only to the believer—the beloved will be physically resurrected and live forever, through death and beyond it. This, at any rate, is the way I have always understood Gabriel Marcel's moving words: 'To love a person means to say: You will not die.' This is certainly 'partisanship for the existence of the beloved'; a more intense partisanship cannot be conceived," *About Love,* p. 23.

103. George Herbert, "Death," *The Metaphysical Poets,* pp. 141-142.

EPILOGUE

And all shall be well and
All manner of thing shall be well
When the tongues of flame are in-folded
Into the crowned knot of fire
And the fire and the rose are one.

T.S. Eliot final lines from *Four Quartets*

In summoning the specter of the Holocaust for the last time, it is important that the reader confront, once again, the content of that mysterious connection between two historical events whose details have so filled these pages, namely the Cross of Christ and the Death Camps of the Third Reich. (Again, treating the latter as this century's most conspicuous symbol of human horror and hopelessness.) For it has been the persisting argument of these pages that between the God-Man who perished in Palestine nearly two millennia ago—the sun-baked Son of the Semite king David—and the six million Semites who perished in this century, profound and intimate links exist. Yes, there is real kinship here, and the quality of it, indeed its very truth and depth, precisely is to be found in that kenosis each has undergone. But only because Christ's infinitely deeper kenosis ("no greater than which can be imagined," to use the Anselmian criterion of the idea of God) carries with it an infinite efficacy to redeem, is it possible to predicate hope and healing in the midst of even the worst horrors of the Holocaust. To put it differently, it is the distinctively Christian content of the faith of Christianity which alone brings with it the power to confer meaning and deliverance to human suffering. "What is uniquely Christian," wrote von Balthasar in 1965 at the end of the Council, "begins and ends with the revelation that the infinite God loves the individual man infinitely. This is most exactly expressed by the fact that for this beloved 'you,' God in human form died the death of a redeemer (that is, of a sinner)."[1]

In other words, we come to know who and what we are in conse-quence of who Christ is and what he did on the Cross for us. As a result of such knowledge, we find ourselves suddenly empowered to see both the weight of our worth in God's eyes—"In a flash, at a trumpet crash, / I am all at once what Christ is, since he was what I am..."[2]—and the infinite distance we were from God before the Son hung on the Cross in order to make it not matter any more. "I first awaken to what it means to be a person by the fact that Jesus Christ takes me so seriously as a spiri-tual person that he gives his life for my eternal salvation, and by dying buries what was evil in me with himself in hell. 'In this we have come to know his love, that he laid down his life for us; and we likewise ought to lay down our life for the brethren' (Jn. 3:16)."[3]

But who really believes this any more? Can those of us who solemnly discharge the great Enlightenment inheritance of the past centuries still be expected to live, and possibly even die, according to so outmoded and disproportionate a meaning? Some twenty years after the Council, Fr. von Balthasar returns to that question and, asking himself what the modern Christian still holds to in the truth of Christ's redemptive act, he confesses sadly that one can no longer be sure that he believes anything at all.

"The idea of Christ's dying for my guilt vicariously before God seems so distant, so unverifiable."[4] And when the theologians are queried, very often the answers are full of duplicity and evasion: "answers in which, as on the continuous color chart, the meaning quite imperceptibly shades from a clear Yes to a clear No. There are many transitions," he says.

> Let us cite a typical illustration. God, it is said, cannot undergo a change of mood, for instance, from an angry God into a reconciled God, on account of a mundane event. Consequently, even before Christ's Cross, God was reconciled to the world and merely made this real disposition evident to mankind by means of the event of the Cross. The Cross is nothing more than a symbol of how much God loves the world....[5]

In short, the whole kenotic ordeal of death and descent, right down to the last dregs of dispossessed Divinity, is reduced to the status of mere epiphenomenon, a redemptive fifth wheel as it were. "This means that in the god-forsakenness of the Cross, in the hellish thirst of him who hung between heaven and earth and died with a loud cry, nothing happened that is essential for us."[6] Is a man to give up his life for a symbol so etiolated as that, von Balthasar asks?

> Am I urged and obliged to give my life for such a symbol? And that perhaps in an extremely painful way, even by having to vegetate on its account for decades in a *gulag* under the most inhuman, humiliating circumstances? Who can require of me something that seems to lack any meaningful proportion?[7]

A man driven to the last extremity of pain and loss, stripped of every outward sign of self, is not likely to leave his bloody witness in anything less than, in his judgment, absolute and transcendent truth. And when the Christian ventures the same risk? He, too, endures a suffering for the sake of which the truth of his life is sustained. And more: "a martyrdom that is not only humanistic, but beyond that truly Christian, witnesses to the unabridged, integral New Testament faith, whose core is the *pro nobis* of the Creed: 'For us and for our salvation he became man; for us he was crucified, died and was buried.' "[8]

How, in the circumstance, could Christian witness be less than an effort at sheer, *anagogical* imitation of Christ's own dying, our participation in which amounting to the truest form of discipleship? "Let me be fodder for wild beasts," implores the impatient Ignatius to the Church at Rome which awaits his arrival, and which may seek to avert the martyr's rendezvous in the arena; "—that is how I can get to God. I am God's wheat and I am being ground by the teeth of wild beasts to make a pure loaf for Christ.... Then I shall be a real disciple of Jesus Christ when the world sees my body no more."[9]

It was this disposition of the martyr to conform perfectly to the model of the suffering Savior—

> A condition of complete simplicity
> (Costing not less than everything)[10]—

which accounts for Fr. Bouyer calling it "the greatest charismatic experience in the ancient Church."[11] Indeed, the importance of so supreme and compelling a witness in shaping a distinctive Christian spirituality, he says, can scarcely be exaggerated. "After the elements of the New Testament, certainly no other factor has had more influence in constituting Christian spirituality."[12]

One thinks at once of the extremely moving account of the *Passio Felicitatis et Perpetuae*, in which the elements of mystic conformity are pressed into a simplicity of form and statement altogether sublime. The young Felicitas is in her prison cell awaiting the cruel torments of execution to commence; but first she must deliver her child which causes her to cry out in pain.

> If you wail like that, one of the jailers said to her, what will you do when you are exposed to the beasts?
>
> "Now," she answered, "it is I who suffer; then, there will be Another in me who will suffer for me, because it is for Him that I will be suffering then."[13]

Can it be any different today? Is it not possible to draw, even from hellish events of our century, examples of that redeeming, transforming grace which Christ has shown us supremely, definitively upon the Cross? That this mysterious and extraordinary affinity between the Founder and his followers, which affinity was perfectly familiar to the early Church, might still be operative today?[14] "There is no question that Auschwitz will always remain for us as a terrifying revelation of the destructive potential of human lovelessness," writes Fr. Hirschmann, S.J., close friend of Blessed Edith Stein. "But there is another revelation at Auschwitz, infinitely transcending the first: that the love which endures the Cross ultimately overcomes all lovelessness. This is the love that says to the Cross: For the sake of the love which has come to men through Jesus' Cross, I love you and I testify: hate is not stronger than love."[15]

Pursuant to this testimony which no amount of hate can efface, I wish to conclude this study with two examples drawn from that hellish place, each in its own way an appendage of understanding joined to that central Christological conviction in which I have tried to steep my subject. Both are, of course, historically verifiable events, and together they succeed, I do believe, in helping to lift the human heart above that setting of vast human wickedness and horror; even to impart something of real spiritual beauty, mysterious and redemptive, to the meaning of Auschwitz and those other places of shame and death. I mean the last hours of Saint Maximilian Kolbe and Blessed Edith Stein, both victims of an insane ideology determined on total destruction of European Jewry.

In Patricia Treece's moving biography of the Franciscan saint, fittingly called *A Man for Others*,[16] she recounts an interview she had with the only Polish Jew to survive Auschwitz who actually knew Kolbe at the time; he was then an orphan of thirteen. Recalling Father Kolbe, whom, he says, "I will love until the last moments of my life," he remembers someone who "used to wipe away my tears. Because of the death of my parents I had been asking 'Where is God?' and had lost faith. Kolbe gave me that faith back. He was like an angel."[17]

But what exactly did he do, this ministering angel of a man who restores, magically as it were, the faith of children? This Roman Catholic priest who, loving God more than himself, is thus able—and free!—to love everyone in God? In one word, Kolbe substitutes himself for another. At the eleventh hour, he takes the place of a grieving husband and father whom the SS have randomly chosen, along with nine or so others, to die in a bunker deprived of food and water. Protracted starvation: a horrible way to die.

"What does this Polish pig want?" demanded the SS officer wearing the dreaded death's head insignia of the Gestapo, when the slight figure of Father Kolbe came forward dressed in his prison garb—the very insignia of man's humiliation, beneath which, in Kolbe's case, shines the unseen holiness of Almighty God. "I am a Catholic priest," he replied. "I want to die for that man. I am old; he has a wife and children."[18] Incredulous, the officer nevertheless permits the substitution, providing thereby the sacramental working out of what Charles Williams, citing St. Paul, was so wont to call the Great Web of Exchange. Kolbe and the others are then led away to die. A fortnight's agony later, all but four have died and of these, only Kolbe remains conscious. Gestapo patience at last having worn thin, an injection of phenol is administered and now Kolbe too is dead. It is August 14, 1941, the Vigil of the Feast of the

Assumption of the Blessed Mother, the Woman clothed with the sun and the moon and the stars, who long before had promised young Maximilian the twin crowns of purity and martyrdom for God. This same Woman, who had herself been schooled in suffering and sorrow, indeed whose mute and anguished consent to her Son's immolation on Calvary became the deepest kenosis of faith in all history, to recall the moving text of Pope John Paul II's encyclical.[19]

Nearly forty years later Poland's Pope would visit that bunker and before a vast crowd declare how "victory through faith and love was won by Maximilian Kolbe in this place, which was built for the negation of faith, and to trample radically not only on love but on all signs of human dignity, of humanity: a place built on hatred and contempt for man in the name of a crazed ideology."[20] And quoting 1 John 5:4, he concluded:

> For whatsoever is born of God overcometh the world, and this is the victory that with faith overcometh the world.

So the Pope reminded the world when, in 1979, he went to Auschwitz to speak of Father Kolbe's victory, of its profound source in the love and the faith of God, and of its continuing relevance to the world.

But it must be understood in all its fullness as a victory for all, for both Jew and Christian alike; otherwise the whole expiatory point of Kolbe's substitution is lost. The victory of the one cannot be denied the other, for the act of exchange is for the other. United thus in the same school of suffering, wedded as one by the One Christ, Jew and Christian stand together as joint beneficiaries of the priestly heroism of Kolbe precisely because, behind it, there stands the universal, infinitely efficacious priestly Sacrifice of the Son of God, broken on his Cross to become bread for the world. Spiritually, then, as Pius XI would tirelessly point out to a world about to witness wholesale liquidations of God's People, *spiritually* we are all Semites.

Why (one cannot help asking) did the Nazis so detest priests? Why, for that matter, did they so frequently identify the two, namely Jews and priests? Were they—are they—kindred spirits? Mieczyslaus Koscielniak, a man who knew Fr. Kolbe quite well at Auschwitz (he would testify at his Beatification), unearths the following story which certainly reveals something of the grounds of that affinity, that mysterious covenant of blood between two peoples whom such suffering had made one:

> In May 1941 we were working in a torn-down house when one of the prisoners found a crucifix. SS Storch got ahold of it and he called Father Nieweglewski.

"What is this?" he asks the priest. Father remains silent, but the guard insists until he says, "Christ on the Cross."

Then Storch jeers: "Why you fool, that's the Jew who, thanks to the silly ideals which he preached and you fell for, got you into this camp. Don't you understand? He's one of the Jewish ringleaders! A Jew is a Jew and will always be a Jew! How can you believe in such an enemy?"

Father Nieweglewski is silent.

Then Storch says, "You know, if you'll trample this Jew!—and he throws the crucifix on the sand—I'll get you transferred to a better job."

When the priest refused, the SS man and the capo threw him a couple of times on the crucifix; then they beat him so badly that, shortly after, he died.[21]

And, finally, there is the testimony of Edith Stein, rendered in blood at Auschwitz extermination camp along with priests and other religious of Jewish descent arrested as a result of Catholic Holland's condemnation of anti-Semitism. She, too, would die, disappearing sometime in August of 1942 into a gas chamber on account of her profound and intimate identification with the Cross of Christ and the martyred blood of her people. Three years before her death, on the feast of Passion Sunday, she had written to her Carmelite Superior asking permission to become a victim soul in order to help atone for the sins of the world. She was not refused. "Dear Mother," she began,

> I beg your Reverence's permission to offer myself to the Heart of Jesus as a sacrificial expiation for the sake of true peace...I know that I am nothing, but Jesus wills it, and he will call many more to the same sacrifice in these days.[22]

By the summer of 1942 her prayer would be answered; Edith Stein was not someone who stumbled blindly into events she would later live to regret. She chose with unblinkered eyes the path which led straight to the end. Beginning with her name, Sister Teresa Benedicta a Cruce, which means Blessed of the Cross, she sensed the mystical resonance it held on account of her Jewishness. "One thing I should tell you," she said to her Superior,

> when I entered, I had already chosen the religious name I wanted, and I received it exactly as I had asked for it. "By the Cross" I saw as referring to the fate of the people of God, which even then was beginning to reveal itself. As I understood it, anyone who recognized that this was the Cross of Christ had a responsibility to bear it in the name of all. I know a little more now than I did then what it means to be betrothed to the Lord in the sign of the Cross. But it's something that cannot ever be understood.[23]

Here, then, were all the elements of that extraordinary kinship in kenosis destined to unfold at Auschwitz; the whole tapestry of motifs: Jew and Christian, Cross and Camp, time and eternity, nature and grace, history and anagogy...all mysteriously convergent upon one single human soul. At the time of her arrest she was, ironically enough, struggling to finish her last theological work, a lengthy study on the life and mystical doctrine of Saint John of the Cross, that tiny little man of sixteenth-century Spain whose towering soul lifted Carmel onto the heights of transforming union with God; but owing to that other Cross, the encounter with which formed the decisive moment of her life, that great work, *The Science of the Cross,* would never be completed. "Right from the beginning," she had told her Prioress, "I've been convinced that it is only by feeling the weight of the Cross that one ever gains a *scientia crucis.* That is why I have said with all my heart: *Ave crux, spes unica!*"[24]

Hail Cross, our only hope! Fewer than forty-five years following her death, Edith Stein would join the truly blessed company of God; on May 1, 1987 Pope John Paul II announced her beatification before thousands at a Mass in Cologne, Germany.[25] "We bow today with the entire Church," he told the assembly, "before this great woman...this great daughter of Israel, who found the fulfillment of her faith and her vocation for the people of God in Christ the Savior." Calling her, in the words of a recent pastoral letter by Cardinal Hoffner, "a gift, an invocation and a promise for our time," the Pope emphasized repeatedly her persisting vision of her own Jewish destiny as something necessarily enfolded within the outstretched arms of Christ on the Cross. She was entirely convinced that the fate of this people, its four thousand year history steeped in a living covenant with God, defined her own fate as well. She who had shared in the strict traditions of their life as a child would not have wanted it any other way than to share in the frightful abjectness of their death as a woman. Wherever the swastika appeared in the streets of Holland, so too would the Cross of Christ loom before her. To her sister Rosa, likewise marked for extermination, she said when they came to fetch them from their convent for deportation and death, "Come, we will go for our people." And in one of her last letters we read of her utter and serene confidence that God will soon gather her up to be that oblation she so longed for: "I always have to think of Queen Esther who was taken away from her people for the express purpose of standing before the king for her people. I am the very poor, weak and small Esther, but the King who selected me is infinitely great and merciful."

The following words from the epistle of Paul to the Galatians were read at her beatification Mass; they seem particularly applicable to Edith Stein. "May I never boast of anything but the Cross of Our Lord Jesus

Christ. Through it, the world has been crucified to me and I to the world" (Gal. 6:14). This woman, whose entire life was consecrated to the pursuit of truth, was destined to see it all come to sublime completion in the same Cross to which, like Paul before her, she found herself conformed with the world. Blessed be Edith Stein, blessed be her Cross, our only hope.

NOTES

1. Hans Urs von Balthasar, "Meeting God in Today's World," *Concilium*, vol. 6, no. 1, (June, 1965), p. 20.

2. Gerard Manley Hopkins, "That Nature is a Heraclitean Fire and of the Comfort of the Resurrection," No. 34, *Poems and Prose*, ed. by W.H. Gardner, (New York: Penguin, 1953), p. 51.

3. Balthasar, p. 20, "And Christ's deed is the proclamation of the eternal love of God, my Father, in that a fellow man, another person, has gone all the way in taking my place, has saved me by standing in my place, and has brought me back to be a child of God. My 'I' is thus God's 'thou,' and can be an 'I' only because God wishes to make himself my 'thou'; and if this is the ultimate meaning of being and if, nevertheless, I am not to become the necessary fulfillment of God (an addition to God himself), then a final conclusion is unavoidable: God must in himself eternally be 'I' and 'thou' and the unity of both in love. The mystery of the Trinity is the irreducible prerequisite for the existence of a world. The mystery of the Trinity is required for the possibility of a drama of love *between* God and the world; it is required if this drama, as an encounter between 'I' and 'thou,' is to fulfill the world's inner need."

4. Balthasar, "Martyrdom and Passion," *New Elucidations*, (San Francisco: Ignatius, 1986), p. 291.

5. *Ibid.*, pp. 291-292.

6. *Ibid.*, pp. 292-293.

7. *Ibid.*, p. 293.

8. *Ibid.*

9. "Letters of Ignatius: Romans," *Early Christian Fathers*, ed. by Cyril C. Richardson, (New York: Macmillan), p. 104. "What distinguishes the martyrdom of a Christian from similar acts of heroism recorded of Jewish witnesses for the law, or of pagan philosophers and teachers of moral virtue, is that the Christian suffered not merely for the sake of loyalty and obedience to the beliefs and practices that he held to be true and inviolable, or because of a principle of world renunciation. Christian martyrdom was all this and more, nothing less than a mystic communion and conformation with One who died for our sins that he might raise us eternally unto a life of holiness and everlasting joy," pp. 141-142.

10. Eliot, *Four Quartets*, final movement of "Little Gidding."

11. Louis Bouyer, *A History of Christian Spirituality I, The Spirituality of the New Testament and the Fathers*, (New York: Seabury, 1982), p. 204.

12. *Ibid.*, p. 190.

13. Cited by Bouyer, p. 204.

14. "It will not do to separate the idea of following Christ from that of imitating him (Paul also speaks of this) in such a way that the one crucified with Christ could not by grace obtain a share in Christ's redemptive work. Otherwise why would Jesus have invited his friends to follow him so closely and foretold for them persecution, rejection, court trials, even crucifixion (Jn. 21)? This close bond between the follower and the 'founder of our faith' (Heb. 12:2) was fully familiar to the early Church. Paul himself speaks of filling up in his body what is still lacking to Christ's sufferings, that is, what Christ in mercy had reserved of his Cross in order to let his Church share in his work and suffering (Col. 1:24)," von Balthasar, *New Elucidations*, p. 290.

15. Cited in Waltraud Herbstrith, *Edith Stein: A Biography*, (San Francisco: Harper & Row, 1985), p. 113.

16. Patricia Treece, *A Man for Others*, (San Francisco: Harper & Row, 1982).

17. *Ibid.*, p. 153.

18. Diane Kewar, *Saint of Auschwitz*, p. 112.

19. See his *Redemptoris Mater: On the Blessed Virgin Mary in the Life of the Pilgrim Church*, (Vatican City: Libreria Editrice Vaticana, 1987) "How great, how heroic is the obedience of faith shown by Mary in the face of God's 'unsearchable judgments'! How completely she 'abandons herself to God'...to him whose 'ways are inscrutable' (cf. Rom. 11:33). ...Through this faith Mary is perfectly united with Christ in his self-emptying.... At the foot of the Cross Mary shares through faith in the shocking mystery of this self-emptying. This is perhaps the deepest *'kenosis'* of faith in human history," p. 37.

20. Dewar, p. 112.

21. Treece, p. 137.

22. Sister Teresia de Spiritu Sancto, O.C.D., *Edith Stein*, (New York: Sheed and Ward, 1952), p. 212.

23. Herbstrith, p. 93.

24. *Ibid.*, p. 96.

25. See his homily, "In Edith Stein we find a dramatic synthesis of the truth which transcends man," *L'Osservatore Romano*, May 18, 1987. Remaining notes taken from his text, pp. 19-20.

BIBLIOGRAPHY

General Reference Works

The Holy Bible, Revised Standard Version, prepared by the Catholic Biblical Association of Great Britain. London: Catholic Truth Society, 1966.

Boadt, Lawrence, C.S.P., *Reading the Old Testament: An Introduction*. New York: Paulist Press, 1984.

Brown, Raymond; Fitzmyer, Joseph; Murphy, Roland, eds., *The Jerome Biblical Commentary*. New Jersey: Prentice Hall, 1968.

Flannery, Austin, ed., *Vatican Council II: The Conciliar and Post-Conciliar Documents*. New York: Costello, 1981.

Johnson, Paul, *Modern Times: The World from the Twenties to the Eighties*. New York: Harper and Row, 1983.

Neuner, J. and Dupuis, J., eds., *The Christian Faith in the Doctrinal Documents of the Catholic Church*. New York: Alba House, 1982.

Richardson, Alan and Bowden, John, eds., *A New Dictionary of Christian Theology*. Philadelphia: Westminster Press, 1983.

Anti-Semitism and the Holocaust of the Jews

Books

Cochrane, Arthur C., "Pius XII: A Symbol," *The Storm Over The Deputy*, ed. by Eric Bentley. New York: Grove Press, 1964.

Cohen, Arthur, *The Tremendum: A Theological Interpretation of the Holocaust*. New York: Crossroad, 1981.

_____, "In Our Terrible Age: The *Tremendum* of the Jews," *Concilium: The Holocaust As Interruption*, ed. by Elisabeth Schussler Fiorenza and David Tracy. Edinburgh: T & T Clark, 1984.

Davies, Alan, ed., *Anti-Semitism and the Foundations of Christianity*. New York: Paulist Press, 1979.

Ecclestone, Alan, *The Night Sky of the Lord*. London: Darton, Longman and Todd, 1980.

Eckardt, A. Roy, with Alice L., *Long Night's Journey Into Day: Life and Faith After the Holocaust*. Detroit: Wayne State University Press, 1982.

Fackenheim, Emil, *God's Presence in History: Jewish Affirmations and Philosophical Reflections*. New York University Press, 1970.

Fiorenza, Elisabeth Schussler and Tracy, David, eds., *Concilium: The Holocaust As Interruption*. Edinburgh: T & T Clark, 1984.

Fleischner, Eva, ed., *Auschwitz: Beginning of a New Era?* New York: Ktav.

Hochhuth, Rolf, *The Deputy*. New York: Grove Press, 1964.

Oesterreicher, John M., *Auschwitz, The Christian, and The Council*. Montreal: A Palm Book, 1965.

_____, *The Bridge: A Yearbook of Judaeo-Christian Studies*, vol I. New York: Pantheon Books, 1955.

Pawlikowski, John T., *Christ in the Light of the Christian-Jewish Dialogue*. New York: Paulist Press, 1982.

Reuther, Rosemary, *Faith and Fratricide: The Theological Roots of Anti-Semitism*. New York: Seabury, 1979.

Steiner, George, *In Bluebeard's Castle*. New Haven: Yale University Press, 1971.

_____, *Language and Silence*. London: Faber and Faber, 1967.

Styron, William, *This Quiet Dust: And Other Writings*. New York: Random House, 1982.

Trilling, Lionel, *The Liberal Imagination*. New York: Mercury Books, 1951.

Tuchman, Barbara, *Practicing History*. New York: Knopf, 1981.

Wiesel, Elie, *Ani Maamin: A Song Lost and Found Again*. New York: Random House, 1974.

_____, *Gates of the Forest*. New York: Avon, 1967.

_____, *Night*. New York: Avon, 1958.

Journals

Dubois, Marcel, "Christian Reflections on the Holocaust," *Sidic* 7, no. 2, 1974.

Evans, John X., "After the Holocaust: What Then Are We To Do?" *Center Journal*, Winter, 1984.

Fackenheim, Emil, "Jewish Faith and the Holocaust," *Commentary*, August, 1968.

Greenberg, Irving, "Judaism and Christianity After the Holocaust," *Journal of Ecumenical Studies*, vol. 12, no. 4, Fall, 1975.

Howe, Irving, "Writing and the Holocaust," *The New Republic*, October 27, 1986.

Maccoby, Hyam, "Theologian of the Holocaust," *Commentary*, December, 1982.

Ravitch, Norman, "The Problem of Christian Anti-Semitism," *Commentary*, April, 1982.

Schwartz, Michael, "Are Christians Responsible?" *National Review*, August 8, 1980.

Sherman, Franklin, "Speaking of God after Auschwitz," *Worldview* 17, no. 9, September, 1974.

Van Buren, Paul, "The Status and Prospects for Theology," *CCI Notebook* 24, November, 1975.

Wiesel, Elie, "Does the Holocaust Lie Beyond the Reach of Art?" *The New York Times*, April 17, 1983.

_____, Interview with Harry James Cargas, *Commonweal*, October, 24, 1986.

Theological Works

Books

Balthasar, Hans Urs von, *Church and World*. New York: Herder and Herder, 1967.
_____, *Convergences: To the Source of Christian Mystery*. San Francisco: Ignatius, 1983.
_____, *Does Jesus Know Us? Do We Know Him?* San Francisco: Ignatius, 1983.
_____, *First Glance at Adrienne von Speyr*. San Francisco: Ignatius, 1981.
_____, *The God Question and Modern Man*. New York: Seabury Press, 1967.
_____, *Heart of the World*. San Francisco: Ignatius, 1979.
_____, "The Last Five Stations of the Cross," *Theologians Today*. London and New York: Sheed and Ward, 1972.
_____, *Martin Buber and Christianity: A Dialogue Between Israel and the Church*. New York: Macmillan, 1961.
_____, *New Elucidations*. San Francisco: Ignatius, 1986.
_____, *A Theological Anthropology*. New York: Sheed and Ward, 1967.
_____, *Truth Is Symphonic: Aspects of Christian Pluralism*. San Francisco: Ignatius, 1987.
_____, *Two Say Why*. Chicago: Franciscan Herald Press, 1971.
Barth, Karl, *Dogmatics in Outline*. London: SCM Press, 1949.
Bouyer, Louis, *A History of Christian Spirituality*, vol. I. New York: Seabury Press, 1982.
Chesterton, G.K., *The Everlasting Man*. New York: Image, 1925.
_____, *Orthodoxy*. New York: John Lane, 1908.
Dalton, W.J., *Christ's Proclamation to the Spirits*. Rome, 1965.
Daniélou, Jean, *Dialogue with Israel*. Baltimore-Dublin: Helicon Press, 1968.
_____, *Prayer as a Political Problem*. New York: Sheed and Ward, 1967.
Dunne, John S., *The City of the Gods: A Study in Myth and Mortality*. London: Sheldon Press, 1965.
Eliot, T.S., "Thoughts After Lambeth," *Selected Essays*. London: Faber and Faber, 1931.
Galot, Jean, *Il Mistero Della Sofferenza Di Dio*. Assisi: Cittadella Editrice, 1975.
_____, *Jesus Our Liberator, A Theology of Redemption*. Chicago: Franciscan Herald Press, 1982.
_____, *Who Is Christ: A Theology of the Incarnation*. Rome: Gregorian University Press; Chicago: Franciscan Herald Press, 1980.
German Bishops' Conference, *The Church's Confession of Faith: A Catholic Catechism for Adults*. San Francisco: Ignatius Press and Communio Books, 1987.
Heschel, Abraham J., *A Passion for Truth*. New York: Farrar, Straus and Giroux, 1973.
_____, *The Prophets*. New York: Harper & Row, 1962.
Ignatius Martyr, "Letter to the Ephesians," *Early Christian Fathers*, vol. I. New York: Macmillan, 1970.

John Paul II (Pope), *Way of the Cross*. New York: Catholic Near East Welfare Association, 1982.

Kasper, Walter, *The God of Jesus Christ*. London: SCM Press, 1983.

_____, *Jesus The Christ*. London: Burns and Oates. 1976.

Kehl, Medard and Loser, Werner, *The Von Balthasar Reader*. New York: Crossroad, 1982.

Kelly, J.N.D., *Early Christian Creeds*. London: Longmans, 1960.

Lewis, C.S., *The Abolition of Man*. New York: Macmillan, 1947.

_____, *The Great Divorce*. London: G. Bles, 1945.

_____, *The Problem of Pain*. London: G. Bles, 1945.

_____, *Undeceptions: Essays on Theology and Ethics*. London: G. Bles, 1971.

Lubac, Henri de, *The Christian Faith: An Essay on the Structure of the Apostles' Creed*. San Francisco: Ignatius Press, 1986.

_____, *The Drama of Atheist Humanism*. New York: Meridian Books, 1963.

Lustiger, Jean-Marie, *Dare to Believe: Addresses, Sermons, Interviews—1981 to 1984*. Boston: St. Paul Publications, 1986.

Lynch, William F., *Christ and Apollo: The Dimensions of the Literary Imagination*. New York: Sheed and Ward, 1960.

Lyonnet, Stanislas and Sabarin, Leopold, *Sin, Redemption and Sacrifice: A Biblical and Patristic Study*. Rome: Biblical Institute Press, 1970.

Maritain, Jacques, "The Innocence of God," *A Maritain Reader*. New York: Image, 1966.

Mascall, E.L., *The Christian Universe*. London: Darton, Longman & Todd, 1966.

Moltmann, Jurgen, *The Crucified God: The Cross of Christ as the Foundation and Criticism of Christian Theology*. London: SCM Press, 1974.

Murray, John Courtney, *The Problem of God*. New Haven and London: Yale University Press, 1964.

Navone, John, S.J., *A Theology of Failure*. New York: Paulist Press, 1974.

Newman, John Henry, *Discourses Addressed to Mixed Congregations*. London: Longman, Greene and Co., 1891.

_____, *The Dream of Gerontius*. London and Oxford: Mowbray, 1986.

O'Donnell, John J., S.J., *The Mystery of the Triune God*. London: Sheed and Ward, 1987.

Pascal, Blaise, *Pensées*. Middlesex, England: Penguin, 1966.

Pieper, Josef, *About Love*. Chicago: Franciscan Herald Press, 1974.

_____, *In Tune with the World: A Theory of Festivity*. Chicago: Franciscan Herald Press, 1973.

Rahner, Karl, *On the Theology of Death*. New York: Herder and Herder, 1961.

_____, *Sacramentum Mundi II*. London: Burns and Oates, 1969.

Ratzinger, Joseph, *Behold the Pierced One: An Approach to a Spiritual Christology*. San Francisco: Ignatius, 1986.

_____, *Introduction to Christianity*. New York: Seabury, 1968.

_____, *Seek That Which is Above*. San Francisco: Ignatius, 1986.

Riches, John, ed., *The Analogy of Beauty: The Theology of Hans Urs von Balthasar*. Edinburgh: T & T Clark, 1986.

Speyr, Adrienne von, *The Cross: Word and Sacrament*. San Francisco: Ignatius, 1983.

Strynkowski, John J., *The Descent of Christ Among the Dead*. Rome: Gregorian University, 1972.

Trinité, Philippe de la, *What is Redemption?* New York: Hawthorn, 1961.

Vann, Gerald, O.P., *The Water and the Fire*. New York: Sheed and Ward, 1954.

Wilhelmsen, Frederick, *The Metaphysics of Love*. New York: Sheed and Ward, 1962.

Willebrands, Johannes, "Christians and Jews: A New Vision," *Vatican II: By Those Who Were There*. Ed., Alberic Stacpoole. London: Chapman, 1986.

Williams, Charles, "The Cross," *Selected Writings*. Ed., Anne Ridler. London: Oxford University Press, 1961.

_____, *The Descent of the Dove*. London: Longmans, 1939.

Journals

Balthasar, Hans Urs von, "Meeting God in Today's World," *Concilium*, vol. 6, no. 1, June, 1965.

Collopy, Bartholomew J., "Theology and the Darkness of Death," *Theological Studies*, vol. 39, no. 1, March, 1978.

Commission Theologique Internationale: Textes et Documents (1969-1985), Preface du Cardinal Ratzinger.

Dupré, Louis, "Jesus Still In Agony?" *Word and Spirit: A Monastic Review*. Still River, Massachusetts: St. Bede's Publications, 1979.

Fessio, Joseph, S.J., "How to Read Adrienne von Speyr," paper presented at an International Colloquy held in Rome, *On the Ecclesial Mission of Adrienne von Speyr*, September 27-29, 1985.

John Paul II (Pope), Address before Jewish Synagogue. *L'Osservatore Romano*, 21 April 1986.

_____, Homily on Edith Stein. *L'Osservatore Romano*, 18 May 1987.

_____, *Redemptoris Mater*. Vatican City: Libreria Editrice Vaticana, 1987.

Moltmann, Jurgen, "The Crucified God," *Theology Today*, vol. 31, no. 1, April, 1974.

Vorgrimler, Herbert, "Christ's Descent into Hell—Is it Important?" *Concilium*, vol. 1, no. 2, January, 1966.

Waldstein, Michael, "An Introduction to von Balthasar's *The Glory of the Lord*," *Communio*, vol. 14, Spring 1987.

Literary Works

Adams, Henry, *The Education of Henry Adams: An Autobiography*. New York: Time Reading Program, vol. II, 1964.

Bergman, Ingmar, *Four Screenplays of Ingmar Bergman*. New York: G.P. Putnam's Sons, 1969.

Camus, Albert, *The Fall*. New York: Random House, 1957.

_____, *The Myth of Sisyphus and Other Essays*. Translated from the French by Justin O'Brien. New York: Vintage Books, Random House, 1955.

_____, *The Plague*. New York: Random House, 1948.

Cheever, Susan, *Home Before Dark: A Biographical Memoir*. Boston: Houghton Mifflin, 1984.

Claudel, Paul, *Coronal*. New York: Pantheon Books, 1943.

Cowan, Louise, ed., *The Terrain of Comedy*. The Pegasus Foundation: The Dallas Institute of Humanities and Culture, 1984.

Dante, *The Divine Comedy*. Translated by C.H. Sisson. Chicago: Regnery Gateway, 1980.

Donne, John, *The Complete Poetry and Selected Prose of John Donne*. New York: Random House, 1952.

Dostoevsky, Fyodor, *The Brothers Karamazov*. Great Books, ed. by Robert Maynard Hutchins. Chicago, London, Toronto: Encyclopedia Britannica, 1952.

_____, *The Idiot*. New York: Bantam, 1960.

Dubos, A., *The Last Worthless Evening*. Boston: Godine, 1986.

Eliot, T.S., *The Cocktail Party: A Comedy*. London: Faber and Faber, 1949.

_____, *Four Quartets*. New York: Harcourt, Brace & World, 1943.

_____, *Selected Poems*. London: Faber and Faber, 1954.

Gascoyne, David, *The Faber Book of Religious Verse*. London: Faber and Faber, 1972.

Greene, Graham, *A Burnt-Out Case*. New York: Penguin, 1960.

Hopkins, Gerard Manley, S.J., *Poems and Prose of Gerard Manley Hopkins*. New York: Penguin, 1953.

James, Henry, *The Complete Tales of Henry James*. Leon Edel, ed., vol. XI: 1900-1903. London: Rupert Hart-Davis, 1964.

James, P.D., *The Skull Beneath the Skin*. New York: Charles Scribner, 1982.

Jarrell, Randall, *Kipling, Auden & Co.* New York: Farrar, Straus and Giroux, 1980.

Jolliffe, John, ed., *Raymond Asquith: Life and Letters*. London: Collins, 1980.

Kafka, Franz, *The Complete Stories*. New York: Schocken Books, 1946.

Le Fort, Gertrud von, *The Song at the Scaffold*. New York: Image Books, 1961.

Mauriac, François, *The Life of Jesus*. New York: David McKay Co., 1937.

_____,*The Unknown Sea*. London and New York: Penguin Modern Classics, 1962.

The Metaphysical Poets, "John Donne," and "George Herbert." London: Penguin, 1972.

O'Connor, Flannery, *A Good Man is Hard to Find*. New York: New American Library, 1975.

Percy, Walker, *Love in the Ruins: The Adventures of a Bad Catholic at a Time Near the End of the World*. New York: Random House, 1972.

Rilke, Rainer Maria, *Translations from the Poetry of Rainer Maria Rilke*. New York: W.W. Norton, 1938.

Scott, Nathan, Jr., *Craters of the Spirit*. New York: Random House, 1968.

Sewall, Richard B., *The Vision of Tragedy*. New Haven and London: Yale University Press, 1959.

Steiner, George, *The Death of Tragedy*. New York: Knopf, 1963.

Wilde, Oscar, *The Complete Fairy Tales of Oscar Wilde*. New York: Franklin Watts, 1960.

Other Works

Aristotle, *Magna Moralia* II. London: Harvard University Press, 1935.

Basset, Bernard, *Born for Friendship: The Spirit of Sir Thomas More*. London: Burns and Oates, 1964.

Buckley, William F., *Odyssey of a Friend*. New York: Putnam, 1969.

Chambers, Whittaker, *Witness*. New York: Random House, 1952.

Clark, Kenneth, *Civilisation: A Personal View*. BBC, 1969.

Dewar, Diane, *The Saint of Auschwitz: The Story of Maximilian Kolbe*. San Francisco: Harper & Row, 1982.

Fabro, Cornelio, "Ch. Péguy: *Il Mistero Dei Santi Innocenti*." Roma: Il Veltro: Rivista Della Civilta Italiana, 1986.

Herbstrith, Waltraud, *Edith Stein: A Biography*. San Francisco: Harper & Row, 1985.

Johnson, Paul, *Pope John Paul II and the Catholic Restoration*. London: Weidenfeld and Nicolson, 1982.

Kushner, Harold S., *When Bad Things Happen to Good People*. New York: Schocken Books, 1981.

Lucretius, *On the Nature of the Universe*. London: Penguin, 1951.

Lukas, Richard C., *The Forgotten Holocaust: The Poles under German Occupation, 1939-1944*. University of Kentucky, 1986.

Péguy, Charles, *Men and Saints: Prose and Poetry*. New York: Pantheon Books, 1944.

Teresia De Spiritu Sancto, *Edith Stein*. New York: Sheed and Ward, 1952.

Treece, Patricia, *A Man For Others: Maximilian Kolbe, Saint of Auschwitz*. San Francisco: Harper & Row, 1982.

Wilson, A.N., *Hilaire Belloc*. New York: Atheneum, 1984.

Wilson, Ian, *The Turin Shroud*. London: Victor Gollanz, 1978.

Wurmbrand, Richard, *Where Christ Still Suffers*. New Jersey: Bridge Publications, 1986.